T0314127

The Weaver's Craft

Early American Studies

Daniel K. Richter and Kathleen M. Brown, Series Editors

Exploring neglected aspects of our colonial, revolutionary, and early national history and culture, Early American Studies reinterprets familiar themes and events in fresh ways. Interdisciplinary in character, and with a special emphasis on the period from about 1600 to 1850, the series is published in partnership with the McNeil Center for Early American Studies.

A complete list of books in the series is available from the publisher.

The Weaver's Craft

Cloth, Commerce, and Industry in Early Pennsylvania

ADRIENNE D. HOOD

PENN

University of Pennsylvania Press

Philadelphia

10   9   8   7   6   5   4   3   2   1

Published by
University of Pennsylvania Press
Philadelphia, Pennsylvania 19104-4011

Library of Congress Cataloging-in-Publication Data

Hood, Adrienne D.
The weaver's craft : cloth, commerce, and industry in early Pennsylvania / Adrienne D. Hood.
p.   cm. — (Early American studies)
Includes bibliographical references and index.
ISBN 0-8122-3735-8 (cloth : alk. paper)
1. Weaving—Pennsylvania—History.   2. Pennsylvania—Economic conditions.   I. Title.   II. Series.

TS1324.P4H66 2003
338.4'7677'09748—dc21   *2003044762*

To
Dorothy K. Burnham, Norman Kennedy, and Lucy Simler

Contents

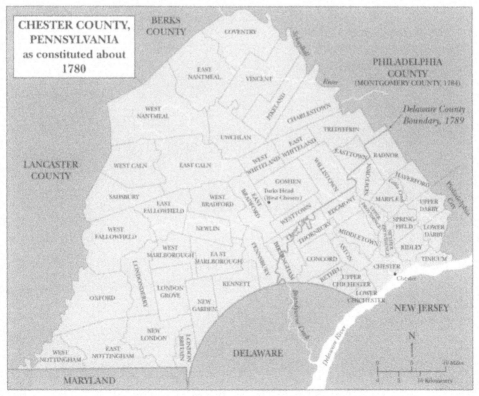

CHESTER COUNTY, PENNSYLVANIA as constituted about 1780

Introduction

Today we take fabric goods for granted despite their importance in our lives. As we put down a credit card at a large department store to buy a new shirt or set of sheets, how often do we stop to think about the work that went into making the finished article: the fiber production, the coloring, the cloth making, and the garment construction? A huge, international industrial process—encompassing sophisticated technology, thousands of skilled and unskilled workers, and complex distribution and marketing systems—goes into producing that item. It is difficult to connect the pastoral image of an eighteenth-century woman, sitting serenely at her spinning wheel, slowly making yarn that will become a shirt for her husband or a new set of sheets for their bed, with the simple act by which we purchase the equivalent objects.

Despite the discrepancies between past and present, there is a continuum in American cloth production and consumption. Then, as now, textiles pervaded the material world. As consumers in an international marketplace, early Americans made choices regarding what they bought and used. What differed were the technology and the place of production in their society. Frequently situated within a household and performed manually by various family members, cloth making was familiar work to most eighteenth-century people of European origin. It would have been an unusual person who did not understand the painstaking labor involved in making the garment he or she wore. Indeed, it would have been surprising if that person had not participated, at least at some stage, in its creation, although no single individual would have performed all of the many and varied tasks required to turn raw fiber into finished fabric. Even in an era when cloth was entirely handmade, the organization and structure of the craft was far more complex and diverse than previously recognized, as was the acquisition and consumption of textiles.

The variety of clothing stolen from Michael Israel's house on Society Hill in Philadelphia in February 1750, for example, suggests not only the range of fabric goods available to mid-eighteenth-century Americans but also their value and origin. In an attempt to recover his property, Israel ran an ad in the *Pennsylvania Gazette* of March 13, where he described what was missing:

a short scarlet cloak, a woman's holland cap, with a cambrick border, a new check apron, a white homespun shirt, a superfine blue broad cloth coat, lined with blue taffety, a scarlet double breasted cloth jacket, with brass buttons, lined with double alopeen, the body with fustian, a black taffety jacket, double breasted, lined with crimson colour'd taffety, without pockets, a man's English velvet jockey cap, a fine Holland shirt ruffled, two linnen petticoats with calicoe borders, a pair of check trowsers, an old long lawn handkerchief, sundry baby cloaths, and sundry things unknown.[1]

Israel assumed that the thief took the clothes to sell rather than to wear and entreated any potential customer to try to apprehend the culprit "so as he may be brought to justice," offering a substantial reward of three pounds. From this short list of garments, we can see that within a single American household the majority of clothing textiles consisted of imported European manufactures—holland, cambric, broadcloth, alopeen, fustian, taffeta, and velvet. In addition, the calico likely came from India, and a local artisan probably made the homespun for the shirt, and the check for the apron and trousers. Soft silk velvet, fine crisp linen, and glossy silk taffeta represented the highest end of the textile scale, while rough, woolen homespun was the lowest.

That such a mixture of used clothing was valuable enough to steal indicates how desirable a commodity it was in eighteenth-century Philadelphia and that there was a demand for secondhand garments of all sorts by those who could not afford to buy them new from a merchant or a weaver.[2] This appetite for articles of dress is not surprising given the increasing role of consumer goods in the creation of individual identities during this period. What could be more visible than the clothes one wore?[3] Eighteenth-century newspaper advertisements further underscore the increasing significance of textiles and clothing to early Americans. Every issue of papers such as the *Pennsylvania Gazette,* the *American Weekly Mercury,* and the *Boston Gazette* brought a proliferation of notices for dry goods from all over the world, imported and sold by local merchants. A bewildering array of cheap and expensive textiles and ready-made clothing arrived at Philadelphia's ports on a regular basis to be sold throughout the province for cash or credit. Although less obvious than the long lists of imported textiles, newspaper ads also suggest the presence of local fabric manufacture. Skilled, immigrant textile artisans could be bought as indentured servants, cloth-making establishments could be purchased or rented, textiles were stolen from the fulling mills that washed and shrank them, and many runaway servants and slaves wore clothing made on local looms. People may have left Europe to establish new homes in America, but they still wanted and needed large quantities of cloth for warmth, for comfort, and, increasingly, for self-identity and fashion. The developing infrastructure of European manufacturing, international trade, and commerce was able to provide the commodities to meet most of those needs and desires.

In some areas of rural America, however, the cloth made by resident weavers supplemented the imports and was a significant component of emergent colonial economies. Many of the farmers who settled in early America came from textile-producing areas of Europe and continued their traditional interspersion of craftwork and agriculture well into the nineteenth century. This book examines cloth manufacture in southeast Pennsylvania, with special focus on the labor involved in its production, to explain how locally made fabric could meet only some of the needs of a large and growing market and the alternatives necessary to augment a supply that was limited in quality, quantity, and variety. The strategies that evolved to meet an enlarging consumer demand were a determining force in the industrialization of America.

My decision to write about cloth and its manufacture is the culmination of a long-term interest in the subject. For about six years during the 1970s, I made a living (of sorts) as a weaver. Many hours spent spinning yarn and weaving cloth gave me a deeper curiosity about historic textiles, the tools used to make them, and the organization of the weaving craft in early North America. After completing a government-funded project to analyze and reproduce early Canadian handwoven fabric using original tools and techniques, I returned to graduate studies in American history to research and write about cloth rather than make it.[4] My subsequent job as curator in the rich textile collections of the Royal Ontario Museum in Toronto provided ten years of close examination of fabrics from many cultures and eras. By applying my practical and historical knowledge to the artifacts, I realized the depth of information embedded in the tools, fibers, color, weave structure, and texture of handwoven fabrics. Over the years, as I handled and exhibited the material and added new items to the collection, it became increasingly apparent that the artifacts could yield a different kind of historical insight unavailable from written sources alone. As a result, I began to understand what it meant to live in "a cloth society" in which, according to Peter Stallybrass, "values and exchange alike [took] the form of cloth."[5] My goal is to share that knowledge, as it pertains to Chester County in southeastern Pennsylvania, with the two groups who helped form my research agenda: practitioners, who will find a lot of interesting historical detail about the processing of cloth, and historians, who will learn more about early American labor, rural life, and industrialization.

A study of spinning and weaving in eighteenth-century Pennsylvania expands our understanding of the work routines of colonial Americans and the technology available to them. It also explains why cloth was such a desirable commodity in this era. Moreover, it shifts the focus away from the well-studied homespun traditions and textile factories of New England, making more apparent the significance of European customs, regional economies, gender roles, and imported manufactured goods in shaping the contours of craft production and industrialization in this era.

The large textile mills that sprang up on the banks of the Merrimack River in Lowell, Massachusetts, during the first decades of the nineteenth century have become the best-known examples of early American industry. Pennsylvania also had a dynamic textile sector that evolved at the same time, although its more urban focus gave it a different look. The key to the variation lies in the structure of local cloth making in the seventeenth and eighteenth centuries. Before industrialization, both Pennsylvania and Massachusetts farm communities produced some of the cloth they consumed locally, initially replicating the European traditions of the immigrant craftsmen. Over time, however, their economic and demographic characteristics diverged, as did the organization of textile production. Although it began in both provinces with a clear division of labor brought over from Europe (women spun yarn, men wove cloth), during the eighteenth century in Massachusetts women took over cloth-making tasks, and along with spinning, weaving became an extension of their informal female economy. In contrast, Pennsylvanians retained the European gendered form of the work that operated on a more commercial basis. As the regions moved away from hand to machine production, entrepreneurs had to operate within the circumstances of their own locality. As a result, early American industrialists dynamically and opportunistically built on indigenous circumstances that allowed both areas to move into manufacturing using available local resources.

Early New England textile mills, in contrast to the situation in Pennsylvania, were concentrated into industrial complexes that dominated a previously rural landscape. In these northern factories, an American-born labor force produced large quantities of utilitarian fabric that entrepreneurs shipped all over the United States. It is not surprising, therefore, that scholars focused on New England as the center of industrial transformation. Most of their research examined the period of obvious technological change during the late colonial years and afterward. They assumed that eighteenth-century New England was the model for industrialization and that it was representative of all early American textile manufacture.[6] These notions fall into what Philip Scranton calls a "textile paradigm" that has dictated our understanding of American industrial development. According to Scranton, the shortcomings of this way of thinking are that the "corporate focus underlying [the textile paradigm's] creation thoroughly blocked perceptions of the persistent alternatives that capitalist inventiveness sustained in the textiles and in other productive arenas."[7] The assumptions that chart the industrial course from handweaving to the domestic weaving of mill-spun yarn to an integrated factory system (where raw materials were made into finished cloth) prevented scholars from understanding that during the colonial era other patterns were leading to industrialization. Because Pennsylvania did not conform to this paradigm, it was not considered a significant force. This book argues differently. Eighteenth-century Pennsylvania, with its highly productive agricultural economy, was more attractive to European immigrants than New England and better able to sustain a European structure of commercial cloth making. These factors generated a very different set of industrial responses within each colony, which combined to shape the process of American industrialization. Understanding the diversity between the two regions is crucial to appreciate fully the shift from domestic to factory production in a developing United States. Why, then, did scholarly investigation stall in New England?

The early years of the twentieth century generated a great deal of scholarship on industrialization in America and on the role of women. This was in part a reaction to the perceived negative aspects of industrialization and in part a justification for giving women the vote. The romance of the spinning wheel, created during the mid-nineteenth century by New Englanders in their town celebrations, provided a somewhat distorted lens through which to examine the past. By the early 1900s, the spinning wheel had become the icon of the industrious colonial housewife, a process eloquently illuminated by Laurel Ulrich.[8] People like Reverend Horace Bushnell of Litchfield, Connecticut, in his 1851 speech "The Age of Homespun," and Henry Wadsworth Longfellow, in his 1858 poem "The Courtship of Miles Standish," did a great deal to transform the spinning wheel from a tool of drudgery into one of romance. Artworks such as Thomas Eakins's 1876 paintings *In Grandmother's Time*, *The Courtship*, and *Homespun* further reinforced the notion, as did late nineteenth-century New England period kitchens where women in colonial dress worked at their wheels. It is not surprising, therefore, to find the spinning wheel as the central symbol for the early twentieth-century Colonial Revival. At the same time, the Arts and Crafts movement, with its nostalgic attempts to recapture the former age of craft production, further iconized the wheel; its adoption by the Daughters of the American Revolution as a patriotic symbol completed the process.[9] Interestingly, the actual tool for cloth making—the loom—was not included in this transformation.

The canonizing of the spinning wheel included romanticizing the labor associated with cloth production and positioning the craft firmly in the female domestic realm. True, spinning had always been women's work, but for many centuries in Europe weaving was the province of men. This traditional gender division of labor was undergoing complex changes by the late eighteenth century on both sides of the Atlantic as industrialization created new work dynamics. A century later, however, when the spinning wheel had come to represent cloth production and women were agitating for suffrage and equal rights with men, what better way to further their cause than by invoking what had become a powerful, gendered symbol of the American past?

At this time, numerous works appeared that examined female contributions to the colonial economy. Cloth making was central to the stories they told, and rural New England became representative of the entire colonial experience. Interpretations by authors such as Alice Morse Earle, Elizabeth Buel, and Carl Holliday, who described New England domestic life, and Edith Abbott, who wrote about women in industry, spawned what scholars variously called the "golden age of women," or the "golden age of homespun."[10] This characterization suggested that colonial households were self-sufficient and that women's labor was essential to their successful operation. As important as the male responsibility to clear land and supply the family's food, for example, was the female responsibility to provide the requisite clothing and household linens. Thus, during the colonial era, yarn spinning and cloth weaving gave women an economic worth and equality with men that was lost during the nineteenth century as the machines of the industrial age removed cloth manufacture from the home to the factory.[11] By the early twentieth century, it appeared that the culmination of this transference was a marked decline in female status and independence.[12] Although there is some truth in this portrayal, it obscures the social, economic, and regional complexity of textile manufacture in colonial America. As a result, we do not understand fully one of the major components of American industrialization. While improved technology was a critical factor in changing the nature of production, people and the social structure of labor were also important.

As long as the focus was on machines, scholarly research overlooked the men and women who operated them. While some early twentieth-century historians were attempting to rediscover women's place in the American past, others were concerned more with the history of technology that was having such a profound impact on their country. Such writers as William Bagnall, Perry Walton, and Arthur Cole concentrated their intellectual efforts on analyzing the history of textile manufacture, in particular how it evolved in the United States. Rolla Tryon and Victor Clark looked more broadly at all industries, but devoted substantial attention to cloth production.[13] Underlying their work was the premise that until technology changed late in the eighteenth century, one could look at textile manufacture at any time or in any place in early America and it would be representative of the era.[14] If females made the cloth and the technology did not change, then there appeared to be no need to reassess this vital element of the preindustrial American economy. Not surprisingly, it seemed logical for later researchers to center their scholarly efforts on a period of obvious transition.

More recently, labor historians have built on the conclusions of their earlier feminist and economic counterparts to examine the late eighteenth- and early nineteenth-century shift from domestic to factory textile production. Topics have included the impact of changing technology on workers, the importance of immigrant labor, alterations in social relations, and the recruitment of a viable work force.[15] In addition, there has been an increasing focus on the declining status of women as spinning and weaving moved out of the home and into the factory. Historians who support the latter interpretation rely heavily on the New England model of the earlier scholars.[16]

Newer research has not neglected colonial craft manufacture entirely. The recent historical emphasis on household production, colonial self-sufficiency, and the transition to capitalism has provided a clearer understanding of early America.[17] Broad works described the existence of colonial crafts, while more focused publications have added detail on labor patterns of seventeenth- and eighteenth-century American wood workers, metal smiths, and shoe makers.[18] Lately, a new understanding of women's role in craftwork has emerged, demonstrating that in trades such as millinery, females were artisans in their own right, and that in cloth making, they provided important support for a family's well–being.[19] We still know more about artisanal work in New England than in other British colonies, however, and more about the post-colonial years than the colonial period. Moreover, the historiographic emphasis on the emergence of capitalism gave production a more sanctified place than consumption, generating the idea that colonial Americans were unwilling participants in the burgeoning consumer culture of the eighteenth century.[20]

In an effort to right the balance, scholars moved the focus of their research away from producers to consumers to analyze how fully enmeshed the settlers were in the wider Atlantic marketplace. The result has been a gradual acknowledgment of an increasing materialism on the part of colonial Americans and that they were an integral part of a trans-Atlantic consumer culture from the late seventeenth century on.[21] This emerging knowledge has profound implications for understanding how the immigrants conducted their daily lives. In addition to exploring the colonists' use of material goods to construct social and political meanings, we can now begin to assemble a more comprehensive picture of the role of consumer demand within local economies. However, the historiographic scales have begun to weight consumption over production and imported goods over those made locally. It is time to consider them in tandem by examining where American-made products fit in the materially expanding world of the eighteenth century.[22] Where better to begin than with the textiles that for so long helped to perpetuate the homespun myth of colonial self-sufficiency and with the long-neglected province of Pennsylvania?

My experience as a weaver and curator made clear that, in early Canada, the German, Scottish, English, and French populations each had visibly different cloth-making traditions; I fully expected to find a similar situation in the American colonies.[23] My museum-based research, however, seemed to be at odds with the conclusions drawn in the pages of American history books. A timely trip to the Archives and Historical Society in West Chester, Pennsylvania, convinced me that there was sufficient evidence for a local study that would move beyond earlier interpretations. Thus began an extensive search for surviving examples of local, eighteenth-century weaving.

Although there was a lot of extant material from the late eighteenth and nineteenth centuries, there was surprisingly little from the colonial period, for three reasons. First, cloth was so valuable that people used and reused it until there was little worth saving. Second, eighteenth-century newspapers regularly advertised to buy linen and cotton rags needed to make paper; undoubtedly much cloth disappeared in this way.[24] Finally, and most significantly, the War for Independence against Britain produced a severe shortage of fabric goods throughout the former colonies. The majority of the colonists' cloth had come from trade with Britain and their own manufacturing ability was small. As a result, the Americans had to find ways to reuse cloth they already had. In 1775 the Committee of Safety beseeched Pennsylvania women to "voluntarily supply the surgeons or doctors who have usually attended their respective families, with as much scraped lint and old linen for bandages as they can conveniently furnish, that the same may be ready for the service of those that happen to be wounded to the Defense of their country."[25] The Continental Army eventually experienced such a shortage of cloth that George Washington appointed James Meese as Clothier General. Meese was to coordinate the acquisition and distribution of clothing and textiles under one department and try to prevent price competition in a country that had depended heavily on textile imports from its present enemy, England. Much of what Meese collected was secondhand; it was cleaned and recycled for military use.[26] Washington also believed that Pennsylvania was capable of providing even more textiles than other regions. Writing from Valley Forge in January 1778 to Thomas Wharton, Jr., president of the Pennsylvania Board of War, he stated: "From the quantity of raw materials and the number of workmen among your people, who being principally against arms [Quakers], remain at home, and manufacture, I should suppose you had it more in your power to cover your Troops well than any other State."[27] Moreover, in areas where there was fighting, the British destroyed or confiscated much of what the Americans failed to requisition, and even the Americans sometimes took textiles by force.[28] Without existing textiles to study, therefore, I had to turn to archival evidence for insight; I especially needed clues to gauge the extent to which early Americans worked at textiles.

In addition to a scarcity of artifacts, scholars' knowledge of early cloth making remained impressionistic because of the difficulty in documenting who made each piece and how much people produced and owned. Yet, as Jan de Vries argues, the household is the essential vehicle through which to understand that the precursor to the industrial revolution was an "industrious revolution," when families changed how they had traditionally allocated their labor resources.[29] The Chester County Archives, with its large number of well-organized and accessible probate, tax, and ledger records, made a domestic-level study feasible. Especially important were the inventories of items listing spinning and weaving equipment and occasionally textiles. These records lent themselves to a computer-assisted quantifiable analysis essential to determine how many households were capable of producing all their own cloth.[30] In addition, I painstakingly combed through legal and business records, diaries, journals, newspapers, and correspondence.

Wills and after-death inventories of household goods, livestock, agricultural implements and products, craft tools, and raw materials frequently shed light on occupations, familial relationships, life-cycle stage, and the disposition of both real and personal property. Because of the large number of probate records (Chester County has approximately 5,500 between 1714 and 1809), I sampled 1,272 of the available records between 1715 and 1831.[31] Sources based on a decedent population can be problematic; they are weighted toward older people who may not be representative of the living community, and property given away before death would not show up in an inventory. Even the season in which a person died could affect whether agricultural products, for example, were inventoried. Moreover, probate records underrepresent or exclude altogether the poor, propertyless, and women.[32] Although it is impossible to correct for all probate bias, sources that are more representative of the living population, such as tax lists and account books, provide some balance.

Tax lists also have problems (women and African-Americans were usually excluded, some assessors were careless, and people could lie about their property holdings), but they provide us with a wider range of the male population than probate because they include many of the young, propertyless men who would not appear in inventories. In addition, often one can use tax records to check probate information of a deceased individual against data from when he (and occasionally she) was alive.[33] Account books supplement both probate and tax data. The weavers' accounts used for this study show the kind of cloth they made, their annual output, the source of their raw material, the people who worked for them, their customers, the costs of their services, the method of payment, and their noncraft activities. The fullers' and dyers' account books shed light on such things as the colors they used, their capital expenditures for repairs to their buildings and equipment, and non–cloth-related services they provided. Occasionally they even contain samples of fiber, yarn, and cloth.

Perhaps the biggest problem with quantifiable sources is that the details and meanings of people's lives, especially of women's lives, tend to get lost in the process (or appear only very superficially). For this reason, this is not the story of many well-identified individuals; however, information from newspapers, journals and diaries, and personal and business correspondence, helps to add stories beyond the numbers. The sources together also reveal the workings of local, regional, and international economies where agricultural commodities supplied both internal and external markets and many farmers practiced a craft. These combined enterprises generated the money with which Chester County residents could maintain their comfortable rural life-style and buy a growing array of imported goods well into the nineteenth century.

Cloth making in eighteenth-century Pennsylvania was not exclusively the work of women for their self-sufficient households. The tasks tended to be gender-specific (women spun, men wove) and the finished product was not usually for household use but sold within a local market. This commercial production is similar to the situation Edward S. Cooke observed in his analysis of furniture and the joiners who made it in eighteenth-century Connecticut—what he calls a "social economy." According to Cooke, such an arrangement involved the decisions artisan households made about how to allocate resources for production and exchange based on local conditions such as the availability of labor, the cost of imported goods, or the annual fluctuation of wheat prices. In this system, manufacturing was as integral to the economy as agriculture.[34] Pennsylvania weavers, like the Connecticut joiners, were skilled craftsmen. Drawing on customs formed long before they crossed the Atlantic, the weavers made informed decisions on how to apportion craft and farming work in their new home. One cannot understand the growth of North America without knowledge of the European craft traditions and consuming patterns. That is where this book begins.

Textiles were vital to England's economy in the early modern period and, because England was also the home to a majority of early American immigrants, I discuss it in most detail. Pennsylvania, however, was a multi-ethnic society; in Chester County, there were large numbers of Germans and Scotch-Irish in addition to the English. Many of these settlers were also involved in cloth manufacture, so I looked at the German, Swiss, and Ulster Irish backgrounds as well. Somewhat unexpectedly, given the focus of much of the literature on British industrialization, it appeared that conditions in these regions were like those in England, with centuries-old work routines, family labor strategies, land-holding patterns, and consumer practices undergoing profound change. By the late seventeenth century, rural cloth-producing districts throughout northern Europe were in the process of transforming themselves from primarily agricultural economies to manufacturing ones. For generations, much of their population had added artisanal work to farming when time permitted. However, as landholdings decreased in size, it began to make economic sense to invest more family resources in craft activities. This transition coincided with an increase in the availability of consumer goods that made it possible for households to purchase items they had once made, freeing up even more time for textile work. Many early Americans came from places that were undergoing this change, but its influence on the structure of their new communities depended on when they arrived and where they settled.

Europeans began to move to Pennsylvania in the late seventeenth century, and over the course of the next few decades their numbers increased. I take a closer look, therefore, at the landholding patterns, occupational structure, and labor strategies established in Chester County. While the situation in Europe was pushing rural cloth workers increasingly away from agriculture into manufacturing, the availability of land in Pennsylvania reversed the trend. Property had always been the most important status indicator for the middling ranks of European society, and its abundance and fertility in the newly opened province gave immigrants opportunities unthinkable in their homelands. Agriculture became the basis of the Chester County economy, and the farmers soon generated enough of a surplus to sell their produce internationally. The ongoing combination of craft work with farming further fueled the emerging market economy; despite their success in agriculture, male weavers continued to make cloth and maintained the European custom of transmitting their skills to their sons throughout the eighteenth century. Labor, however, was always in short supply, so early Pennsylvanians developed a number of strategies that allowed them to maintain the kind of flexible labor force they needed to sustain and expand their market production. Their success meant that they were able to participate as both producers and consumers in the increasingly complex eighteenth-century Atlantic economy.

Having established the critical interaction among agriculture, craft, and labor in Chester County, I take a closer look at the textile raw materials wool and flax, demonstrating further the interconnectedness of agriculture and manufacturing. Tracing the fiber from the sheep's back (wool) and the planting of seed (flax) to the first stages of processing highlights how central textiles were in the lives of rural people and the deep cultural roots embedded in the vocabulary used to describe the tools and processes involved. It also demonstrates that even the production of raw materials operated within both local and international markets; Pennsylvanians grew flaxseed for their own use, but they also exported large quantities of it to Ireland. In addition, fiber processing highlights the early indications of a gender division of labor. Finally, toward the end of the eighteenth century hand production begins to coexist with newly emerging textile technology, factors that surface even more strongly in the subsequent discussion of spinning and knitting.

In both Pennsylvania and Europe, spinning and knitting by hand were women's work, while men operated the knitting machines. Despite the importance of female work to the household economy, this type of labor lacked the status of the men's jobs of framework knitting, weaving, and cloth finishing. Still, some females did earn money through these time-consuming occupations throughout the colonial period. When the late eighteenth-century mechanical improvements moved hand spinning out of the home and into a factory, they actually liberated women from these labor-intensive jobs and freed them to do other things. The early mills also provided needed employment for New England women.

The yarn women spun provided the raw materials for the cloth woven and finished by men, further delineating the gendered nature of the work. These final stages in textile manufacture also begin to point out emerging differences in the structure of the craft in Pennsylvania and New England, despite their shared European roots. Over the course of the eighteenth century in Pennsylvania, men continued to weave on a small-scale commercial basis, selling cloth on order for a local market. In New England, women gradually took over the traditionally male work and wove primarily for their own households. Whether men or women made cloth, however, local production was not enough to meet the needs of the colonials.

The textiles made in the northern colonies tended to be relatively plain and functional and could not satisfy the demands of the population in quantity, variety, or quality. This shortfall did not pose a problem, though, because both luxury and functional fabrics were easily available as imports. The ability to generate cash through a variety of commercial activities gave early Americans, especially Pennsylvanians, the money to buy these imported goods. As a result, there was little need, during the colonial period, to expand local fiber production or to reallocate labor resources, which limited the growth of American textile manufacture. The American Revolution, separation from Britain, and industrialization would begin to bring change.

Moving into the nineteenth century, local cloth-making patterns determined the nature of industrialization in regions like Pennsylvania and Massachusetts. Rural Pennsylvania continued to have a thriving agricultural economy throughout the eighteenth century, with the result that its textile production remained relatively static and close to its European craft structure. In contrast, on New England's smaller and less fertile farms, a growing number of females began to weave some of their own cloth. It was an easy transition, therefore, to bring these women first into a system of outwork (weaving for an employer from home) and later into the factories that sprang up along rivers in the countryside. The absence of an equivalent work force in Pennsylvania meant that the textile mills that did emerge in the early nineteenth century were either small, local enterprises or urban factories that depended on recent immigrant labor to do the work.

The regional structure of craft organization and its utilization of labor was one of the most important components in the process of American industrialization. The new United States needed vast amounts of cheap and functional textiles. Rural Pennsylvania, still involved in market agriculture, lacked a surplus of native-born workers to move into factories on a large scale. Moreover, the male weavers in Philadelphia (many of them newly arrived immigrants) were skilled artisans whose labor was costly. As a result, Pennsylvania provided them with a choice of making specialty handwoven fabrics in Philadelphia or moving into the suburban mills of Manayunk. Early on, only the rural New England industrialists had access to an existing local female labor force that allowed them to manufacture large quantities of plain cloth at prices that could compete with English imports.

When one considers American textile manufacture and use from its roots in pre-industrial Europe, through the early nineteenth-century United States, as part of a continuum, it is no longer possible to view industrialization as a dislocating process that tore unwilling workers from their land and moved them into factories. The story begins, therefore, in Europe—a continent in transition that provided an important model of agriculture, production, and consumption on which the Pennsylvanians could draw as they established their new world.

Chapter 1

European Origins

No matter how small the community or where it was located, making and using fabric integrated seventeenth- and eighteenth-century Americans into a wider international economy. Chester County, Pennsylvania, bordering Maryland and Delaware, with its rich soil, abundance of rivers, and proximity to the urban port of Philadelphia, attracted a diverse group of settlers from England, Wales, Germany, Switzerland, and Northern Ireland. From the arrival of the first Europeans in the late seventeenth century and throughout the next hundred years, many people who came to the new province came from parts of Europe where textile manufacturing was beginning to replace agriculture as the prime source of income. England led the way in this process, and its expanding production spawned a newly emerging consumer society.[1] Other parts of Europe—for example, Germany and Northern Ireland (areas that also provided large numbers of immigrants to Pennsylvania)—underwent a similar evolution, although scholars know less about the non-English. Because transatlantic migration did not dissolve long-standing traditions, it is important to examine the developing European context of textile labor and consumer behavior to understand its impact in North America. Regardless of their country of origin, all migrants were experiencing the early stages of changing economies that involved larger numbers of farm families in a nexus of production and consumption; the distance of a large ocean could not suspend forces already in motion in Europe.

The English dominated the landscape of Chester County, comprising approximately two-thirds of the population throughout the colonial period. In the first decades of European settlement the Welsh were the next most populous group, but their relative numbers declined over the century, while the Scotch-Irish and Irish population grew; the Germans were never a proportionately large group, although their numbers steadily increased. The county maintained this heterogeneity throughout the eighteenth century.[2] English domination extended to more than the size of the population, however, for regardless of national origin, everyone arrived in a colony well positioned to fit into England's developing mercantile economy and expanding empire.[3] As the newcomers settled the land, they successfully replicated the structure of their former environments by combining agriculture and crafts. Nevertheless, while the products of the weavers' looms, and even their tools, likely retained a distinctive ethnic look, national origins were less visible in the organization of their craft because of some shared characteristics of the old and new environments.

Settlers arrived from societies that were gradually shifting from a system of wealth based on property to wealth based on capital, a process that altered in Pennsylvania where land was abundant. In addition, labor was in short supply in the new colony, so as it matured, its social and economic structure evolved differently than in the residents' homelands.[4] The European background of the North American weavers—in particular, the English—allowed them to maximize the potential of their new surroundings and position themselves to participate in the increasingly complex eighteenth-century Atlantic economy. At the same time, the colonists established a pattern of production and consumption that would help determine the course of industrialization on both sides of the ocean.

English immigrants departed a country where textile production had always been central to the economy, and by the mid-seventeenth century, when the Pennsylvania settlement began, England was in the midst of profound transitions.[5] To outline these changes broadly, until the fifteenth-century weavers made wool cloth solely for local consumption, only wool fiber was exported. During the sixteenth century, undyed white broadcloth superseded raw fleece as the major export. By the end of the seventeenth century, a growing variety of dyed and finished wool textiles had become the major component of trade. Over the course of two hundred years, therefore, the main export of the English economy was transformed from raw materials that were finished in other countries to fully manufactured goods.[6]

The expanding English textile markets employed a growing proportion of the population in some facet of the industry. Depending on the type of fabric, anywhere from twelve to forty people could be involved in making a single piece of cloth—more if all the finishing processes were included. In the 1580s in Yorkshire, for example, the labor of approximately fifteen people went into making a piece of short broadcloth measuring twelve by one and three-quarters yards (by regulation, broadcloth was to be twenty-four yards long and two yards wide). According to D. C. Coleman, it took one week for a weaver to weave this sort of simple cloth, with at least five or six people carding and spinning to produce the yarn he needed. More complex fabrics could require a work force of from twelve to forty to keep a single loom operating.[7] Given that 127,000 pieces of this cloth were exported from London in 1614 alone, it takes little imagination to see how much of England's population was involved in textile manufacture.[8] Such a vast number of workers had to be coordinated to ensure efficient production. By the sixteenth century, for many reasons, labor arrangements were changing from the urban-centered guild structure of the Middle Ages to one that was based in rural households.

Craft guilds were primarily artisanal organizations that focused on making cloth, not marketing it, while the more powerful mercantile guilds often controlled distribution. The craft guilds neither financed production nor bothered themselves with technological innovations; they concentrated on the maintenance of high, uniform standards of their products and the social and religious well being of their members. They also guarded long-standing craft traditions and carefully governed the entry of workers into their organization in an effort to sustain reasonable wages and a good standard of work.[9] The formal exclusion of females from the cloth-making and finishing sectors of textile manufacture was one important stricture (women had always participated as spinners in yarn-making processes), with the exception that a widow of a weaver could officially take over her husband's work and tools as long as she did not remarry.[10] From the twelfth until the sixteenth century, urban organizations dominated English cloth making, although this did not mean that there was no rural fabric production. On the contrary, even though country weavers were not guild members, their numbers and economic importance were gradually increasing.

An early catalyst for the steady transference of England's textile manufacture from the city to the country in the mid-fourteenth century was the introduction of water-powered fulling mills for the first stage of cloth finishing. After weaving, woolens were shrunk to make them denser and warmer (the fulling process); brushing the wool to bring up a nap and shearing the surface to give it an even texture completed the finishing process. Because the new fulling mills used water-driven mechanized hammers to pound the cloth to wash and shrink it (instead of pummeling it by hand or feet or with wooden mallets), they required running water and large plots of land on which to stretch the drying cloth.[11] As the export of finished cloth became more important to England's economy, the base of textile manufacturing gradually moved from urban to rural areas, to be closer not only to the power supply but also to sources of wool.

Access to free and unorganized labor was another advantage.[12] Because the guild system restricted the number of members, it was unable to meet the growing demand for artisans. Labor accounted for between 55 and 65 percent of total textile production costs, so supplies of workers became the prime incentive for change, surpassing access to raw materials or waterpower.[13] As a predominantly agricultural nation whose population was growing, sixteenth-century England could expand its work force to accommodate the labor-intensive manufacture of finished textiles. The seasonality of agriculture meant that many cotters (people who lived in a cottage with a small plot of land), rural laborers, and farmers had periods when their primary work did not take all of their time. Fabric processing, with its numerous stages of production, was well suited to a division of labor within a farm household and to domestic manufacture—the women and children could card and spin the wool and the men could weave it into cloth.[14] Among the many factors that combined to change the structure of England's cloth-making industry, therefore, were access to waterpower, a growing underemployed population, and increased demand for larger quantities and varieties of finished cloth for new international markets. By the seventeenth century, the continued primacy of textile production for England's economy depended on its location in the countryside.

As the rural household challenged the urban workshop, the organization of the textile trades changed fundamentally. Increasingly, cloth was made in pastoral regions of mixed agriculture where farmers with small landholdings had become accustomed to combining farming and industry and using their families as the primary wage-earning group.[15] In a domestic setting, therefore, it was possible for women and children to participate informally, although the more customary gender divisions of labor, with women doing the spinning and men the weaving and cloth finishing, continued to be the norm. A weaver's wife might even become as skilled as her husband, though her craft status would remain unacknowledged.[16] To extend their work force, many householders hired what Ann Kussmaul calls "servants in husbandry," who usually negotiated an annual, renewable contract that included payment and lodging.[17] Dwelling with their employer protected live-in workers from fluctuations in the cost of living experienced by wage laborers. Much of the servants' employment was agricultural, but if they had craft skills, they would use them. Most were young and viewed their service as a transitional period between youth and adulthood, hoping that once they saved enough they could find a cottage with common grazing rights and a garden with which to supplement their agricultural wages. The most fortunate might even become smallholders, but all recognized the need to cobble together whatever opportunities arose in their rural communities. Such a system had several obvious advantages. Servant mobility permitted an efficient allocation of agricultural and/or artisanal labor: Employers had only short-term obligations to their workers and could expand and contract their labor force as needed (often in relation to the changing needs and size of their families), and servants could search for better opportunities when their contractual responsibilities ended.

The interconnected development of English agriculture and industry prior to the seventeenth century was most prominent in counties like Wiltshire, where there was a concentration of small, independent landowners or tenants who had difficulty supporting themselves through farming alone. Cloth making provided the opportunity for many to supplement their agricultural income, and the family, not the village, became the cooperative working unit.[18] Unlike the urban guild weavers, these farmers derived status not from their artisanal pursuits but from agricultural production and the land that sustained it. Consequently, any profits that might have accrued from their craft work went back into the land, not textile-related activities.[19]

Toward the end of the seventeenth century, the development of cloth production followed different paths, depending on region, population density, and the availability of land.[20] Enclosure (the fencing of land that until that time had been open to common use) and partible inheritance (the division of property among all sons rather than just the firstborn) combined to decrease the size of agricultural holdings and increase the population in many parts of England, especially the Midlands, where a growing landless population emerged.[21] Many small-scale, independent artisan cloth producers, or clothiers, no longer owned land and just leased a small plot with a house and garden. Instead of participating in the flexible system of farming and craft production found earlier and in other regions, these clothiers became dependent on their craft work to sustain them. In the eighteenth century, they eventually became wage-earning workers employed by capitalists.[22]

In woodlands and pastoral and mixed agricultural regions, the domestic system of production flourished, and clothiers continued the lucrative combination of agriculture and industry. As a result, farmer-weavers had more opportunities to accumulate capital to consolidate larger land holdings or expand their textile manufacturing operations.[23] Independent as they were, however, clothiers did not operate as a monolithic group of equals. In late seventeenth-century Yorkshire, the domestic system included two categories of people who were involved in the production and distribution of cloth in addition to the

clothier: the merchant and the manufacturer. Merchants were not involved in the production of fabric; some brought raw materials to a
cloth-making region and others sold locally made textiles in external
markets. Manufacturers operated on a larger scale than did the clothiers, using hired labor from outside their families to produce bigger
stocks of cloth.[24] The domestic system most closely resembled the
structure of textile production that developed in Pennsylvania. The
autonomy of the artisans was at the core as they acquired their own
raw materials, used the labor of their families (perhaps extended by
hired servants) to work it up, and sold the product in local markets.

Regardless of any inequality among the participants, everyone—
manufacturers included—was part of a similar, independent, artisanal
culture within the English domestic system. The first clothiers who became manufacturers did not incur substantial debt to increase their
output. Rather, using the local systems of debt and credit available to
all, they gradually expanded their textile operations.[25] Growth could
be attained through a reallocation of the productive resources within
a household by converting leisure time to work time, for example,
or by adding more labor from women and children. By the mid-
seventeenth century, the stage was set for an "industrious" revolution,
where families chose for themselves how to allocate their hours of labor and spend their household income.[26] For flourishing manufacturers, the critical element in their success was a fundamental modification
of their investment strategies. Whereas previously an artisan might
have been most inclined to acquire agricultural equipment or to improve or expand his property holdings, now the weaver would funnel
any extra money back into the cloth operation. This in turn allowed
the craftsman to acquire more raw materials and to hire more people,
all of which resulted in a larger stock of finished cloth to sell on the
open market.[27] The availability of land in North America meant that
few New World farmer-weavers took this step.

Not surprisingly, the industrious revolution was predicated on an
increase in consumption as well as production. Local demand for
manufactured goods was equally, if not more, important to England
than its international markets. Since the mid-sixteenth century, the establishment of a series of small industrial and agricultural enterprises
had triggered new patterns of spending, resulting in a gradual rise in
employment and a dispersal of cash through all classes of society and
to all corners of England.[28] By the end of the seventeenth century,
many projects had become established industries and spawned important export goods as well. Items originally produced for home markets, such as knitted woolen stockings and caps, felt hats, iron cooking
pots, frying pans, knives, sword blades, daggers, nails, pins, glass bot-

tles, gloves, earthen pots, and copper wares, were part of Britain's expanding international trade. Originally meant for domestic consumption, the manufacture of these products, along with textiles, provided supplemental employment for many rural families, adding to the income generated from their land and giving them more money to buy the newly available consumer goods. They not only had more cash, they also had more things on which to spend it. As the seventeenth century progressed, many new occupations further encouraged domestic trade and stimulated the manufacture of a wider array of consumer goods. Thus, commercial networks expanded and money circulated more speedily. By the second half of the seventeenth century, England was becoming a consumer society.[29]

The middle ranks of English society and prosperous artisan classes became the largest new market for consumer goods in the early eighteenth century—precisely the group most likely to seek advancement by moving to the New World.[30] Interestingly, independent craftsmen and tradesmen and their families often owned more stylish and decorative goods than the gentry, including Far Eastern imports, new kinds of cooking and eating utensils, and well-furnished dining rooms and parlors.[31] Such middle-class consumerism suggests that emulation was not the primary motivation behind people's desire to acquire new household possessions. How one dressed was visible to everyone, however, and clothing comprised the third-largest family expenditure after food and utensils for its production.[32] Clothes (both new and used) gave everyone, even people from the lower ranks of society, the opportunity to indulge in a growing sense of fashion or simply to use them as a form of self-expression.[33] In the rural north of England—for example, an area like the American colonies that was long thought to consist of self-sufficient households—relatively poor women paid specialists to fabricate many of their outer clothes rather than make them themselves. These fashion-conscious but economical consumers wanted to ensure that no fabric was wasted and that their garments fit properly.[34] More than just fashion, emulation, or status drove the demand for commodities manufactured outside the home; a growing number of rural dwellers had no choice in the matter because their changing labor patterns meant they now had to purchase many of the staples they once had made themselves. If we think of the early modern English household as "a unit of co-residence and reproduction, of production and labor power, of consumption and distribution among its members, and of transmission across generations," as Jan de Vries has described it, then at its heart was the ability to allocate and reallocate its resources.[35] The overall shift from agriculture alone to agriculture combined with industry had less social and economic impact on a household than did the intensification of craft production. As growing numbers of families chose to expand the amount of household labor expended on textile production, not only did leisure time diminish, so did the more broadly based productive activities of women. When merged with shrinking property holdings, this shift of resources compromised a family's ability to grow and make food, for instance, leading to an increasing dependence on purchased necessities. As a result, females in the household went from being producers of staple goods to consumers.[36]

Early Chester County residents were familiar with the prevalent English system of farming and craftwork, in many cases as it pertained to cloth production. A majority of the individuals who responded to William Penn's recruitment attempts came from this dynamic English environment. Significantly, for the purposes of this book, the highest proportion were from the middling ranks of society and originated from major cloth-making districts such as Yorkshire and Wiltshire.[37] Moreover, they migrated largely as families, seeking to better their lives. They also tended to be among the group that was more focused on the status and wealth associated with agriculture and land owning than with manufacturing. Farming was to be their main occupation in the new environment, but craft work remained central, providing additional money for capital improvements, new land, or the consumer goods to which they had become accustomed in England.

Although the English comprised the main group of Pennsylvania's early settlers, there were significant numbers of Germans and Irish as well. German-speaking emigrants to the province came from the lower and middle Rhine Valley and Switzerland.[38] Like the English, their primary reason for leaving their homeland was economic rather than religious; both farmers and artisans had trouble making a living in Europe. According to Aaron Fogleman, migration from the region had a long history, and after factoring in active recruitment of Germans to the colonies, about 80,000 Germans moved to the New World between 1717 and 1775.[39] In the Rhineland, heavy taxes levied by lords of war-torn territories caused economic stresses, which were exacerbated by a system of primogeniture that demanded an eldest son buy out his siblings' claim to the family estate to keep the land together. Younger sons, therefore, were used to migrating to make a living, and the move to Pennsylvania promised economic opportunities unavailable in their homeland. This did not mean the migrants were destitute. The majority of German emigrants, like their English counterparts, had moderate means and many moved as families.[40]

Cloth-making districts of Germany and Switzerland in the late seventeenth and early eighteenth centuries were also undergoing change. As in England, in the regions from which many people chose to emigrate, urban guilds were losing their control over craft production beginning in the late sixteenth century when a growing export trade made it desirable for country households to engage in textile manufacture. In central Europe, rural residents chiefly wove linen cloth—a textile that was even more labor-intensive to make than wool in both fiber production and weaving and finishing.[41] Under the domestic system of production that developed in the countryside, a farmer could accommodate the many tasks of linen processing by using family labor when agricultural demands were low. With women and children as an extended work force and income from agriculture to fall back on, rural weavers could undercut urban craftsmen by selling their cloth for far less. Over time, the threatened urban guilds responded by restricting females' access to independent artisanal status. By the mid-seventeenth century, just before Germans began a large-scale movement to America, craftwork was fully identified with men, as it was in England, while women were relegated to household tasks.[42] Different regions of Germany experienced variations in the establishment of rural cloth production, so a closer examination of Switzerland and the Rhineland provides more insight into the traditions the German emigrants took with them to Pennsylvania.

In the countryside around Zurich in the late seventeenth century, a growing demand for textiles drew rural families into craftwork. Privileged urban burghers (citizens of a corporate town) monopolized rural production by controlling the distribution of raw materials and the sale of finished textiles. For generations, peasants in the Zurich area, like those in the Rhineland, had used impartible inheritance (deeding their property to the eldest son) to maintain land holdings of sufficient size to preserve the fragile balance of subsistence agriculture. This practice began to alter with the possibility of income from a nonagricultural source. Early on, spinning (and some weaving) generated sufficient earnings to permit peasants to sustain farming operations through their manufacturing endeavors. Over time, this practice created a more equal division of land among family members who no longer needed to support themselves fully by farming.[43] The long-term problem, however, was the creation of a landless group of laborers whose textile wages alone were insufficient to live on and who no longer had access to land on which to grow food.[44] Moreover, as with the English, new consumer goods had come to play an essential part in the existence of both urban and rural households in the Zurich region, making the population in the country even more dependent on wages. As one eighteenth-century observer lamented about what he saw as very negative changes occurring in Germany,

A nation that earns its living by agriculture and by dealing in coarse local produce ... [,] a nation that has not yet been seduced beyond the bounds of moderation and restraint by the lengthy enjoyment of refined manufactured products, such a nation is in a quite different situation to a commercial state, in which the pursuit of an injurious industry has turned a thousand seductive pleasures into essential necessities through the power of habit and custom, and where the feeling for simplicity and innocence has been altogether removed from the range of domestic duties.[45]

The obvious biases of this commentator aside, the growing industrialization of the Zurich countryside transformed the rural people from a group that lived on the land to consumers who depended on nonagricultural activities.

Sections of the Rhineland, too, were experiencing the growing commercial incentives to use as large a work force as possible. Part of a pastoral zone that had traditionally supported an abundance of cattle and sheep, the Rhineland began to develop a market economy in the wake of gradually loosening feudal bonds as early as the fourteenth and fifteenth centuries.[46] By the fifteenth century the preconditions important for industrial production were already established in the countryside around Cologne, in part because the land tenure system had evolved into a kind of hereditary tenancy, creating a large group of independent landholders much like those in Wiltshire, England. In the Wupper Valley, for instance, a two-tiered system composed of an elite group of tenants and yeomen had evolved. Below them were cotters, who could barely support themselves on their minimal property holdings. Wealthier peasants, with their larger dispersed land holdings, gradually diversified their economic activities to include cattle raising, dairy farming, and timber and woodcutting. Much of their produce supplied the city of Cologne with food and raw materials. In the process of selling their goods on the open market, many peasants became entrepreneurs. The urban guilds' restrictive measures, enacted to protect their monopolies, furthered rural business activities. As in other parts of Europe, the guilds' limitations resulted in newly forged manufacturing partnerships between urban traders and rural households, assisted additionally by rising demand for manufactured goods and the inability of guilds to provide the quantities needed.[47]

Linen textiles were among the increasingly desired commodities for international markets (including the new American colonies), and it was a logical step for wealthier peasants to grow the flax required to make the cloth. An underemployed cotter class provided the labor needed to transform the flax into spun linen yarn. Brown linen also had to be whitened, and by the early seventeenth century linen yarn bleaching had become another important activity in the region. Finally, access to world markets through Amsterdam made it profitable to begin producing finished linen cloth, a move that made great sense given the abundant supply of high quality yarn. By the seventeenth century, rural Rhinelanders added linen weaving to their list of manufactures. Although Dutch weavers protested loudly, income from cloth making had quickly become too important for the poorer residents of the Wupper Valley to eliminate it. In fact, linen textile production expanded at this time largely because of the efforts of the peasant manufacturers, who continued to diversify and expand their entrepreneurial activities.[48]

The English and German emigrants to Pennsylvania left similar rural worlds in which combining agriculture and craft (often textiles) was the norm; for a growing number it was becoming the only way to make ends meet. By the end of the seventeenth century, many households in England and Germany had moved well beyond subsistence, purchasing a growing array of consumer goods to replace those formerly made at home. Although women's work was critical for textile production, most women only spun yarn, an activity deemed to be part of the female domestic world. In contrast, male weavers received the formal recognition of craft status. Finally, as land holdings continued to decrease in size, even farmer-weavers found it difficult to make a living. A natural response to these conditions for some was to look beyond Europe's borders in search of a better life.

The Irish, the other large group of emigrants to Pennsylvania, were leaving a situation that resembled England and Germany in some respects, but it was distinct in other ways. The first great wave of immigration to Pennsylvania from Northern Ireland—in particular, from Ulster—began in 1717–1718 and peaked in the 1720s, as did the German arrivals. In both cases, people traveled mostly in family groups with enough resources to establish their own ethnically homogeneous communities in Chester County, along with the many English who were already present.[49] The Ulster immigrants were mainly Scottish Presbyterians who had earlier migrated to Ireland, where, living among both Irish and English, they created what Nicholas Canny calls the "first truly British settlement." This mixture of national groups, according to Canny, would "serve as a prototype for what would develop in North America, and particularly in Pennsylvania, in the decades after the restoration."[50] The Ulster Scots' motivation for moving to the New World rather than back to Scotland was, like that of the English and Germans, primarily economic, although religion was also a factor. In Ulster, an exploitative land system generated by absentee landlords, exorbitant rents, and short leases made life difficult for the Scots. The expiration of leases (granted earlier on easy terms to attract settlers), combined with a series of bad harvests, gave people the impetus to move.[51] In the first quarter of the eighteenth century, most of the individuals we have come to know as the Scotch-Irish arrived in the middle colonies in groups with enough resources to settle the land immediately; later migrations also included a number of single men.

In the Irish regions of Ulster, the Protestant Scots combined linen weaving and farming, unlike the Irish Catholics, who generally lived on smaller land holdings and traded cattle and property.[52] The climate and soil of Ireland have always been well suited to grow flax, and linen production for domestic use had occurred for centuries. Not until the late seventeenth century, however, when external textile markets expanded—first in England, later in America—did linen cloth manufacture become a flourishing industry. At this time, the English government made a concerted effort to curtail the wool production, which, for the second half of the seventeenth century, had been almost as important as linen, and to foster the large-scale manufacture of Irish linen. In 1698, the English eliminated the duties on plain linen shipped to England and, in 1704, the American colonies could also obtain it duty-free.[53] Although slow to take off, this branch of cloth manufacture grew steadily in importance to the wider Irish economy during the eighteenth century.

Ulster was the center of the linen industry, largely because of the presence of the Scots and the favorable conditions for flax cultivation. For many years, the people of Ulster, like the peasants in Rhineland's Wupper Valley, had grown high quality flax and spun fine linen yarn that they sold to textile manufacturers in Manchester, England. The Scotch-Irish cloth workers did not have to contend with urban guild controls, as did producers in England and Germany, so the weavers who had moved to Northern Ireland hoping to rent cheap land and take advantage of the availability of good yarn settled in the countryside, not in the towns. Rural weavers combined their craft with small farming operations that provided a safety net for when the ever-varying cloth prices fell below subsistence levels. In addition, their ability to feed themselves allowed the artisans to sell their linen for the most competitive prices.[54]

The home was the base of the textile industry in Northern Ireland from the beginning, with the family as the unit of production, comparable to the system that was evolving in England and Germany. Similarly, the various tasks were gender specific: women harvested the flax and spun the yarn that men wove into cloth.[55] Family labor resources fluctuated, however, depending on the number of children and their ages. At times, there might be an adequate supply of workers within the family, but if there were too few members or the children were too young to contribute, it might be necessary to hire a journeyman weaver to help. Usually, young single males, these journeymen functioned much like unmarried farm servants; generally hired on a six-month contract, they received both cash and commodities as pay. In the first half of the eighteenth century, many of these young artisans could expect to save enough money to become independent artisans or, if they were so inclined, to migrate, some to the New World.[56]

Ulster weavers made both fine and coarse linen that created a hierarchy within their class. Fine cloth required a great deal of skill and training to make and, because the weaver had to keep his hands smooth in order not to damage the textile in his loom, hard agricultural labor was not compatible with his craft. These artisans could make enough money by linen weaving, however, to lease their own farms and hire other people to do the agricultural work. Coarse linen cloth took less skill to produce and brought these weavers much lower remuneration. Members of this group, often unable to lease their own lands, became part of a cotter class by renting a cottage with a garden from a wealthier tenant farmer in exchange for cash, cloth, or agricultural labor, a system that was replicated in eighteenth-century Pennsylvania. These cotters also had to rely on external sources for their raw materials, either another weaver or wealthier tenant farmers (who might also be weavers).[57] Women spun the yarn needed to make cloth, usually for use in their own household, but some worked on a commercial basis. Many independent artisans grew a portion of the flax and made some of the yarn they needed, but if there was a shortage of females in their families, a relative might assist or they would hire an itinerant spinner in exchange for board and wages. The other alternative was to purchase yarn from a traveling yarn jobber.[58]

Whether making coarse or fine cloth, spinning their own yarn or buying it, the linen weavers of Ulster were much more prosperous than people in other parts of Ireland where the craft did not exist; their houses were more substantial and they were able to dress better. Even the poorer cotter weavers, according to Vivienne Pollock, enjoyed "a much higher degree of commercial integration and consumer power than is popularly supposed to have existed among this section of society," buying craft tools, textiles, and farm implements, in addition to having their clothing tailor made.[59] Clearly, the system of farming and cloth making transformed the linen-weaving district from subsistence to a commercial economy in ways similar to the weaving areas in England and Germany.

Abundant labor and access to land were the essential components of the Ulster system. Because weavers carried out most stages of cloth production within their own households, a large family was a real asset. One of the ways a weaver increased his work force was to ensure that adult children continued to contribute to the family's production. As weaving gradually superseded farming as the primary source of income in Ulster, many fathers subdivided their property among siblings, rather than follow the system of primogeniture or impartible inheritance that prevailed in some parts of Germany (although even in Germany the system was breaking down). With journeymen and cotter weavers further extending the labor force, the conditions were right for a thriving Irish industry to supply a growing external demand.[60]

Despite its relative success, however, the domestic system was not firmly established until the mid-eighteenth century. Before that time, religious persecution and economic instability induced many to move from Northern Ireland to the New World. For the Scots Presbyterians, religious factors were of greatest concern between 1700 and 1720, when Queen Anne made a concerted effort to reinforce the presence of the Church of England in Ireland, a policy that also affected the Irish Catholic population and a smaller group of Quakers. Pennsylvania, with its religious tolerance, was an attractive destination for all these groups. In addition, many Ulster weavers had difficulty making a decent living in the first half of the eighteenth century because of long-term economic stagnation; periodic downturns caused by erratic climate conditions, bad harvests, famine, and low cloth prices provided even more incentive to move.[61]

When the Scotch-Irish emigrated to America, they brought their textile and farming skills with them and joined an established English population and incoming German settlers who had similar patterns of production and consumption. Although each group may have had a distinctively ethnic material culture (textiles, clothing, tools, architecture, and household objects, for example), manifested most clearly by the Germans, this was not visible in their agriculture or work routines. Moreover, the conditions the immigrants encountered in Chester County, where there was an abundance of land and a shortage of labor, reinforced the similarities among the groups; all drew on their earlier experiences of land holding and labor strategies to become successfully integrated into the dynamic Atlantic economy.

The founding of Pennsylvania in the late seventeenth century created a province perfectly situated to contribute to Britain's growing mercantile empire. Liberal land policies, which encouraged the selling of small farming lots as well as larger tracts of land, combined with a climate of religious tolerance to attract ambitious settlers from all over Britain and Europe. Most important for Pennsylvania's successful integration into the international trading network was the existence of an external market for agricultural products. In this respect, much had changed since the Great Migration (1630–1640) to New England, and by the late seventeenth century, cereal products were in demand not only in Europe but also in the staple-producing regions of the West Indies and the Southern plantation colonies. Pennsylvania, with its growing number of prosperous small family farms, adaptable labor system, and proximity to the port city of Philadelphia, was ideal for supplying the provision trade while becoming a market for an increasing array of international commodities, including cloth.[62]

By the time William Penn sought settlers for his new colony, the long-term change in Europe made Pennsylvania an attractive destination for people seeking better circumstances than they could obtain in their homeland. Urban guild members were losing control of their crafts as increased demand for consumer goods required more people to make them.[63] All over Europe, cloth production moved to the countryside, where it was closer to sources of labor, raw materials, waterpower, or land. Even more important, the numerous underemployed rural households not only became producers of cloth with clearly defined gender divisions of the work, but they also turned into consumers of an increasing array of new goods. Access to land was becoming difficult, and inheritance practices meant that many would find it impossible to own property. A move to the New World could reverse that trend for those who chose to leave. At the same time, the move across the Atlantic did not alter drastically the impulses of these people to combine agricultural and textile work. A closer look at the settlement patterns, land holding, and work structure of Chester County, Pennsylvania, demonstrates that despite national differences among a diverse group of settlers, they drew on a shared experience of land holding, labor strategies, and consumer patterns to establish a successful system of market production in their new home. The former Europeans encountered an abundance of land, a shortage of labor, and a steady stream of immigrants following them over the course of the eighteenth century. These factors took production and consumption along a different course in America than in Europe, ultimately creating a distinctive industrializing process.

Chapter 2
Landholding and Labor

Many Europeans who immigrated to Pennsylvania during the early waves of settlement arrived with their families and possessed sufficient capital to purchase land and begin working it.[1] These early farmers retained much of the agricultural, occupational, and household organization with which they were familiar in the homeland.[2] Chester County, with its proximity to Philadelphia, was among the first counties settled.[3] Although the majority of its population was English (and, early on, Quaker), throughout the eighteenth century the region also attracted numbers of Welsh, Presbyterian Scotch-Irish, and Lutheran Germans. At first, the various groups established their own ethnic communities, but, over time, only the Germans maintained a clear cultural identity among the dominant English culture by virtue of their language, religion, and folk and material culture. The need to participate in the English legal and economic system of the colonies, however, meant the Germans were not isolated from the rest of the community. As A. G. Roeber maintains, the "Dutch- and German-speakers had shared with English-speakers considerable common ground in religious, commercial and political heritage that facilitated their exchanges with British North America."[4] Aside from European immigrants, some African slaves arrived unwillingly during periods of labor shortages, and, by the late 1700s, there was also a small but separate community of free blacks.[5]

The British and European groups came from rural areas where craft and farm work were the norm and where they expected to buy and sell goods in a wider market. They settled and used the land in similar ways, and had a common approach to textile production. Drawing on their European traditions, the newcomers established a system of landholding and labor that made the best use of their agricultural and artisanal skills. Their ultimate success allowed them to take full advantage of their easy access to Philadelphia in order to participate in an international marketplace that wanted their agricultural surplus and provided them with goods to buy.

Despite its international connection, Chester County remained predominantly rural well into the nineteenth century, and, over time, the ethnic concentrations dissipated somewhat.[6] Regardless of national origin, the vast majority of residents lived on dispersed farms in a region that was composed of a series of contiguous townships with almost no towns or villages; the exceptions were Chester, the first county seat, which became part of Delaware County in 1789, and later West Chester, which took over the county's administration.[7] The responsibilities of the landowners within a township included civic responsibilities such as superintending (or "overseeing") the poor, maintaining roads, keeping peace, and levying and collecting taxes; all males who qualified to vote were expected to serve in the various public offices of tax collector, constable, overseer, or supervisor, at some point. Through their public service or their ethnic identity, people developed a sense of community despite the distances between the households and the absence of such centralizing influences as villages or town halls.[8]

From the beginning of European settlement until about 1715, the number of landowners in Chester County remained stable because land elsewhere in Pennsylvania was still plentiful and cheap. In the 1720s, householders proliferated rapidly, however, mainly because of the influx of German and Irish families. Growth continued steadily until the 1760s, after which the number of rural landowners leveled off until the beginning of the nineteenth century, when it began to decline.[9] Throughout the eighteenth century, although the size of most properties in the county decreased, the cleared and arable acreage remained fairly constant, averaging between 100 and 125 acres per owner, with a sharp decline after 1800.[10] According to James Lemon, the stability of farm size can be explained by agricultural and inheritance practices. Until farming became more intensive (with the addition of fertilizing, crop rotation, and selective breeding, for example) in the eighteenth century, a family needed at least 125 acres to feed itself, and developed a flexible method of inheritance to ensure this. Instead of dividing his land equally or leaving it to his firstborn son, a father might deed a larger portion to his oldest son and less to the younger boys; he might also sell the entire farm and use the proceeds to ensure that his male offspring could acquire land elsewhere.[11]

Agriculture sustained the rural inhabitants of Chester County, and most of them engaged in mixed farming, with an emphasis on wheat production for the Atlantic market. They grew a variety of vegetables, fruits, grain, and fodder crops such as hay, grass, and clover, in addition to raising cattle, sheep, horses, and swine; some grew small quantities of flax and hemp.[12] The generally strong international demand for grain from 1700 to 1830, combined with the surplus produced in Chester County, allowed local farmers to move quickly beyond subsistence.

For the residents of this region, the booming wheat market meant higher incomes, resulting in an increased ability to save money and to purchase consumer goods, both imported and locally made. Many of the early English imports were not just luxury items but also consisted of what S. D. Smith calls "producer" or "capital" goods, such as alum (a chemical used in cloth dyeing), wool cards for processing fiber, and iron for making tools, all of which contributed to the growth of colonial manufacturing.[13] Given the availability of a wide range of trade goods, however, a potential local market was not in itself sufficient to establish crafts; artisans had to be capable of making a competitive product, and a number of these individuals lived in Chester County. Because so many immigrants arrived with a craft skill in addition to their farming abilities, almost from the beginning people produced goods locally.[14] As domestic production began to expand and diversify, however, Pennsylvanians needed an efficient medium of exchange to facilitate internal trade.

In the early decades of the eighteenth century, the method of payment for goods and services used within Chester County was what Mary Schweitzer calls "commodity moneys." According to Schweitzer, this form of exchange was not a system of pure barter where one good was simply traded for another. Rather, it was more like "near barter" in which "a chosen item is accepted as money generally because most consumers feel that others will also accept it in trade."[15] Specie (gold, silver, copper) was most desirable, but any good in high demand that could be traded, such as tobacco or sugar, would serve the purpose. For Pennsylvanians, agricultural products, especially those traded internationally, such as flour or flaxseed, proved best. The cost of using commodities as money was high, however, because it included transportation and storage charges. As their internal trade expanded, therefore, Chester County residents needed a less cumbersome and costly way to pay for goods. By the 1720s, the Pennsylvania Assembly responded to their demands with the first of many issuances of paper money (Pennsylvania currency). The resulting increase in the supply of cash decreased the costs embedded in commodity exchange and prices went down, which raised the income of many in the colony. Moreover, because Pennsylvania currency lowered the cost of doing business and could only be used locally, inhabitants ended up with more money to spend within their communities, agricultural production expanded, and people began to engage in craft specialization that ensured the maintenance of a small but important artisanal base throughout the eighteenth century.[16] All this agricultural and manufacturing growth required land and labor in addition to money, however, and Chester County residents drew on Old and New World strategies to create effective structures to meet their needs.

We tend to associate the opening up of a new colony with an abundance of land and, in the first decades of Chester County's settlement, many new arrivals acquired property. In this early period, immigrants of all nationalities tended to migrate as families, often in groups, and they were relatively well off.[17] Subsequent waves of immigration, consisting of more single, less affluent people, created a significant group who were not landowners, and, as in Europe, they lived on the property of others. Their numbers increased over the colonial period although their status varied.[18] Those who arrived in the province with very little could rent land that they then farmed for themselves or earn money by living with and working for a family in the hope of eventually buying their own property. Many new immigrants tended to move into existing settlements, where there were better employment opportunities, rather than frontier areas.[19] Moreover, as in Europe, a variety of working arrangements provided a fluctuating labor force to support the rapidly growing economy of the region.[20]

African-Americans did not figure largely in this system. The institution of slavery was ill suited for Chester County's seasonal and fluid demand for agricultural workers and skilled artisans. Although a few rural households had slaves, most African-Americans lived in Philadelphia. The investment of capital in purchasing slaves and the need to supply permanent shelter and food made them less attractive as laborers.[21]

During the 1700s, as land became more difficult to acquire because of scarcity and high prices, and immigration and the native-born population increased, several categories of nonlandowners evolved: farm and smallholding tenants, cottagers (similar to the European cotters), servants, inmates, and freemen. Traditionally, these people were all identified as landless, but such a grouping hides important distinctions.

In the early decades of settlement, numerous married men became landholders by working as tenants on others' property. Under a lease agreement, tenants were often responsible for clearing the land, erecting buildings and fences, and maintaining the property until the owner wanted to take it over. In return, tenants structured their own time, had control over their produce and labor, voted, held public office, and paid taxes. This system freed property owners from the obligations attendant on hiring laborers to live in their household and provided them with cleared land more quickly than if they did it themselves. Tenants, who usually worked holdings the size of the average farm of 100 to 125 acres, tended to devote most of their energies to agriculture and could expect to make enough money eventually to buy their own land. In addition to tenants, smallholders rented smaller properties of twenty acres or less and more frequently combined farming with another occupation. This secondary employment (or by-employment) was not limited to smallholding tenants, however, as numerous property owners and farm tenants also had an occupation besides agriculture.[22] Landowners, tenants, and smallholders, therefore, can all be categorized as "landholders" and, like their European counterparts, they often had labor needs that family members alone could not meet.

A variety of work-force arrangements evolved over the course of the eighteenth century to accommodate Chester County's market agriculture and craft production. In the early years, landholders used bound labor in the form of indentured servants and some slaves. Germans as a group preferred not to use slave labor, however, and Africans never comprised a significant proportion of the county's population.[23] Once farmers had cleared their land and planted their crops, they needed more flexibility to adapt to the seasonally intense cycles of mixed farming dominated by grain production. Thus, by the 1720s, the use of bound workers sharply declined in rural areas in favor of free labor provided by inmates and freemen.[24]

Before 1740, inmates (who were usually married) and freemen (who were single) were live-in servants hired on a short-term contract by a landowner in return for lodging and some additional pay. They were also at liberty to work for others if they had extra time. Like tenants, some inmates and freemen were able to save enough money to purchase their own land. By mid-century, however, rising rents and intensified market farming meant that while some people in Chester County enlarged their property holdings, many families could no longer expect to buy land, becoming part of an emerging group of cottagers (similar to the situation in Europe). Rather than working as servants who lived in their master's household, inmates and their families lived in a small separate cottage, usually with a garden, on someone else's land. A contract specified the obligations and responsibilities of inmates: terms of occupancy, including wages, work to be done, privileges, and so on. Generally, the agreement was for a period of one year or less, after which a person could renew it or move on to employment with someone else if he was still unable to acquire his own land. Within the limits of their contracts, cottagers were at liberty to hire themselves out to work when they were needed, while maintaining their own small plots of land and practicing their trade or craft during slack periods.[25] Freemen usually continued to live with their parents or in the household of their employer under a contractual agreement that exchanged work for room and board.

The increasing use of a cottager system freed landholders from the responsibilities and expense attendant on housing, feeding, and keeping employed its resident workers. It also permitted many former inmates and freemen to become householders during a time of rising land prices and continued to provide the kind of elastic work force needed to support the Chester County economy. Most inmates were artisans, as were some freemen, although many of the single men were unskilled.[26] The status of these two groups was above that of bound laborers (indentured servants or slaves), below that of smallholders, and even further below that of farm tenants. Nonlandowners of these various levels were essential for entrepreneurial activity within the region, and the possibility of making a living while accumulating capital to buy land one day ensured that it remained an attractive destination for immigrants.[27]

Whenever possible, Pennsylvanians preferred to employ workers with renewable contracts, because many landholders, in particular those of British background, were accustomed to hiring people on a short-term basis to live in their households and assist them with their work. If the employer were also an artisan, it became particularly important to hire someone who could supplement the family's agricultural or craft labor pool, or more likely both.[28] In addition to servants who resided with them, many landholders employed people living in their own cottages whom they paid on a daily basis or for doing a specified task.[29] As the demand for labor increased, Chester County farmers began to use a work force that looked increasingly like that of their homeland.[30]

Just as many Pennsylvanians re-established familiar European labor strategies, some continued to practice their family's traditional occupation. The variety of evolving land-holding and labor arrangements permitted an array of trades and crafts to thrive throughout the eighteenth century, contributing to the county's flourishing economy and influencing the region's move into industrialization.

Tax lists and inventories demonstrate that in Chester County, as in Europe, when propertied men became less involved in craft production, their landless counterparts took over the work.[31] Probated wills and inventories alone suggest that the number of artisans within the inventoried population declined steadily over the eighteenth century, from a high of 16 percent prior to 1720 to only 5 percent by the end of the eighteenth century; by 1830, only 1 percent was designated by a craft occupation. Probate data further imply that while there was an assortment of artisans such as blacksmiths who worked in metal, cord-wainers who made shoes, tanners who processed leather, and wheel-wrights who made wheels and vehicles with wheels, they were so few in number that, with the exception of textiles and woodworking, there was little craft specialization. The majority of people in a sampling of 1,275 inventories did not have a specified occupation, making it diffi-cult to assign them to agricultural or artisan categories, as they may have done both types of work. Furthermore, a higher degree of craft production occurred than the probate records indicate, as many peo-ple owned and used specialized craft tools. In contrast, the tax lists show both an increase in the artisan population in the second half of the eighteenth century (from 8 percent in 1765 to 21 percent in 1799 and 1810) and greater occupational diversification. Although textiles and woodworking appear in tax and probate records, wills and inven-tories hide the expansion of those in the building trades, such as car-penters, masons, and nailers, who were providing for a growing population that needed to be housed in the late eighteenth and early nineteenth centuries. The confusing and contradictory data from these two sources make it necessary to reconcile them by looking be-yond the simple numbers.

Because inventories and probate records concern property, they ig-nore the poorer elements of the population who were often younger, more mobile, and owning few personal effects and no real estate. Dis-crepancies between information in the tax and probate documents be-gin to make sense, therefore, if one separates landholding artisans from those identified as nonlandholders on the tax lists.[32] The num-ber of men taxed for both land and a trade declined steadily between 1765 and 1800, with a noteworthy drop in the first decade of the nine-teenth century. There was a proportionate and significant rise in the number of landless craftsmen.[33] Weavers reflected this trend, though less dramatically.[34] The proportion of weavers who owned land, 25 percent in 1765, rose to over 35 percent in 1781, only to fall to 18.5 percent in 1799 and drop to less than 4 percent in 1810. The sta-tus of nonlandholding weavers shifted over time in tandem with the change in land ownership—their numbers increased as the number of propertied weavers declined.[35] Factors such as mobility and wealth meant that many of these men would appear only on the tax lists and not in probate records.

Chester County did not tax trades until 1758, however, so we must rely on wills and inventories for evidence of early craft production. In the first decades of the eighteenth century, in fact, a higher propor-tion of county residents had the designation of artisan than in any subsequent period, probably reflecting their former way of life in Europe. Of the people with specified occupations in 1715, more than half were agricultural workers (husbandmen or yeomen), while over one-third were artisans.[36] By the 1730s as agriculture expanded, the occupational proportions began to shift. Approximately 80 percent of those identified by status were in the agricultural sector, a number that remained constant over the rest of the century. The proportion of inventoried artisans fell to 20 percent in the 1730s and to 10 percent in the 1750s and 1770s. Moreover, if weavers are any indication, the craft designation was not merely a formal remnant of a European occupation. All the men so identified in 1715 and 1734 owned the requisite tools of their trade. Although they may have done some farming, these men were also skilled, working artisans as indicated by their occupational title; the quantity and variety of their tools; and the presence of yarn, woven cloth, or both in their inventories.[37] Given the early presence of craft production, clearly increasing population and a decreasing availability of land were not the reasons for Chester County's diversified economy.[38] The impetus arrived with the dual farming and craft traditions of the first settlers, combined with a prosperous agricultural economy, a situation that remained unaltered until the 1790s, when the number of farmers began to decline and non-agricultural occupations multiplied.

As Chester County matured, artisan production became more extensive, especially in cloth-related and woodworking crafts. Because the textile trades comprised the single largest group, a closer look provides important detail about labor in the county. Although occupational designation reveals the extent of farm work, the presence of craft tools—in this case, the loom—offers another way to gauge its prevalence. Although the number of households owning looms slowly rose over the first half of the eighteenth century, it leveled off at between 8 and 10 percent for the second half.[39] The quantity of looms listed in inventories and probate records (some households had more than one) jumped from six looms for every hundred households between 1710 and 1720 to eleven per hundred households in the 1730s, after which the numbers remained constant until 1800.[40] The general agricultural stability over the period was mirrored in the cloth-making equipment—as long as farming remained lucrative, there was little need or time for farmers to expand their craft operations.[41] There was, however, a growing pool of workers who could maintain the productivity of the looms if it proved more advantageous for farmer-weavers to devote their energies elsewhere.

The number of propertyless young people, some of whom were native-born, others immigrants, expanded in the second half of the eighteenth century and with it the available labor force. Many of these men were trained artisans and needed access to the tools of their trade and a market, both of which they obtained by working for landholding weavers who owned the appropriate implements and acted as the agents for selling the cloth.[42] Once a propertied loom owner (who usually had been a weaver himself or related to one) could afford to hire journeymen to use his cloth-making equipment, he was free to spend his time elsewhere while still sharing the profits from weaving. In 1765, there was a ratio of one landowning weaver for every one without property; in 1781, there was one weaver with land to every 2.5 weavers without it, a proportion that was unaltered in 1799.[43] Because propertyless weavers may have worked longer hours at their craft than men who also had to farm, the per capita cloth output of the county may have risen slightly. The increase would not have been substantial, however, because the percentage of households owning tools with which to make fabric did not grow. Given the availability of workers, many practicing weavers with land became employers, with one group of artisans substituting for another. Seasonal agricultural demands further contributed to an expanding population of periodically unemployed workers who, if they had the skill, could be kept busy during slow times with artisanal work.[44] For these men without property, the combination of craft production and agricultural labor made it possible to earn a living and either stay in the region where some of them had grown up or to hope for a better life than in Europe.

Looking at textile production, we see that very early in the history of Chester County several essential ingredients needed for nonagricultural work existed: skilled artisans from Europe who quickly set themselves up in Pennsylvania, a strong economy that provided the residents with money to buy goods they did not make themselves, and an evolving monetary system that facilitated internal trade. Also important in sustaining the artisanal base was the mixed farming practiced by most of the population; the variation in labor needs by season provided the time to pursue a variety of crafts, even those as labor intensive as the tasks involved in cloth manufacture. Some of the factors responsible for establishing and maintaining craft production, however, hindered its expansion. Continued agricultural growth and the availability of labor provided little impetus for the eighteenth-century population to move toward product specialization within the textile crafts, or to expand their markets. This situation—agriculture both sustaining and impeding the growth of manufacturing—was further maintained by easy access to a variety of cheap and luxury imported cloth goods with which local production could not compete (but provided the cash to buy) and which satisfied the growing consumer inclinations of the population. While a shortage of land in parts of Britain and elsewhere in Europe forced many regions into full-time, specialized manufacturing during the eighteenth century, the ongoing success of Chester County's market agriculture meant that craft production continued to take second place to farming.

Eighteenth-century Chester County presented immigrating Europeans with two features that differed radically from their past experience—a lot of fertile land and a need for labor. Interestingly, they adapted to their new home using European systems developed to accommodate precisely the opposite conditions—a declining ability to make a living through farming and a shift to large-scale manufacturing. William Penn's decision to sell small plots of land, combined with the early implementation of landholding systems that involved both ownership and tenancy, ensured the early settlement and cultivation of Chester County. Local, regional, and international demand for the county's agricultural produce provided residents with a comfortable livelihood. At the same time, creative labor solutions, first in the form of bound workers, later as a variety of contractual systems, guaranteed the continuing success of agriculture and small-scale manufacturing. These employment opportunities also made Chester County an attractive destination for immigrants throughout the eighteenth century and kept a native-born population in place. When land became prohibitively expensive, young men could stay in the region with the expectation of making a decent living. As Lucy Simler points out, the "wage laborer, working within the framework provided by the cottager arrangement, enabled rural Pennsylvania to move on to the early years of industrialization."[45] The nature of the industrializing process, however, was determined by the landholding and labor systems developed over the course of a century.

Local fabric manufacture persisted well into the nineteenth century despite its labor intensiveness and the availability of imported textiles. The raw materials consisting of wool, flax, and hemp were agricultural products that had a variety of uses and, because the early stage of their processing was an extension of farm work, weavers could obtain them locally. Many farmers raised sheep and grew flax; if the labor of their own families was insufficient to process the fiber, they had an effective structure of landholders or tenants on which to draw for assistance.

Chapter 3

Flax and Wool:
Fiber Production and Processing

Agriculture was central to Chester County's rural economy throughout the eighteenth century, and as long as farming predominated textile manufacture remained relatively stable. The dual traditions of
agriculture and craft work among an immigrant population, a flexible
labor system that divided the work along gender lines and accommodated people of all generations, and the availability of domestic and
international markets ensured the continuation of small-scale fiber
and cloth production. Flax, which could be made into linen cloth, flaxseed, which could be pressed for oil or sold for cultivation, and wool,
which could be made into woven, knitted, or felted goods like hats,
were the two principal fibers the residents cultivated. Cloth fed only
local demand, however, while flaxseed became an important international trade commodity. During the eighteenth century, the extent
of fiber production remained much as it had at the beginning of
settlement—part of the mixed farming of the majority of the rural
population that only changed with technological innovations late in
the century.

Following the seasonal cycle of production and processing of flax
and wool on one farm provides a window through which we can view
the complex set of social relationships and business transactions involved in textile production in eighteenth-century Chester County.
On April 5, 1788, George Brinton, a farmer from Thornbury Township, paid Caleb Temple a day's wage for plowing ground for the season's flax crop.[1] Several weeks later, Brinton sowed the flaxseed
needed for the annual yield of fiber and seed. In late May, he washed
twenty-five sheep and sixteen lambs in advance of shearing them the
following week. About the middle of July, workers pulled, dried, and
rippled the flax to remove its seeds.[2] On September 28, he "put out
the flax in the Old field on the Clover Lot" to rot the stalks in order to
loosen the fibers for further processing, and on October 26, Brinton
paid Obadiah Dingy to "take it up." During the months of January
and February 1789, Dingy earned two dollars a month working for

Brinton and spent a total of twenty-six days breaking and dressing the flax to prepare it for spinning.[3]

Several local women helped Brinton transform his fiber into yarn. He hired John Rock's wife, Margaret, to do both indoor and outdoor work at 3s 6d per week. Among her tasks, Margaret spent two days in June "in the House picking Wool & Carding wool." The female members of Brinton's family may have had the sole responsibility of spinning the prepared wool fiber into yarn, but they had the assistance of several local women to spin the flax.[4]

Once he had sufficient yarn, Brinton took it to weaver Levi Pyle, who, in return for goods such as meat and cheese, wove him a variety of cloth, including linen, tow for bagging, woolen for cloth, coverlets, blanketing, "a Coverlid Wove out of Wrags," linsey, worsted, and "flaxen Twilled for Bed ticks."[5] Finally, Brinton would have taken the wool cloth and blanketing to the fuller's to be washed, napped, and possibly dyed, and the linen fabric may have been professionally bleached and/or dyed.[6]

Neither Brinton nor his family undertook the entire process of converting raw fiber into cloth. Different individuals performed each task, and nonfamily members were paid for their service. The cycle of fiber, yarn, and fabric production on the Brinton farm also exemplifies the intersection of textiles and agriculture. In addition to the work described here, Brinton raised cattle and sheep for sale as well as for himself; he had an orchard; and he grew wheat, barley, clover, corn, and potatoes.

Wool and flax provided the raw materials for cloth making, but they were also profitable agricultural commodities. Many farmers raised sheep and planted flax whether or not they worked up the fiber because there was an external market for their by-products. A closer look at the processing of these fibers reveals their importance within Chester County's rural economy and helps explain the stability of eighteenth-century cloth manufacture in the region.

Five kinds of fiber were grown with varying degrees of success in the American colonies: flax, hemp, cotton, wool, and silk. European settlers cultivated several types of plant fibers, the most important of which in Pennsylvania were the bast fibers—flax, used for linen clothing and household textiles and, less extensively, hemp, which was coarser than flax and used for rope and canvas.[7] Cotton is a shorter fiber than flax or hemp and comes from a different type of plant. By the mid-eighteenth century, the warm climate of South Carolina induced farmers to cultivate cotton for domestic use in lightweight clothing and household textiles; by the end of the century, cotton had become an important staple crop and an item of export. Wool from sheep to make warm bedding and clothing was found most extensively in the colder, northern colonies, and the production of silk from a silk worm and used for luxury fabrics was attempted on an experimental basis throughout British North America. Because silk was even more labor-intensive to manage than the other fibers, it was not commercially successful until well into the nineteenth century.

In Chester County, wool and flax predominated. Until the 1740s, the fibers were about equal in importance, although the number of households owning the raw materials almost doubled between 1715 and 1737 as the settlers cleared more land and established working farms.[8] At the same time, many were setting up the textile activity that had been an integral component of their past life in rural Europe. The first third of the eighteenth century witnessed the largest increase in the number of looms, paralleling the trend in fiber ownership. In 1715, there were only six looms per one hundred families, a figure that almost doubled by the mid-1730s, after which it remained relatively stable for the rest of the century.[9] The market for locally made textiles was limited, and weavers did not specialize, as they did increasingly in Europe, where an entire region might devote itself only to woolen or linen goods, for example. Rather, small-scale, general production allowed some residents to meet a modest proportion of their textile needs, while imports provided the rest. After all, a field of flax could be integrated into the seasonal crop plantings, a few sheep could be combined with the general animal husbandry of most farmers, and trained local weavers could work up the fiber during quieter periods in the agricultural calendar. By 1740, therefore, cloth production was established in the province on a scale that it would maintain until late in the century.

Wool was inventoried in approximately the same number of households as flax until about 1740, after which there was a noticeable change. By mid-century, the ownership of wool leveled off until the mid-1770s, when it declined steadily, reaching comparatively insignificant proportions by 1830. In contrast, possession of flax fiber increased dramatically beginning in 1737, peaking from 1773 to about 1800, after which it declined until 1830.[10] The seeming contradiction in the growth in the number of households with wool and flax fiber and the relative stability of the number with looms (indicating the ability to transform fiber into cloth) can be understood by recognizing that flax and sheep provided important commodities other than fibers and that agriculture was central to the local economy.

The cultivation and use of flax is a particularly good example of how local agriculture and manufacturing integrated the rural community of Chester County into the larger eighteenth-century Atlantic world; it further demonstrates the opportunistic spirit of many farmers. Once they had established their local, internal economy, landholders could capitalize on the products they had been growing for their own use through trade. Surplus wheat had quickly become an important export commodity in the form of flour and bread, and the most valuable by-product of flax—its seed—was not far behind.

Early on, farmers used flaxseed, also known as linseed, for local oil production and livestock fodder; some even produced enough seed to sell to their neighbors. In addition, by the 1730s, Philadelphia merchants shipped both linseed oil and flaxseed to the West Indies.[11] When the British opened Irish ports to direct colonial trade in 1731, Pennsylvanians quickly took advantage of the market and transported small quantities of seed to Ireland for growers to plant for the expanding linen industry.[12] In 1742, Philadelphia merchant Samuel Powel commented, "the call for flaxseed to Ireland continues & increases. It puts our people on sowing a great deal & they must work up the flax or let it perish as we have no export for it."[13] Despite this early activity, it was not until the middle of the century that flaxseed export became a significant component of Pennsylvania's economy as farmers responded to the increased demand from Ireland.[14]

Although North American flax and its products had important local uses, the burgeoning Irish linen industry required large amounts of imported seed. In order to produce good quality linen cloth, one had to harvest flax plants before the seed was ripe, in the process sacrificing the seed. Even though not all linen was of the finer qualities, Irish flax-growing regions had to use their limited land resources judiciously for producing fiber, not seed.[15] Prior to 1750, the Irish imported the majority of their flaxseed from the Baltic and Holland. The British government, however, passed several acts in the 1740s that provided bounties to encourage the export of Irish linen, causing a dramatic rise in cloth output and a need to find new sources of seed.[16] As a result, flaxseed distribution became more organized through specialized agencies in Dublin and Belfast, and seed from America became an important commodity for both the Irish and Americans. In return, the British North American colonies provided the largest markets for Irish linen cloth.[17]

It is possible to measure the mid-century growth of flaxseed production at the most basic level, the household, as well as through export figures. Before 1737, few Chester County households recorded flaxseed. By mid-century, however, 10 percent of households had flaxseed, at which point it became Pennsylvania's third-largest export commodity after flour and bread.[18] Farming households throughout the county produced the seed, so it is not surprising that it became a significant component of the external Pennsylvania economy.[19] Ownership rose steadily so that by 1800, flaxseed production was thirty-three times what it had been during the first third of the eighteenth century. The nineteenth century reversed the trend as American linen manufacture began to decline and with it flax growing and seed production.[20]

The export figures support the trend of flaxseed production evidenced in the inventories. Exports peaked in early 1770, then fell steadily, probably because the price of seed was high before the American Revolution interrupted trade across the Atlantic. In the mid-eighteenth century, the province exported approximately 70,000 bushels of seed annually; the exports reached a high of 110,412 bushels in 1771; after which they tapered off to about 71,050 bushels in 1791–1792.[21] Frequently, entrepreneurs from Philadelphia advertised that they would buy flaxseed "for Ready Money," and throughout the 1700s, people published directions for growing high-quality seed "for the Good of the Province."[22] A 1765 letter in the *Pennsylvania Gazette*, encouraging the growing of flax and hemp, highlights the demand for flaxseed (although the real purpose was to get people to grow flax and hemp fiber for export to Great Britain, thereby giving British manufacturers a cheaper fiber supply than was available from the Baltic and Europe):[23]

The price of flaxseed is so high, that that alone might encourage the raising of flax, nor is there any danger of its ever becoming a drug, for the quality of our flaxseed (owing, it may be presumed, to the warmth of our sun, which matures and ripens it to a greater degree of perfection) is so much superior to Flanders, Dutch, or any other, that Ireland and Scotland, the great markets for it, will never buy any other flaxseed, while they can have ours.[24]

Hyperbole aside, the local farmers recognized and heeded the call for flaxseed. Chester County residents did not, however, respond to the bounties offered for export of undressed flax to Great Britain because they had their own small, stable market for serviceable fabrics that used the raw material produced in the county.

Pennsylvania was not the only British colony engaged in the Irish flaxseed trade. For Connecticut, the commodity was also an important component in its developing economy. Small-scale seed production provided Connecticut farmers with credit in London merchant houses that permitted them to buy needed imported goods. Chief among the desired items was rock salt, used as a preservative for meat and fish in the growing provisioning trade, and fine Irish linen to supplement the coarser linen cloth that was produced locally in both Connecticut and Pennsylvania. The principal ports for shipment of Connecticut flaxseed to Ireland were New York and Philadelphia. From Connecticut farms, seed was transported via coastal vessels that took it to whichever city had a scheduled transatlantic shipment.[25] Interestingly, Boston was not part of this commerce, nor did other New England colonies participate in it on a scale equivalent to that of Connecticut. In Essex County, just north of Boston, for example, farmers produced only negligible amounts of flaxseed.[26] Among the reasons for the participation of Chester County and the communities along the Connecticut River in the flaxseed trade was their proximity to merchant groups in New York and Philadelphia who had tight connections with Ireland. In exchange for the seed, the regions around these ports provided markets not only for fine Irish linen cloth but also for migrating Irish indentured servants who could find ready work in economies such as these where commercial agriculture and craft production coexisted.[27]

Unlike flaxseed, hempseed was not a major export product. Less than 4 percent of the Chester County population produced hemp fiber either for sale locally or for their own consumption as cordage or cloth.[28] This situation remained unchanged throughout the eighteenth century, with the exception of a brief increase in the mid-1770s, perhaps because of the period of nonimportation before the Revolution when Americans tried to increase local manufacturing as they boycotted British imports to protest growing trade restrictions. Generally, however, despite the frequent exhortations and bounties offered to colonists to produce larger quantities of hemp for export to Britain, Chester County farmers, like their counterparts in other colonies, failed to respond.[29]

Bounties to encourage flax and hemp production were not sufficient incentive for the colonists to make major changes to their agricultural habits. Any shift in their output had to be justified within increasingly established colonial economies, independent of Great Britain. In Pennsylvania and Connecticut, where flax was already an important agricultural product, the growing Irish demand for seed, coupled with access to merchants eager for something to trade for needed imports, made it a logical and easy step for nearby farmers to begin harvesting the seed. Hemp was less important to these local economies, and no amount of bribery could increase its value. Moreover, while Pennsylvanians valued the linseed oil and seed produced by the flax plant for their external trade, flax fiber and, on a smaller scale, hemp provided raw materials that local weavers could make into cloth and cordage, despite the considerable time required to process them.

Flax and hemp require similar agricultural management and processing to transform them into fiber. To encourage local production (and perhaps to reinforce the bounties offered by the British), several treatises on growing and handling flax and hemp in North America appeared in the 1760s.[30] At the turn of the nineteenth century, as the newly formed United States sought to create an independent manufacturing base using its own raw materials, combined with a new emphasis on scientific farming, other tracts appeared. Of particular interest are a pamphlet simply called *Hemp*, written by John Beale Bordley of Maryland in 1799, and a document handwritten by Thomas Aldred of Chester County about 1801.[31] These accounts, combined with evidence from local sources, provide insight into the knowledge, labor, equipment, and time required to extract fiber from flax and hemp.

All the treatises began with the soils best suited for growing the plants, fertilizing and plowing methods, and appropriate fallow periods, thereby demonstrating the high level of agrarian expertise involved in successful management of flax and hemp. Noting that the choice of seed affected the quality of linen fiber, Aldred asserted, "Connecticut seed is Better than Pennsylvania but Dutch seed is probably best." If a farmer did not have his own flaxseed from a previous year's crop, he could buy it from a neighbor or a local merchant.[32] In addition to the international market for flaxseed and linseed oil, therefore, there was a steady local demand for it as livestock feed or to be planted for fiber.

The first stages of flax and hemp production had to be incorporated into the busy schedules of American farmers. Depending on the weather, one could sow flaxseed or hempseed from mid-March to the end of April; George Brinton, for example, began his plowing on April 5 and planted his seed about the middle of the month.[33] Flax fields generally ranged in size from one quarter of an acre to an acre and a half; hemp fields, where they existed, were slightly smaller. According to Bordley, a quarter acre of hemp "would give [a farmer] more than he would want of traces, leading lines and other rope."[34] As a rule, an acre of flax fiber crop required two to two and a half bushels of seed, but seed production required only one and a half bushels of seed per acre.[35] Bordley further suggested that two bushels of hempseed per acre be planted for rope production and three for cloth.[36] Thus one had to have a clear idea of the ultimate use of the plants before sowing the seed.

Depending on the amount of land to be planted, a person could either do all the work alone or hire someone to do the job.[37] Men were responsible for plowing the flax and hemp fields, which they did in conjunction with their other agricultural activities, but women as well as men sowed the seed.[38]

Throughout the growing period, the flax required regular weeding to ensure long, strong fiber. Even this seemingly simple job required skill. As it was in Europe at the time, weeding was probably the job of women and children. Aldred urged caution in the kind of workers one employed, however, and warned against the use of "young and unskillful persons [as they] frequently pull up and spoil the flax," and if children worked at this task "they ought to be mixed with those [people] of more experience."[39]

When flax was harvested, sometime near the end of July, and slightly later if the plant was to be used for seed, the entire plant was pulled up by its roots, sorted into bundles according to length, and stacked immediately to dry (Fig.1).[40] In Pennsylvania, men and women shared this work, but because pulling the plant out of the ground required strength, children were not involved at this stage except to assist in removing weeds before the plants were stacked.[41]

Following a two-week drying period, laborers, who were usually men, rippled the stalks to remove the seed. Rippling involved pulling the stems of the plant through the teeth of a rippling comb (a slab of wood set with coarse teeth made of wood or iron); the action caused the seeds to drop onto a winnowing cloth. The workers then winnowed or threshed the seed by beating it with flails. (A flail is a tool with a wooden handle to which a shorter piece of wood is attached so that it moves freely.) This process allowed air currents to remove the chaff from the seed. The men further cleaned the seed by passing it through special sieves, after which they spread it to dry in a barn loft. These first processes in flax production required specialized equipment in the form of rippling combs, flails, sieves, and winnowing cloths. A farmer could purchase these implements from a local artisan, make them himself, or buy imported tools from a nearby retailer.[42]

Aldred noted that there were different qualities of flaxseed, suggesting that the poorer seed combined with husks made good fodder for livestock, but the seed to be used for the following year's harvest should be rippled and winnowed indoors to prevent it from blowing away. All the instructions for flax processing advocated that even if the timing was inconvenient, rippling to remove the seed should be done before the plant was set out to rot. Indeed, one of the complaints from Irish growers was that "a considerable Part of [Pennsylvania] Flax-Seed is found not to grow by Reason that many Persons do rott the

STRAPPARE IL LINO.

Piante di Lino.   5. Fascetto di due Case
Mode di Strapparlo.   6. Birla di Fascetti a
Casolle dopo Strappato.   causa di pioggia
Due Casolle distese.   7. Modo di farla

Figure 1. This man is pulling the flax plants up by the roots. After tying them in bundles, he stacks them or spreads them out to dry. In the foreground are individual flax plants that show their length (approximately two to three feet), seeds, and roots. *Strappare il lino* (plate 2). From G. B. Trecco, *Coltivazione e Governo del Lino Marzuolo con Dodici Tavole in Rame* (Vicenza, 1792). Permission of the American Textile History Museum, Lowell, Massachusetts.

Flax before they Thresh the seed."[43] Although this practice might have saved time in the short and agriculturally busy period between harvesting and watering the plant, it obviously harmed the seed.

Once dried, the seed could be stored until ready for market or sowing. Flax, however, according to Aldred, should never be laid up before it was rotted (or retted) because that rendered the fiber harsh and coarse. Besides, the water in spring or summer was "not so soft and warm as in harvest," and one would lose a year before the linen could be used. The labor-intensive job of rotting the plant, therefore, had to occur during the busy harvest period. Many authors writing about flax and hemp processing agreed that this step required great skill and luck in order not to destroy the fiber.[44]

Men were responsible for the heavy and dirty work involved in rotting the outer stem of the plant to expose the fiber. Pennsylvanians "dew retted" the flax and hemp more frequently than they water retted it, despite the advice of such authorities as Quincy, Aldred, and Bordley that the latter method produced the finest fiber. Dew retting involved spreading the plants on the ground for a period of twenty to thirty days, watering them to keep them wet, and turning them frequently to expose all the surfaces to moisture from dew or watering.[45] During this process, the plants had to be monitored closely to prevent fiber destruction.

Water retting was more laborious and filthy because the plants had to be submerged in a pool, preferably a trough especially dug for the purpose, lined with clay, and filled with water. Once in the trough, the plants were weighted with heavy stones and covered with sod. During submersion, if all the steps had not been carefully executed, the crop was subject to infestation by vermin and small reptiles that could damage the fiber.[46]

Water retting was faster than dew retting, taking only a week or two, but the initial preparation was more complex and time consuming and required access to a water source. Moreover, once the process was completed, the water was so polluted that fish could not survive in it.[47] If the farmer was more concerned with seed production than with the quality of the flax fiber, or if he was intent on producing only coarse goods, dew retting was the better alternative, as it required less expertise and labor.

After dew or water retting, the drained stalks had to be dried in a field. According to Aldred, women and children under the supervision of a male farmer could do this work. Once rotted and dried, the flax or hemp could be stored until the farmer had time and/or the appropriate help to process it further. Usually work on the fiber occurred from early winter until late spring after the agricultural season had ended and people had more leisure to engage in the time-consuming chores of flax or hemp dressing. John Bordley under-scored the seasonal rhythms of farm work when he noted that "hirelings" were more easily available in winter so that was when the heaviest work could be done.[48]

Although the operations involved to this point were labor intensive and time consuming, they required only the general agricultural knowledge most eighteenth-century farmers and their families pos-sessed and had brought from Europe. If the farmer's relatives could not handle the workload, he hired wage laborers, most of whom had no special training, a situation that changed very little during the eighteenth century.[49]

The next stages of processing, however, required sufficient expertise that some men specialized in these areas. Three major steps were in-volved in transforming rotted plants into fiber ready to be spun into yarn: breaking the plant to loosen the rotted outer stalk; scutching (also called *swingling*), which removed the bark and separated the fibers; and hackling, or combing the fibers, which aligned them for spinning.

Workers who broke flax and hemp most commonly used a wooden tool called a *break* (or *brake*) (Fig. 2, top), which they might have made themselves or bought from a skilled woodworker.[50] In 1765, Edmund Quincy suggested, "As the use of the common Hemp-brake is a laborious exercise, and consequently the labor is a great addition of the charge of preparing the Hemp for a market, it might be a great saving to the Farmers, in any town or place where much Hemp may be produced" to build a mill to do the work.[51] At the end of his treatise, he included plans for the construction and operation of such a mill (Fig. 3). There were a few water-powered hemp mills indicated in Chester County tax lists but none specifically designated for flax (although one could have been used for both).[52] Not surprisingly, the hemp mills were situated in the areas in which hemp fiber was present in the household inven-tories.[53] There were too few mills for most of the inhabitants with flax to have had access to them, thus the majority used hand tools to dress the fiber.[54]

Once the bark had been loosened, scutching removed it. A worker laid the fibers over a board and beat them with a blade-like device called a *scutching knife* that also began to separate the fibers (see Fig. 2, middle, and Fig. 4). Some evidence suggests that the onerous work of breaking and scutching was becoming somewhat mechanized by the last decades of the eighteenth century in flax and swingling mills.[55] Al-though the plans for Quincy's hemp mill indicate it only broke the fiber, swingling mills went one step further. According to Patri-cia Baines, the "breaking was achieved by passing a handful of flax

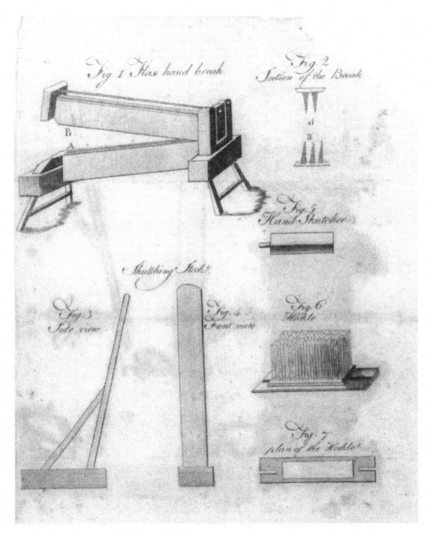

Figure 2. The tools required for flax dressing are the flax break (Figs. 1 and 2) to loosen the outer bark of the plant; scutching stocks (Figs. 3 through 5) for removing the bark; and hackles, or heckles (Figs. 6 and 7), for combing the fiber to make it tangle-free for spinning. From "The Manner of Raising and Dressing Flax, and Hemp," in *Dictionary of Arts and Sciences*, Doctor Tobias Smollett, trans. (Philadelphia, 1777). Permission of the Library Company of Philadelphia.

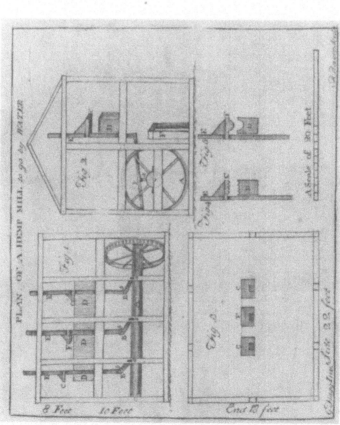

Figure 3. Flax and hemp processing required a lot of time and physical strength. This plan for a water-powered mill would have made the initial stages of breaking the stalks of the plant to loosen the outer bark much easier and faster. From Edmund Quincy, Esq., "Explanation of a Hemp Mill," in *A Treatise of Hemp-Husbandry* (Boston, 1765). Permission of the Library Company of Philadelphia.

Figure 4. The men on the left are preparing the dried flax plants for seed removal. The man in the center is beating the seeds off the stalk by holding the stems over a scutching board and striking them with a scutching knife. Once removed, the seeds fall to the floor onto a winnowing cloth that facilitates easy collection. "Hand Scutchers at Work," from *Great Industries of Great Britain*, vol. 1 (London: 1877–1880?), 212. Permission of the American Textile History Museum, Lowell, Massachusetts.

between fluted rollers, and the scutching by replacing the bat [scutching knife] with a wheel of four or twelve wooden blades" (Fig. 5). These mills would have reduced the physical labor required, sped up the dressing process, and increased the output substantially.[56]

The final step in flax or hemp preparation was hackling, or heckling, a process that straightened the fiber and separated the short strands from the long. The tool required was called a hackle, or heckle, and consisted of a board into which long, sharp iron or brass prongs were set; the hackler would need two or three hackles in graduated degrees of fineness (see Fig. 2, bottom, and Fig. 6).[57] William Lindsay (d. 1773) of Uwchlan Township had "10 Baggs of Cut Wire for Hackle Teeth" in his inventory, along with "63 plates Tin," suggesting that he was a tinsmith who made the hackles or sold the teeth to others to make their own tools.[58] Although some people might have

Figure 5. This eighteenth-century flax mill, or "machine," would have eased the labor associated with scutching. Replacing the scutching stock seen in Fig. 2, the twelve rotating blades protruding from the wheel would remove the broken bark from the fiber as the worker held it over the curved board and turned the wheel by hand. Acc. # 1992.5564. Permission of Chester County Historical Society, West Chester, Pennsylvania.

made the implements after buying the wire for the teeth, most would have purchased them from a local merchant or one of the specialized hackle makers working in the province.[59]

After hackling, the longer fibers were ready to be spun into linen yarn. The shorter fibers, called *tow*, required further processing with imported tow combs to align the tangled fibers, after which they could be used to make coarse goods such as bagging, rough sheets, or cordage.[60]

Although it is difficult to know to what extent the people who performed the breaking, scutching, or hackling of flax and hemp did so as a profession, at least some individuals in Pennsylvania considered themselves specialists in this area of fiber preparation. *Dressing* was a term used at the time to encompass all three operations. Newspaper advertisements show that men coming to the province as servants for sale were flax or hemp dressers by profession, and servants employed in that capacity worked in the rural areas.[61] In addition, county tax records identify "hemp workers," "flax hatchellers," "hemp hecklers," and "hemp dressers," most of whom would have worked with both fibers.[62] At least some of the men who specialized in hemp processing worked in mills, but the flax dressers would have operated as independent, often itinerant, artisans.[63]

In the first half of the eighteenth century, a majority of households with flax fiber did not have the appropriate equipment with which to process it. In these cases, the grower might have taken the fiber to a mill to be dressed or to the farm of someone who had the equipment with which to break and hackle it.[64] More likely, however, because flax and hemp processing was "the work of leisure winter," householders hired dressers or hacklers to live with them for several months while processing the flax and hemp that had been harvested a season earlier; some farmers also sold it undressed.[65] Breaks, scutching implements, and hackles were not overly large or unwieldy pieces of equipment, making it possible for skilled workers to carry their tools to a job, finish the work, and move on. If the farmer with flax fiber had processing equipment, the itinerant dresser could also use his employer's tools. As the community became established, and with it cloth manufacture, gradually more households that grew flax acquired the equipment with which to process it.[66] The ownership of flax-dressing tools peaked just prior to the American Revolution, as did possession of flaxseed. It is difficult to gauge to what extent this reflects the region's attempts at increased cloth production because of the nonimportation movement, however, or just the continuation of a trend that began in the 1730s and was spurred on by the strong grain and flaxseed prices in the decades before the Revolution.[67]

Although it was presumably a profitable specialization for some, flax

Figure 6. The last stage of flax dressing was hackling or combing the flax to make it smooth for spinning, using implements like these. The top hackle is simple and functional and would be used during the first stage of combing or to produce a coarse fiber. The long, sharp teeth are set comparatively far apart and the cover would offer protection from injury when the tool was not in use. The lower hackle has smaller, closer-set teeth and would create a fine fiber that was ready to spin. The decoration, including the initials "R. C." and the date "1769," suggests that this was probably made and used locally by someone of German background. Acc. #1987.1054.1-2 (top) and 1987.4571 (bottom). Permission of Chester County Historical Society, West Chester, Pennsylvania.

dressing did not require the same amount of skill as weaving or cloth finishing. Indeed, strength and stamina were as important as mastery in working up flax and hemp for spinning.[68] Furthermore, dressing fiber was too labor intensive and the specialists too few in number to be the only people doing the job. For the most part, there were more nonspecialists (including some women) working with flax and hemp than their more skilled counterparts.[69] These people were casual laborers and in most cases they also did such jobs as "work at wood," clear brush, and work "at flax and corn."[70] Finally, older children in a family could have done the needed fiber dressing without outside assistance. Households in other colonies that grew flax would have operated in a similar manner.[71]

Raising and processing flax and hemp required horticultural knowledge, an investment of time to make the requisite equipment or money to purchase it, and a substantial amount of labor. Moreover, the entire operation of planting, harvesting, rotting, and dressing flax and hemp occurred in conjunction with all the other labor- and time-intensive agricultural activities of Pennsylvania farm families. Among these was the processing of wool, the other major fiber used in Pennsylvania textile manufacture.

Unlike flax, American-grown wool did not figure directly in the Atlantic trade, but raising sheep had as varied and important a role as flax in the local economy beyond fiber production. The mixed farming practiced by most Chester County residents, for example, necessitated the use of fertilizers after the first decades of settlement. Cow manure was in short supply, and sheep dung was important enough as a fertilizer to render wool a by-product.[72] William Keith, a former governor of Pennsylvania, noted in a report to the British Board of Trade in 1728 that the colonists kept sheep primarily for fertilizing purposes, but rather than waste the wool, they employed their servants to work it up during the winter months.[73] One of the other major reasons for keeping the animals was as a source of food. The English had been eating sheep in quantity for more than a century. This practice was not limited to old mutton available only after the animal was beyond producing good quality wool but included meat from sheep in their prime.[74] Despite suggestions to the contrary, throughout the eighteenth century, Chester County account books show that inhabitants continued to share the English taste for mutton and lamb.[75] Early Americans also used wool for products other than cloth making. Unprocessed fiber, especially the lowest grades in the form of discarded wool and rags became stuffing for mattresses known as flocks beds, and hat makers needed a great deal of unspun wool to make felt, a nonwoven fabric that used heat and pressure to mat the fiber together. In addition, parchment and clothing such as artisans' leather aprons were made from sheepskin.[76] Sheep were important enough to Chester County's rural economy to justify keeping them even if there was no local cloth industry. For the weavers who did practice their craft, the animal's fleece provided the raw materials to make into warm clothing and bedding.

Although wool was not as labor intensive to work up as flax and hemp, its processing was yet another task to add to the busy routine of rural life. Farmers who kept sheep had to grow the grain, maize, and hay necessary to feed them when cold weather rendered grazing impossible. Even if the animals roamed freely, they still required shelter and feeding in the winter, which was also the season for the intensive work of lambing; starting in February, the ewes bred the previous September produced their offspring.[77]

In Pennsylvania, and in North America more generally, the wool produced by most sheep was uneven in quality until the end of the eighteenth century, partly because lack of tending meant that debris that accumulated in their fleece made it difficult to clean and also because living in a climate of hot, humid summers and cold winters was detrimental to the animals' health. Moreover, because sheep were just as, if not more important for meat, farmers generally did not try to improve the breeds until very late in the eighteenth century when they imported merino sheep.[78] As with flax cultivation, if fiber had been the sole reason for keeping sheep, farmers would have thought more about how they cared for the animals.

However mediocre the wool, it had to be removed regularly, usually annually and sometimes twice a year, by shearing, a task of prime importance because unshorn animals could become ill in the heat of the summer. Pennsylvania farmers like George Brinton usually sheared their sheep in late May, having washed them a week earlier by driving them through a fast-moving stream, dunking them under the water, then turning them into a clean, enclosed pasture to wait a few days for the wool to dry.[79] After the sheep dried, the shearer clipped the fleece off the animal using iron shears either bought from a local blacksmith or imported (Fig. 7).[80] Less than 10 percent of the population owned a pair of shears, and, given that about half the households kept sheep, either they shared their equipment or, more likely, a small group of men skilled in sheep shearing moved around the community working for wages.[81]

Clipping was considered a man's job given the required strength and skill. Indeed, one expert on sheep states, "without a doubt the shearing of the sheep . . . is the most arduous and dirty of the animal husbandry tasks."[82] The shearer had to hold the struggling animal immobile while cutting off the fleece. Men who were proficient at this task could clip about forty sheep a day. The average number of sheep owned by individuals was about twelve, so a farmer would have had to hire a shearer for less than a day. If a farmer did the job himself it might have taken slightly longer.[83] A skilled shearer would remove the fleece in one piece and roll it to be stored until sold or sorted; someone less skilled might have simply collected sections of the fleece in baskets.

Because wool is an animal fiber and is shorter than flax and hemp, it requires different skills and equipment to transform into cloth. The sorter, who might have also been the shearer, or perhaps the farmer or spinner, separated the fleece into its varying qualities, depending

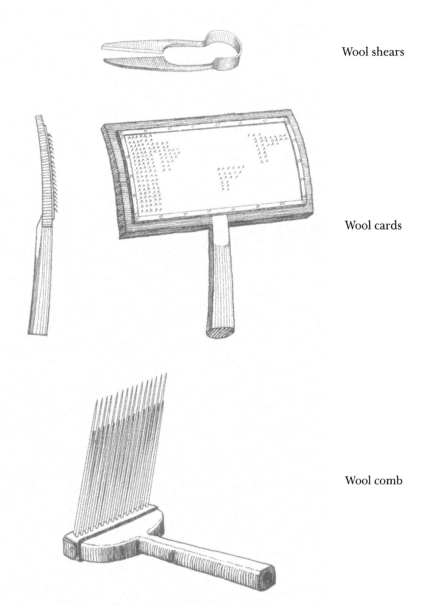

Wool shears

Wool cards

Wool comb

Figure 7. For much of the eighteenth century, wool-processing tools—shears, cards, and combs—(or the materials to make them) were imported from Britain. By the end of the century, the tools were made locally. From Marion L. Channing, *Textile Tools of Colonial Homes* (Marion, Mass., 1969), 10–12.

on the ultimate use of the wool: fine for inner clothing, coarser for outerwear and some household textiles. After sorting, the wool had to be washed again.[84] To avoid damage while cleansing the sheared fleece (which could easily become felted and useless if handled too much), the fibers first had to be separated, immersed in large tubs of warm water, turned occasionally, and then rinsed. Once washed, the wool had to be picked, a job performed by women who did the work for pay as well as for their own households.[85] The most efficient method of picking quantities of wool was to spread it on a hurdle (a table with openings for the dirt to fall through) set on trestles, beat it with sticks, and separate the fibers with forks.[86] Because Chester County wool was not intended for large-scale commercial production, pickers would have dispensed with the hurdles, sticks, and forks, and simply pulled the fiber apart with their fingers.

Depending on the final use for the wool, dyeing might occur at this stage. In Pennsylvania, there were numerous professional dyers, many of whom either worked with a cloth fuller at his mill or combined the skills of fulling and dyeing.[87] Although such artisans usually dyed finished cloth, they also colored fleece, as dyeing at this stage allowed a different blend of hues than dyeing yarn or cloth (Fig. 8).[88]

After picking the wool but before spinning it into yarn, the worker aligned the fibers so the spinner could make a smooth, even thread. There were two ways of doing this, depending on the length and quality of the fiber—shorter, finer fibers were carded to make woolen yarn, while longer, coarser fibers were combed for worsted yarn.

Workers carded most wool fiber using a pair of implements called cards. Each card consisted of a piece of leather with rows of closely set bent wire teeth inserted into it, the whole of which was attached to a piece of wood approximately ten inches wide and six to eight inches long with a handle (see Fig. 7). The need for wire made it difficult for farmers to make their own cards. Because most owners of these tools had more than one pair and because the cards wore out after processing about forty pounds of wool, they had to be replaced at regular intervals. Most people would have bought the tools from a local shopkeeper who obtained them from Philadelphia merchants throughout the eighteenth century. With the establishment of the local wire mills, cards also could have been available from Chester County manufacturers.[89]

Until the creation of mills to do the work late in the eighteenth century, carding was a household task performed by women and children when time permitted.[90] Unlike weaving, which required good lighting, carding could be done in the evening when other work had ceased because of darkness. One traveler to the United States in 1794

Figure 8. The professional dyers who operated in eighteenth-century Chester County kept track of their dye recipes in books like this one. In addition to the recipes, the book contains samples of raw fleece attached with sealing wax (such as those shown on this page), yarn, and fabric that would be useful for showing a customer the finished color. This is an unusually early example of such a book. Dating originally from about 1710 and likely belonging to John Pim, the book contained information that was valuable enough to be handed on to subsequent generations of dyers; it seems that William Chambers was still using it in 1792. Pim Papers, 1710–1714, Ms. #13785, Chester County Historical Society, West Chester, Pennsylvania. Photograph by author reprinted with permission of the Chester County Historical Society, West Chester, Pennsylvania.

commented that "every housewife keeps a quantity of these cards by her to employ her family in the evenings when they have nothing to do out of doors."[91] Hector St. John de Crèvecoeur suggested that the women carried out this work during the summer in the barns where the "neatness of our boarded floors, the great draught of air caused by the opened doors . . . and their breadth afford them an opportunity of spinning long threads, of carding at their ease."[92] In the barns, the residual dirt left in the fleece after washing could fall on the floor during carding without the same need to worry about cleaning up as in the house. Not only did women perform and supervise the carding of their own family's wool, but some, like Margaret Rock, who carded for George Brinton at his home, hired themselves out to do the work.[93]

Wool combing was the other method of preparing wool fiber for spinning a strong, smooth yarn called "worsted." Contrary to carding, which was the work of women and children, wool combing was a job done by professionally trained men. It required specialized equipment in the form of a pair of combs with long, tapered teeth made of tempered steel, a post to which one comb was fixed, and a small stove for heating the teeth of the comb (see Fig. 7). Like flax hacklers, a wool comber either purchased imported tools or assembled them from materials fashioned locally by a blacksmith or in a wire mill.[94] To prepare fiber for spinning worsted yarn, the worker hung warmed wool onto one heated comb attached to a post, drawing the other comb through the long wool; the heat melted the lanolin oil present in wool, making it easier to comb. This action separated out the short fibers, which could be used as mattress stuffing, for example, or for spinning coarser yarn, and laid the long ones parallel.

Only long-fibered wool could be combed. To obtain this type of fleece, sheep had to be very well fed and cared for—an uncommon occurrence in eighteenth-century North America. Despite the dearth of long wool, some worsted production did occur, with less than 2 percent of the population in Chester County, most of whom were British, owning wool combs or worsted yarn.[95] The small amount of worsted present in the inventories suggests that wool combing was rarely if ever performed by unskilled members of a household and was done almost exclusively by professional artisans.[96] The majority of wool combers were inmates who would have worked either for a set wage or with an agreement to share their earnings with their landlord.[97] Americans did not produce enough worsted wool to be a threat to the British industries, but officials perceived the more extensive woolen production as worrisome.

Because England needed flax and hemp to supplement its own pro-

duction of naval stores such as ropes and canvas for sailcloth, it offered the colonists incentives to grow flax and hemp with the expectation that if the fiber went to England, the products would not be
manufactured in the colonies. Wool was another story. The poor
quality of the American wool made it undesirable for English manufacturing, so it followed that where there were sheep (as there were
throughout the northern colonies) there would be local cloth making.
As Arthur Cole notes, British wool manufacturing was "popularly considered the backbone of the country's strength, the source of her
greatness. Hence any threat or possible misfortune to that enterprise
was to be warded off by the most effective measures available." As a result, rather than the bounties offered for colonial flax and hemp production, the British enacted numerous laws to curb American wool
manufacture.[98]

Regardless of their value or threat to Britain's imperial economy,
flax and sheep were essential components of the agricultural system
developed by early Americans. When demand for Irish flaxseed increased, farmers already growing flax for their own use could harvest
and sell its seed. Hemp, with its more specialized uses, was less pervasive, and British encouragement was no inducement to produce more
of it. Conversely, discouragement of sheep raising and wool production did not curtail this activity for the simple reason that fiber was
only one aspect of the animals' importance to the colonists. Despite
their many uses, however, sheep and flax provided the needed raw
materials for local cloth production. The seasonal nature of the cereal
agriculture practiced by many Pennsylvania farmers provided the
time to process the fiber. In addition to time, this resource-intensive
craft needed an abundance of workers, some of them skilled, and the
evolving labor systems of the region meant that manufacturing grew
alongside farming.

In Pennsylvania, trained workers employed by a farmer to do their
specialized jobs performed some of the work, such as flax dressing
and wool combing. Even the operations requiring less skill, such as
sowing seed, harvesting flax, and carding wool, often used the labor of
men and women hired from outside an individual household. The intense work involved in flax management and sheep husbandry had to
be carried out along with all the other farm work, much of it during
the busiest agricultural periods. Moreover, although each tool individ-
ually may not have been expensive, collectively the equipment—ripples,
flails, sieves, breaks, scutching knives, hackles, tow combs, sheep shears,
wool cards, and wool combs—represented a considerable investment
in either capital or labor. As Mary Schweitzer points out, on the farm,

investment "consisted of taking time away from income-producing activity" to do such things as make tools.[99] These tools were often evaluated as part of a group of items, making it difficult to assign individual worth, but wool cards, shears, and flax breaks were valued at roughly one shilling whereas a loom was about £2, or forty shillings. As a result, regardless of whether textile tools were made or purchased, they represented an important outlay of resources that enabled a family to produce goods for their own use, or for sale or trade.

Given the skill, money, and time needed for fiber processing, it is not surprising that many of the eighteenth-century North American households did not own either fiber or the equipment with which to process it. Fewer than 40 percent of inventoried estates included flax fiber; at its peak, fewer than 25 percent had wool; and ownership of hemp fiber never passed 5 percent.[100] Even adjusting the numbers upward to account for the seasonality of the labor, workers who may have used their own tools, fiber that might have been disposed of or sold prior to death, or the existence of fiber quantities too small to be recorded by an assessor, it is still true that a majority of Pennsylvanian households did not engage in flax, hemp, or wool production.

Of all the fibers used, flax was the most common and took the most time and labor to produce. Compared to the 30 percent of Chester County households with flax, only 20 percent had wool, although more than half had sheep. With the exception of the early years (1715–1718), the percentage of the decedent population owning sheep stayed relatively static throughout the eighteenth century, as did the percentage of those possessing wool fiber. Although fiber production and processing experienced early growth followed by comparative stability during the eighteenth century in Chester County, the nineteenth century witnessed dramatic transformations in some aspects of these early stages of cloth production.

Several factors converged at the end of the eighteenth century to modify the nature of fiber production in rural areas and with it the connection between local and international economies. Advancing textile technology triggered these alterations. At the most basic level, farmers experimented with breeding their sheep more carefully to obtain higher quality wool. In addition, increasingly available Southern cotton began to replace flax. By 1820, North American cloth production had undergone a significant transformation.

Water-powered carding machines had the earliest affect on woolen production. By the first decade of the nineteenth century, they dotted the New England and Pennsylvania countryside as grist- and fulling-mill operators added carding to their operations. Initially, this helped female domestic spinners by eliminating the onerous job of hand carding the wool.[101] Beginning in 1810, small woolen mills began to replace home production, however, and the new machinery required a better caliber of raw material. No longer was it sufficient to grow generic sheep suitable for both meat and fiber; the fledgling woolen industry obliged farmers systematically to breed sheep with adequate fleece for use with the new machines.

Early in the nineteenth century, a few enterprising individuals imported Spanish merino sheep into the United States and bred them with local stock. By the 1830s, an animal with wool suitable for the new carding machinery and for the production of medium- and low-quality cloth for the American market had replaced the less satisfactory American sheep that had been raised in the eighteenth century.[102] This shift to careful breeding led to increased agricultural specialization on the part of sheep farmers. Beginning in the 1790s, the number of Chester County households owning a few sheep declined (as it did in Essex County, Massachusetts), while the average number of sheep per sheep owner increased, suggesting that for the first time since settlement wool fiber production for local mills could be a lucrative but specialized activity.[103]

Flax growing, too, underwent a significant change, but only because it was supplanted by cotton, not in response to new flax processing technologies. Although cotton had been grown in South Carolina since about the middle of the eighteenth century, the cotton gin, patented in 1794, took over the time-consuming task of removing the seeds from the fiber. This in turn provided an abundance of raw material for the new cotton spinning mills established in the north during the 1790s.[104] Cotton could easily be substituted for most items that had previously been made of linen—it was easier to wash and dye, and it was far less labor intensive to grow and process than flax. Cotton had to be planted, tended, and picked, but slave labor kept these costs relatively low, and the gin removed the most painstaking task of seed removal. The impact was profound. By 1830, flax production, which had been a significant component of the agricultural work cycle of both New England and Pennsylvania in the eighteenth century, had all but disappeared. Moreover, in Chester County, as linen manufacture declined, so did flaxseed production, despite its former value as an export commodity.

Although North Americans did not universally produce and process fiber within their individual households, the work engaged many in the community at one stage or another and highlights the growing complexity of the rural economy. At the household level, those who grew fiber could use it for their own textile needs or sell it locally. At the community level, the presence of various specialists (who may have been itinerant professionals or simply skilled neighbors) in Chester County allowed people who chose to do other things or who may not have had access to land or tools not to have to undertake the work. In addition, it provided employment opportunities for both skilled and unskilled men and women. Finally, flaxseed production yielded an export crop that tied rural regions of Connecticut and Pennsylvania into the international Atlantic trading network, bringing cash into the local economy and permitting participation in the growing consumer culture of the period.

Despite the ability of some farm households to buy imported goods, chief among them cloth, most colonists continued to supplement imports with items they made themselves.[105] Indeed, the very act of manufacture gave both the internal and external economy a dynamism that permitted responsiveness to the technological and economic changes during the Early Republic period. Although North American textile manufacture did not emerge full-blown at this time, cloth making remained, as it had always been, an integral component of northern American rural life. Moreover, during the early period of industrialization, new technologies and old traditions coexisted.

Chapter 4

Spinning and Knitting

On October 16, 1794, Elizabeth Drinker, a wealthy Quaker from Philadelphia, had lived at her new country home about six miles from the city for "one third of a year," as she put it. That day, during a walk with her daughter Nancy, she stopped to rest at a place where she had an encounter so noteworthy she described it at length in her diary:

[T]he place I stop'd at belongs to one John Shields, who does not live there, there was no body but an old Dutch woman, name'd Nany White, she was busy spining tow, about three score and ten years old. I ask'd her if she was spining to make cloath for her own ware, on no! I take it in, at a 1 1/2 d a cut, how many cuts dost thou spin in a day? she was not willing to tell, can thee spin twelve? oh no! six? No. 3 then? maybe so, then thee earns 4 1/2 d a day? yes some times;—I had but a nine penny peice in my pocket which I gave her, and say'd if she would except of it, she might venture to take a days rest, as that was two days earning, she was much pleas'd and gave me many thanks. Well, thought I . . . , to be delighted with so trifling an acquistion.[1]

Nany White could move her small spinning wheel outdoors to work on a fine day. An accomplished spinner, she could instinctively feel the size and quality of the yarn she made, so a chat with a passerby did not interrupt her work. In contrast, as an affluent urban woman, Drinker did not spin yarn, although she did sew and knit for the use of her own household. She would have purchased all the sewing thread and textiles she needed and even her servants would not have spun. In both Pennsylvania and Europe, this was rural, not urban women's work. Although Drinker was surprised that Nany White spun to make money rather than for her own use, she was more aghast at how little Nany earned for her labors. What Drinker seems not to have realized was that the work of the "old Dutch woman" was familiar and common to many rural females.

In cloth-making regions of North America and Europe, women's labor was critical in transforming processed fiber into the yarn required for textile production because such large quantities of yarn were needed. Yet, even when females received payment for spinning, and

regardless of the skill involved, Europeans saw it as simply an extension of domestic work that lacked the craft status of the male-dominated
tasks of weaving, dyeing, and finishing. Although gender divisions of
labor in textile production were not rigid, before the nineteenth-
century introduction of the industrial spinning mule (a heavy machine of multiple spindles that had to be physically pushed back and
forth), which required male strength to operate, spinning was
women's work (Fig. 9).[2] Indeed, people deemed the early modern European social order completely turned on its head if men took over
this operation.[3] In the New World, until industrialization in the early
nineteenth century, as long as spinning was done by hand, women did
it, whether slave or free and regardless of where they lived. As we
have seen, not all early North American females made yarn, however.
Factors such as wealth, stage of life, and whether their home was in
the city or the country determined who engaged in the work.

Hand knitting, too, was the domain of women, and much of the
yarn they produced in early North America they also knit into garments. In late sixteenth-century England, however, an enterprising
gentleman by the name of Reverend William Lee had invented a knitting machine, or frame.[4] By the time settlers moved into Pennsylvania,
framework knitting, which required great physical effort, had become
a male-dominated craft that knitters transplanted to their new homes.
Although it never completely supplanted women's hand knitting, it
was another area where European traditions continued.

Spinning and hand knitting may not have had equal status with the
weaving and finishing processes done by men, but that did not preclude females from becoming an integral part of the growing local
economy. Many women were paid for their spinning or used it as a
medium of exchange in commercial transactions with local storekeepers or artisans. In addition, some hired themselves out to do the work,
and a few were apprenticed to learn the skill. In Pennsylvania, spinning (and sometimes knitting) provided a means for females to earn
an income, to make spending money, or to increase the economic well
being of their households.

Beginning in the late 1700s, technological innovations altered
women's role in textile production and ultimately in their household
chores. As water-powered spinning mills replaced work in the home
and cotton substituted for flax yarn, rural women no longer had to
spend long hours making yarn and could devote themselves to other
tasks. Prior to the mechanical improvements, however, women's participation was essential in providing the raw materials needed for knitting or cloth making.

Figure 9. The invention of the spinning mule altered which gender did most of the spinning. Shown here in an English factory about 1835, the mules consisted of hundreds of spindles that had to be moved back and forth on a track. The strength involved meant that men became the spinners; women assisted them by repairing broken threads while children often worked under the machines to keep the dust and lint to a minimum. "Mule Spinning/Fisher Son & Co. London 1835." Drawn by T. Allom/Engraved by J. W. Lowry. Plate 11 from Edward Baines, Jr., *History of the Cotton Manufacture in Great Britain* (London, 1835). Permission of the American Textile History Museum, Lowell, Massachusetts.

Spinning involves the creation of a long, continuous yarn by twisting (spinning) the fibers of wool, cotton, or flax that have been separated and aligned during carding or combing. The twisting action gives the fibers strength and can be accomplished most simply by rolling them between one's thumb and forefinger. A spindle performs this action more efficiently and, when a drive wheel turns it, the process becomes even faster. Textile specialist Dorothy Burnham describes the spindle as "a stick or rod which is rotated causing attached fibers to adhere to each other and form a thread. A hand spindle is usually weighted at one end with a spindle whorl. The spindle can be held in the hand, supported in various ways, or dropped to spin freely; it can also be mounted and turned by wheel or machine."[5] Although it may initially seem difficult to make yarn that is lump free and a consistent size, once learned, spinning becomes almost intuitive, based on a sense of feel. Unlike the more complex work of weaving (described in the next chapter), yarn production requires little concentration—a spinning wheel can fit into the corner of a kitchen, and the work can be done while watching children, waiting for a stew to cook, or visiting and chatting. As a result, spinning was a job suitable for women to work into their household routines, although some, like Nany White, earned money for it.

The spinning wheel has become the icon for the colonial era, although it was by no means a ubiquitous tool.[6] As we have seen, the majority of households did not have fiber, and those who grew it had to either sell it or make further investments in equipment and time to spin it into yarn. Moreover, although yarn making was the responsibility of women, not all were proficient at the task, nor did all households have the spinning and yarn-winding equipment with which to perform the work. Averaged over the eighteenth century, about 60 percent of Chester County decedents had these devices listed among their personal property. That so many households (40 percent) did not have these tools was partly because not all women knew how to spin or they were wealthy enough to hire others to do it, and partly because spinning equipment required a lot of expertise to make and usually had to be purchased. Some women inherited their wheels, but, like any items used regularly, the tools needed replacement as they wore out. When this happened in Chester County, people could buy imported wheels, purchase them from Philadelphia artisans, or obtain them from the professional spinning-wheel makers working in the county.[7] In any case, as with fiber processing devices, spinning equipment represented a further capital investment.

Spinning wheels were specialized tools. Most wheels were designed and built to accommodate the different properties inherent in flax and wool. In addition, another apparatus, a reel used for winding and measuring the finished yarn, usually accompanied spinning equipment. Finally, the majority of the households engaged in spinning had more than one wheel on which to spin both fibers, or to allow several people to work at the same time.

Three types of wheels were consistently noted in the probate inventories—big (or wool) wheels for wool, little wheels for flax, and the more generic spinning wheels on which both fibers could be spun. The wool wheel consisted of a large wheel with a single drive band attached to it at one end and a spindle at the other (Fig. 10). Because this type of wheel was best suited for shorter fibers, one could also use it to spin cotton or tow (the residual, short fibers left after combing flax). The spinner turned the wheel with her right hand while drawing out the thread attached to the spindle with her left. As the yarn

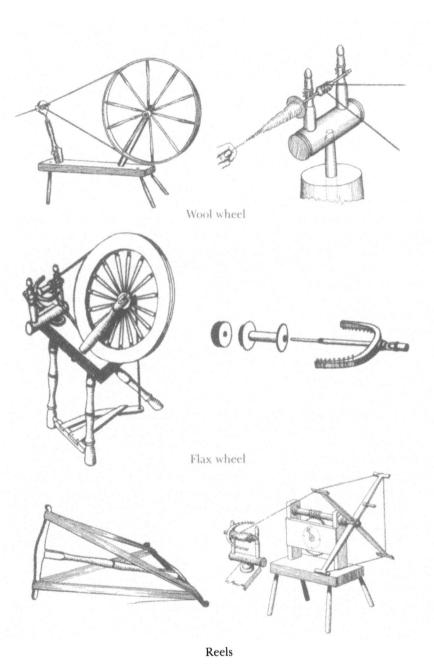

Wool wheel

Flax wheel

Reels

Figure 10. The long fibers of flax and the shorter wool fibers required different amounts of twist, making it desirable to have specialized spinning wheels for each. Reels wound the spun yarn into skeins for knitting or weaving. From Marion L. Channing, *Textile Tools of Colonial Homes* (Marion, Mass., 1969), 20–21, 28–29.

lengthened, she walked backward until she could no longer turn the wheel, walked forward while she wound the thread on the spindle, and then repeated the process. Using this wheel, a proficient spinner could spin two to three ounces of blanket yarn an hour, or about a pound a day, working continuously.[8] Because most women, especially if married with young children, would not have had the time to spin for extended periods unless they had help, the accumulation of the six to eight pounds of yarn required to make a blanket could take quite a bit of time—up to a week if working constantly, more if not. The large size of the wheel (approximately thirty-six inches in diameter) and base (approximately thirty-six inches long), which when fully assembled might be as large as five feet high and five feet long, combined with the room required for the spinner to move back and forth, meant that wool wheels took up considerably more space in a home when in use than little wheels or spinning wheels. They could, however, be disassembled by removing the wheel and stored when idle. Despite their size, in Chester County there were more wheels designated for wool than for flax.[9]

Flax, or little, wheels had a much smaller drive wheel (approximately nineteen inches in diameter), with a doubled drive belt attached to a mechanism consisting of a flyer and a bobbin that replaced the spindle of the wool wheel (see Fig. 10; Fig. 11). The spinner was seated and turned the wheel by means of an attached foot treadle, freeing both hands to manipulate the fiber to form the yarn. The independent motion of the flyer and bobbin caused the thread first to be spun, then pulled in and wound on the bobbin automatically. Because the smaller size of the drive wheel gave less twist to the yarn, this device was more suitable for spinning longer, stronger fibers such as flax and hemp (technically, one could spin wool on this type of wheel, but there would be a tendency to underspin the yarn, causing it to be less strong). In addition, flax wheels (approximately two and a half feet high and wide) took up much less space in the home than their wool-spinning counterparts. Using a small wheel, a good spinner could produce the two pounds of flax needed to make a coarse shirt in about five days of concentrated work; finer yarn would take much longer.[10]

The term *spinning wheel* specifically referred to wheels that could be used for both wool and flax. They were similar to flax wheels, although larger (approximately three and a third feet high and wide, with a wheel diameter of twenty-six inches). Because the operators sat, spinning wheels did not require the same amount of space for walking back and forth as the wool wheel. As a result, flax and spinning wheels could have been kept in a kitchen and used when time permitted,

Distaff

Flaxwheel

Orifice

Bobbin and flyer
mechanism

Maidens

Flyer

Tension device

Bobbin

Spindle

Entire unit is called "mother of all"

Figure 11. Hackled flax was spread onto a distaff to keep the fibers in place
for even spinning. The traditional association of females with spinning is reinforced by the nomenclature of the various parts of the spinning wheel: the
distaff, "maidens," "orifice," and "mother of all." This Chester County flax
wheel with its attached distaff was made in the late eighteenth century and
stamped by its maker, J. Fox. Acc. # 72 TT 59. Courtesy of Chester County
Historical Society, West Chester, Pennsylvania. The flyer and bobbin mechanism is from a flax wheel owned by the author; photograph by author.

while big wool wheels might have needed a designated space like an upper chamber in the house or perhaps the barn; they might have been specially assembled for more extended periods of use.[11] Issues of space and versatility may help account for the fact that most of the households with spinning implements owned the generic kind.[12]

Yarn spun for weaving required measuring to produce the desired length and width of cloth; for knitting, yardage was less important than weight, but yarn had to be plied (two or more strands of thread twisted together to make a thicker stronger yarn).[13] In both cases, yarn had to be removed from the spinning wheel for further processing. Reels permitted a spinner to wind the yarn off the spindle or bobbin into skeins for weighing and measuring to determine value and quantity (see Fig.10; Fig. 12). A reel could be a simple hand-held device (often called a *niddy-noddy*) around which a spinner wound the yarn, or a more elaborate piece of equipment called a *check* (or *clock* or *click*) *reel*, which counted each revolution to measure the length— essential knowledge for the weaver who would use the finished product. If a spinning wheel appeared in an inventory, it was very likely accompanied by a reel.[14]

All of the wheels and reels described here could have fit easily into the houses of most eighteenth-century North Americans.[15] In fact, throughout the eighteenth century, a majority of the people who owned spinning wheels had two or more. The presence of several wheels suggests that people spun both wool and flax and needed the appropriate tools. It also could indicate that there were several females available in a family to do the work or that the householder hired people to do it. Whatever the reason, it took about six to ten people spinning to manufacture enough yarn to supply one weaver.[16]

Spinning formed a major component of what historian Laurel Ulrich calls the "female economy," and in Pennsylvania this operated on two levels: some women produced yarn for home consumption only, some for commercial purposes, and some for both.[17] It was generally understood that a spinning wheel "belonged" to the woman who used it, either because a father, husband, a female relative, or a friend had given it to her, or she purchased her own. In 1718, almost 38 percent of decedent Chester County households had at least one spinning wheel and this number grew steadily throughout the century so that by 1795, 67 percent had one; female spinning-wheel owners mirrored this trend. By the 1770s, well over half the inventoried women had wheels; later, the numbers began to decline.

Women could acquire spinning equipment in different ways. Frequently, a husband bequeathed the household spinning wheel to his wife, either because she owned it prior to marriage or because he had

Figure 12. These reels are used to wind yarn from the bobbin of the spinning wheel into skeins. The small tool in the foreground is a hand reel, also called a "niddy-noddy." It is held in one hand and moved in a pattern that ensures the yarn is wound on the appropriate ends of the crosspieces. The larger reel, called a click or check reel, is turned by hand. As the yarn is wound onto the spokes, the gear-and-peg mechanism clicks against the wood piece below it to signify the number of revolutions, thereby measuring the length of the skein—essential information for a weaver. These tools were made in Chester County, but similar equipment exists wherever hand textile production occurred. Acc. # 1992.5218 (click reel) and 1994.2640 (niddy-noddy). Permission of Chester County Historical Society, West Chester, Pennsylvania.

acquired it for her afterward and she continued to need it. Margaret Boyd's husband, in his 1754 will, gave her "her Little Wheel She brought."[18] Samuel Maxfield, who died in 1774, left his daughters the spinning wheels that had been theirs while he lived. Women also specified in their wills that their spinning equipment be given to other females. Some, like Mary Sharp of Easttown, kept it within their families by leaving her "grand Children Viz Rachel and Mary the Children of my son Thomas my wooll and flax wheel and Reel" in 1779.[19] Others, like Jean Simontown of Tredyffrin, left in 1794, "to [her] Negroe woman Betty and to [her] Negroe Woman Dinah each a Spinning wheel and the Reel & Big Wheel between them."[20]

In addition to inheriting tools, single or widowed females might have to buy their own yarn-making equipment. Robert Todd, a spinning-wheel maker in East Whiteland Township, made wheels and reels that he sold to both men and women in the late 1790s.[21] Several vendue (auction) lists that delineate property sold from decedent estates show, for example, that in 1752, Jane Power bought flax, a flax wheel, and a reel, and, in 1773, Sarah Guthery bought a spinning wheel. Both women were widows whose household goods were being sold, likely to pay off debts; they probably purchased wheels that had been theirs before their husbands died.[22] Although it may seem surprising to have to pay for what had been one's own property, the law was less favorable to Pennsylvania widows than to widows in other colonies. If their husbands died suddenly, in debt and without a will, creditors were first in line for payment—regardless of the needs of the widow and her family. Personal property was sold first, but if that could not erase the debt, real estate followed. This left women like Power and Guthery no alternative but to buy back their own equipment (if they could afford it), perhaps in the hope that it would provide them with some means of support.[23] This pattern of bequests and purchases of yarn-making equipment suggest the gendered associations with it on both an emotional and practical level; spinning wheels were simultaneously a means of support and an emblem of womanly skill and industry.

Spinning was one of the core components of female training and culture, transmitted from generation to generation. Indeed, even the terminology for various parts of the wheel reinforces the gendered nature of spinning (see Fig. 11). Most obvious is the *distaff* that holds the flax for spinning—a word now associated with a woman's side of the family. But the names for the spindle and bobbin mechanism were also female oriented; the uprights that held it were called the *maidens,* the yarn was threaded through an *orifice,* and the entire unit was called the *mother of all.* Today we forget the age-old entwinement between fabric production and daily life, yet many words we now use derive from the tools and processes involved in textile manufacture.

Women could learn how to produce serviceable yarn in several ways. The most common method was for a mother to train her young daughters, for as soon as her children could operate a wheel, they expanded the family labor force. Some women became apprentices, with formal indentures, to learn the skill from people outside their families. Elizabeth England "put her Daughter Apprentice unto Nathaniel Jefferies of East Bradford . . . to Learn to Sew, & Spin." As part of the agreement, Jefferies was to teach the girl to read and write and give her "Two Suits of Cloths one intire New."[24] Because he failed to comply with these terms, England took him to court in 1772.[25]

Once trained, females would spin for their own use, for wages, or for both, regardless of their marital status. Women who could spin, with access to the appropriate equipment, would have performed the work when they could fit it around other household duties. If yarn was required for a specific item in a hurry, they might devote a block of time to the endeavor. Unlike weaving, however, which demanded the full attention of the artisan, a spinning session could be interrupted easily.[26] If the wife of a householder had female help (indentured servants, slaves, or hired labor), she could have them assist her with spinning jobs or relegate the work to them entirely. Similarly, any female relatives living in the household would also have helped.[27]

Both married and single women in Chester County made money by spinning. Some went into the homes of others, used their equipment and fiber, and earned a wage for their labor, as in the case of Margaret Rock, who worked "2 Days in the House" of George Brinton, and the wife of Harold Chiffrow, whom Brinton also hired to spin tow yarn for him.[28] In most account records, single and widowed women transacted the work in their own behalf, while married women either did so in combination with their husbands or were totally subsumed under their husband's names. Other women, like Nany White who was introduced at the beginning of this chapter, spun at home for recompense, using fiber produced on their own farms, purchased from others, or provided by their customers. The income they generated might pay for needed goods like agricultural products or for services like weaving or finishing cloth, for example.[29] Married women customarily disposed of their earnings in this manner, while single women—who did not need to contribute directly to household finances—tended to spend their money on finery for themselves.[30]

As in Chester County in general, bound labor, especially before 1760, could assist with household tasks like spinning. Many of the female slaves and servants coming into or already living in Pennsylvania were proficient at the task—clearly a desirable asset in a woman worker. Some African women had lived long enough in North America to learn how to make yarn on a spinning wheel. In 1730, for example, the *American Weekly Mercury* advertised the sale of "a very likely Negroe Woman, who has lived in Philadelphia from her Childhood, and speaks very good English, she can do all Sorts of Housework . . . ; she can Knit and Sew, Spin Flax, Cotton, Worsted, and Wool, very well."[31] European female servants whose spinning skills were highlighted mainly came from Holland, Ireland, and Scotland.[32] Whether a servant or a slave spun wool or linen or both, her proficiency with a spinning wheel was a marketable commodity, especially for households that produced fiber but needed extra labor to spin it. After 1760, although the use of bound labor in Pennsylvania declined substantially, this was not because of a decreased demand but because of a change in the nature of the work force. For rural Pennsylvanian householders, the increasing availability of free workers prepared to work on a short-term basis in the last half of the eighteenth century, provided a more elastic labor supply than indentured servants or slaves and gave local female spinners increased wage-earning opportunities.[33]

Even though some women received special training as spinners and some spun for pay, in general spinning was regarded as a household task rather than a professional craft. The designation of "spinster" during this period is solely in wills and refers to the unmarried status of a woman, not her occupation. Occasionally, women appeared on tax lists, but even in the years for which occupation taxes were levied, they were never taxed as spinners. Thus spinning did not have the formal (and therefore taxable) occupational status of such male-dominated crafts as weaving.[34] As in Europe, even if activities such as sewing or spinning were done for pay, they continued to be defined as "domestic work" or as "housekeeping." In contrast, similar activities were considered "production" when carried out by men for consumption outside the home. Thus, throughout the colonies, as in Europe, what defined labor status was not whether one worked in the home or what one did, but whether it was performed by a man or a woman.[35]

There was a difference between the eighteenth-century Pennsylvania experience, however, and that of New England.[36] In New England, especially before changes triggered by the Seven Years' War in the 1760s, families were far less likely to use an extended labor force of indentured servants or wage laborers, making the region less attractive than Pennsylvania for immigrant workers. Instead, rural households depended on their own nuclear families, supplemented by an arrangement of neighborhood exchange, for most of their labor needs. For women, this might mean going to the home of a neighbor or relative to assist with spinning in the expectation that the favor would be returned if needed.[37] The dearth of immigrant workers meant that when women did spin for pay, however, their wages were higher than those of their Pennsylvania counterparts.[38] In contrast, many rural Pennsylvanian females spun for wages, in addition to those who made yarn for their own use.[39] The market orientation of Pennsylvania farmers and the availability of an extended labor force of female slaves, servants, or, later, contract wageworkers, liberated some Pennsylvania women, especially the wealthier ones, from the work. Moreover, with the exception of hand knitting, women's role in cloth making (excluding the post-production activity of sewing) largely ceased after spinning was completed, as they handed over their yarn to a skilled male artisan whom they paid to weave it into cloth—the subject of the next chapter.

Knitted textile production allowed women another way to participate in their household economy. Most women could knit serviceable garments from any yarn not designated for weaving—for example, much of the worsted yarn produced locally was knit into stockings. Laurel Ulrich describes young New England girls working at home, knitting goods only for themselves and their families, while they were more likely to spin at a neighbor's "as part of an exchange of work."[40] For Pennsylvania women, too, hand knitting was likely to be more a domestic activity than spinning, but both were female jobs. In contrast to spinning, however, men were also knitters, but they worked on a piece of equipment called a *frame* that facilitated the commercial production of knit goods (mostly stockings). The division of labor with framework knitting also resembled that of other European textile traditions: Women used simple knitting needles to work by hand, while men operated knitting frames to make goods for the market.

Whether or not spinners sold the yarn they made or kept it for themselves, they usually knew if it would be used for knitting or for weaving clothing or household fabrics. Knitting was one of the simplest ways to create a functional textile, requiring only two knitting "pins" or needles, and yarn. Stockings and mittens comprised the majority of items made by hand and machine, but knitters also created more elaborate articles of clothing, including men's breeches and women's shawls; although difficult to quantify, these latter garments were also imported from England.[41] The extent of hand knitting is also hard to determine, but it is likely that members of a household or professional knitters used a great deal of the yarn spun in early America for knitted goods.[42]

When knitting needles appear in inventories, they always belonged to women, further underscoring the female association with hand knitting. As we have seen, throughout the eighteenth century, the skill was among the desirable assets of female slaves and servants.[43] Women in a family and those who worked for them could readily incorporate it into their daily activities. Because a ball of yarn and knitting needles were easily portable, one could carry a project about, working on it when time allowed, perhaps while waiting for a baby to be born, minding a child, or visiting a neighbor. The metal or wooden needles could be imported, purchased nearby, or made oneself. Local retailers sold large quantities of British-made metal needles, although after the 1760s this seems to have declined.[44] Alternatively, an individual could whittle needles out of wood or perhaps obtain them from a local blacksmith or wire mill.

In addition to the women who hand knit as part of their household work, professional male knitters in Chester County operated "stocking looms," or frames (Fig. 13).[45] Invented in the sixteenth century, knitting frames became more widely used and versatile during the eighteenth century, when adaptations made it possible to knit a variety of stitches and advances in cotton spinning meant that cotton, as well as linen, worsted, and silk yarns, could be knit. Although the technology and products of a knitting frame were quite different from looms and the woven cloth made on them, the work was structured in a similar manner. Sitting in front of a heavy iron carriage supported on a wooden frame, the knitter needed a great deal of strength, using both arms to move the carriage, and both feet to work the treadles. While the male of the household operated the frame, the women and children might have assisted by winding the yarn onto bobbins and seaming the stockings he made.[46] A few "stocking weavers," or "framework knitters" as they were also called, operated in Chester County throughout the eighteenth century.[47] Working in the 1720s and 1730s, John Camm practiced his craft with the help of an indentured servant who learned the trade so well that, drawing on Camm's good reputation, the servant later sold stockings that he falsely claimed were the work of his master.[48] Like the weavers in Chester County, Camm combined his artisan skills with farming.[49] Later in the century, when land was more difficult to obtain, stocking knitter John Graves had only a house and a garden lot and devoted more of his time to his craft, using three stocking looms that comprised 15 percent of the value of his personal estate at his death.[50] His surviving account book shows that Graves knit stockings made predominantly of linen but also of cotton, wool, and silk, for the most part with yarn provided by his customers. Graves' formal records indicate that he made about

Figure 13. Males operated the knitting machines, or "stocking frames," on which they produced quantities of knit stockings. Their wives or daughters often assisted in the work by spinning the yarn or winding skeins. Several stocking weavers practiced their craft in Chester County. Plate 314, "The Stocking Frame," Charles C. Gillespie, ed., *A Diderot Pictorial Encyclopedia of Trades and Industry: Manufacturing and the Technical Arts in Plates Selected from "L'Encyclopédie, ou Dictionnaire Raisonné des Sciences, des Arts et des Métiers" of Denis Diderot,* vol. 2 (New York, 1959).

four hundred pairs of stockings a year.[51] Unfortunately, however, it is almost impossible to compare his output with that of female hand knitters given the informality of their work.[52]

Despite the presence of male professional knitters in Chester County, many inhabitants made their own knitted goods or purchased imports from local retailers. According to contemporary traveler Andrew Burnaby, a large stocking weaving industry in nearby Germantown (northwest of Philadelphia), which produced about 60,000 pairs in 1757, provided another source of knit stockings for rural Pennsylvanians.[53] Both hand and frame knitting continued relatively unchanged in this region into the nineteenth century, but new spinning technologies drastically altered and soon eliminated the yarn making that had been such an important component of some women's domestic work routine.

Beginning in the 1790s and continuing into the nineteenth century, new machines transformed women's role in the processing and spinning of yarn. By the 1830s, machine-spun wool and cotton eliminated the need for women to do this time-consuming work in most communities, with the exception of newly opened frontier societies. As this occurred, spinning equipment, once of central importance, was either discarded, sold, or became so irrelevant it was no longer noted in inventories. In some instances, spinning wheels were simply relegated to an attic to be resurrected by later generations as romantic symbols of the industriousness of their foremothers.

Just as European craft traditions shaped the structure of domestic cloth production in the New World, European immigration was crucial for the early establishment and development of the textile industry that began late in the eighteenth century. Early on, individuals arrived from Britain with technical knowledge that Americans lacked. Later, immigrant workers filled the need for a growing labor force.

British textile mechanic Samuel Slater is perhaps the best-known example of the importance of immigrant expertise. Working with his American partners, William Almy and Smith Brown, only Slater could provide the technical knowledge needed to establish one of the earliest and most significant American industrial textile ventures (although by no means the first)—a cotton-spinning mill in Pawtucket, Rhode Island, in 1793.[54] Coupled with the perfection of the cotton gin a year later and the opening of numerous other small cotton-spinning factories all along the eastern seaboard, machine-spun cotton yarn soon replaced flax and linen. Woolen mills, too, began to appear, making it easier for people to take wool from their own sheep to be carded mechanically and/or machine spun. With the introduction of the water-driven loom in Waltham, Massachusetts, in 1815, it was not long before integrated factories took over fiber and cloth production completely. This was not an evenly distributed or instantaneous process, however, as it was determined by local economic and demographic patterns.

By the mid-1790s, Almy and Brown had a surplus of yarn that they wanted to sell. They developed aggressive (and successful) marketing strategies in New England and the middle colonies, advertising in both urban and rural newspapers "a large assortment of Cotton Yarn suitable for Warp and Filling, and also of Two and Three Threaded [ply] Yarn, suitable for knitting or weaving Stockings, of equal quality to any in America."[55] Their clients were rural storekeepers who sold the yarn to locals who might have previously spun their own, and professional weavers, who would no longer have to rely on their customers to provide the raw materials. Notations in the account book of Pennsylvania weaver Joseph Eldridge, for example, show that he began buying yarn from Rhode Island in 1810.[56]

The availability of yarn from New England mills and, more important, the persistence of local manufacture and agriculture, helps to explain why Chester County still had no spinning factories and only two carding mills as late as 1810. During the next decade, however, this region began to industrialize and, by 1820, the county could boast three carding mills, four cotton mills or factories, two woolen mills, and one hemp mill.[57] Machine-spun yarn, whether available from local mills or through interstate commerce, would soon change women's work and indeed the household economy. New textile factories, regardless of location, eventually made hand spinning obsolete.

After the early 1790s, spinning-wheel ownership steadily declined in most areas, including Pennsylvania. In Chester County, the decrease was much less dramatic than in Essex County, Massachusetts, for example, probably because the former was less urban and less industrialized than its New England counterpart. Although spinning was fading in these regions, there was an even more marked decline in the ownership of specialty wheels. After a steady increase into the 1790s in the number of Chester County households with wheels designated to spin wool and flax, their numbers then decreased noticeably, a trend that continued for thirty years, while the number of generic spinning wheels rose.[58] In addition, fewer nineteenth-century households possessed more than one spinning wheel than had been the case in the later 1700s.[59] This decline in spinning-wheel ownership and number of wheels per household suggests that the newly available mill-spun yarn had an immediate impact, almost eliminating the need for flax-spinning equipment by the 1830s and substantially reducing wool wheels as well. Households with wheels at this point were most likely to have only one on which they could spin either fiber, if they spun at all.

The elimination of the time-consuming work of yarn spinning left some women with new options for how they spent their time. New England women, for example, especially those who were young and single, might choose to go to work in the new textile mills. In rural Pennsylvania, where many women had used spinning to earn money, there were fewer mills with opportunities for them, but other options existed. Beginning in the 1750s, Pennsylvania farmers began to expand their market agriculture in response to an increasing demand for dairy products (especially butter) from abroad, and from Philadelphia's growing population, giving women the option of butter making as an income-generating activity to replace spinning.[60]

The eighteenth century witnessed a proliferation in the number of households involved in spinning and a growing investment in skill and equipment for the more specialized production of wool and flax yarns. This trend reversed in the nineteenth century as water-powered carding and spinning mills removed the need for women to make their own yarn. Females who had made money with their handiness or who had simply spun yarn for their own use, later had to find other activities with which to generate income. Market dairying was an option for the still very productive farms in the middle colonies, while working in the new textile mills was an alternative for many New England women. Less changed was the activity of knitting. Women still plied their knitting needles to make stockings and clothing, although they no longer had to make their own yarn. A local storekeeper or mill could provide all the machine-spun yarn they could knit. The male framework knitters, too, saw little variation in the structure and nature of their work before the 1830s, when the first successful water-powered knitting mills were established in the United States.[61] The most important early change of the new spinning industry for the mechanical knitters, as with their brother weavers, was the liberation from relying on their customers for the yarn. Following deeply ingrained European traditions, early Americans changed little in the production of fiber, yarn, or knit goods over the eighteenth century. Weaving and cloth finishing, too, continued in Old World grooves. As the next chapter will demonstrate, however, in these areas of production, technological innovation combined with the local structures of cloth making to determine the nature of industrialization. Rural Pennsylvania, with its continued reliance on agriculture and craft followed a different path than did New England.

Chapter 5

Weaving and Cloth Finishing

In 1794, weaver and farmer James Garrett bequeathed to his nephew, Joseph Eldridge, his property and "the whole of my Stock, farming Utensils and household furniture what ever that I am now possessed of," including looms.[1] James had never married, but when his sister Mary Garrett Eldridge died in 1775, he took her ten-year-old son Joseph to live with him. Over the years, James taught his nephew the intricacies of the weaving trade and as his skill grew, Joseph was able to take on more work for his uncle. Once Joseph, too, became a fully trained weaver capable of working on his own, he represented the fifth generation in an unbroken chain of male weavers living and working in Chester County, Pennsylvania (see Garrett family tree, page 86).

Joseph Eldridge was twenty-nine years old when he became a property owner. At that time, he had been living with James for nineteen years, was married, and had a young son. The apprenticeship Joseph served with his uncle differed very little from the training of preceding generations. In 1794, however, the long-practiced traditions of their trade were about to be displaced by major industrial and mechanical innovations. Technology was not the only driving force of change, though, as labor conditions, craft practices, and people responding to transformation, all combined in North America, as in Britain, to shape the industrializing process.

The advent of spinning mills altered the nature of rural women's work, whether they lived in England, New England, or Pennsylvania. Once factory production eliminated the time-consuming task of making yarn, female family members and their children could take on other duties. New technology also transformed the entire process and structure of cloth making, first by providing large quantities of yarn and later by replacing hand looms with power looms. Unlike spinning, however, local cloth manufacture in Pennsylvania and New England had followed different developmental courses over the eighteenth century, despite common early European roots. These regional variations in pre-industrial craft structures of weaving and cloth finishing were the

Garrett Family Tree, Chester County, Pennsylvania

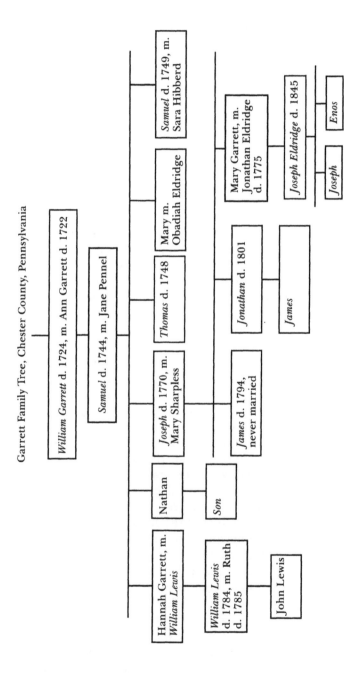

This partial family tree highlights generational involvement in cloth-making crafts. Italicized names were identified as weavers, owners of weaving equipment, or both.
Source: Chester County Wills and Inventories (Chester County Archives) and J. Smith Futhey and Gilbert Cope, *History of Chester County Pennsylvania* facsimile reprint edition (Evansville, Ind: Whipporwill Publications for the Chester County Historical Society, 1986).

forces determining that in Pennsylvania, large-scale industrialization was an urban (or suburban) phenomenon, while in New England it began in the countryside. The eighteenth-century hand-weaving enterprises in rural Chester County evolved into a series of small textile mills in the early nineteenth century that continued to serve much the same clientele as the earlier hand weavers.

With the exception of hand knitting, the transformation of yarn into a finished product demanded higher levels of skill and training than the preceding stages and a far larger outlay of resources for equipment. In Pennsylvania, the specialization of weaving and machine knitting separated the work from the day-to-day operations of a farming household and the realm of women. Skilled male weavers and cloth finishers, working in the European tradition, made textiles to sell in the local market. Seventeenth-century New England experienced a similar situation that would persist for the few skilled male weavers who continued to practice their craft throughout the colonial period. As the eighteenth century progressed, however, women began making cloth for their own household use in increasing numbers, breaking down the traditional craft structure.[2] As a result, fundamental differences developed between textile manufacture in the two provinces as New England household industry evolved into homespun production.[3] This transition did not occur in Pennsylvania, where cloth work continued to be divided by gender, and production was for a larger market.

In Chester County, the cloth making that was established in the early years of settlement on a small scale grew little in proportion to the population over the eighteenth century, limited by regional factors such as demographics, immigration and economic conditions. Fewer than 10 percent of the inventoried households ever possessed the tools needed to make cloth, and weavers comprised fewer than 2 percent of the designated occupations.[4] Substantially fewer people owned looms than spinning wheels, reflecting the relative number of spinners required to keep a weaver supplied with raw materials.

Depending on the quality of the finished product, as mentioned in Chapter 4, various European estimates put the number of spinners needed to provide yarn for a single loom at between six and twelve.[5] Viewed from this perspective, in Chester County, the number of weavers was to some extent related to the ability of the residents to produce sufficient yarn to supply them. Throughout the eighteenth century, there were about twelve spinning wheels to every loom, with the highest ratio in the years immediately preceding the Revolution (perhaps reflecting the attempt to increase domestic cloth manufacture because of the conflict with Britain).[6] Given that most spinning wheels would not have been in use at all times and that spinners also made yarn for knitting, the numbers can be adjusted slightly downward, bringing them into conformity with estimates of spinners to weavers in Britain and France. These ratios suggest the relative stability of textile production in Chester County during the period and the inability of most farm families to make their own fabric; more households would have to have spinning equipment and even more would require looms in order to manufacture even small quantities of cloth for themselves. Given the ratio of wheels to looms and that only a maximum of 60 percent of households had wheels (see Chapter 4), the "soft occupation" of spinning was very clearly demarcated from the work of weaving in this rural area.[7]

Fabrics that are evenly constructed and attractive require much equipment, skill, and stamina. Spun yarn can tangle easily, and the quantities needed for weaving must be kept snarl-free, in sequence, and under even tension to produce a uniform product with straight edges that does not bulge or sag. Regardless of pattern or design, any woven cloth consists of the basic elements of interlocking strands of warp and weft. The warp threads (ends) are the longitudinal strands of yarn placed on the loom, and the weft threads (picks) interlock horizontally with the warp, usually carried across it with a shuttle; in the most simple weave structure (plain weave, or tabby) the weft passes over and under alternate warp ends (see Glossary). Not only do weavers need a great deal of training to make anything but the plainest cloth, they also require numerous specialized tools and the space to use and store them.[8] The following description of the assorted equipment required by weavers and how each fits into the weaving process provides a necessary understanding of the complexity of cloth making and the investment required to do it properly. This information is essential for determining the nature and extent of textile manufacture in early America.

First, a spinner removed spun yarn from the wheel by winding it onto a reel to make a skein. If the yarn was designated for weaving, the reel had a device that measured it. Next, the weaver, or more likely an assistant, placed the skein on a swift, which allowed the yarn to be unwound as it was rolled onto spools with a spooling wheel (a spinning-wheel-like tool turned by hand) (see Fig. 14 for illustrations of this and the following weaving accessories).[9] The quantity of spools to be filled was controlled by the number of warp ends per inch that determined the cloth's density (Fig. 15). For example, wool blanketing with twenty ends per inch might require twenty spools, but ten would also work as a half-inch unit. The spools, when filled with a measured

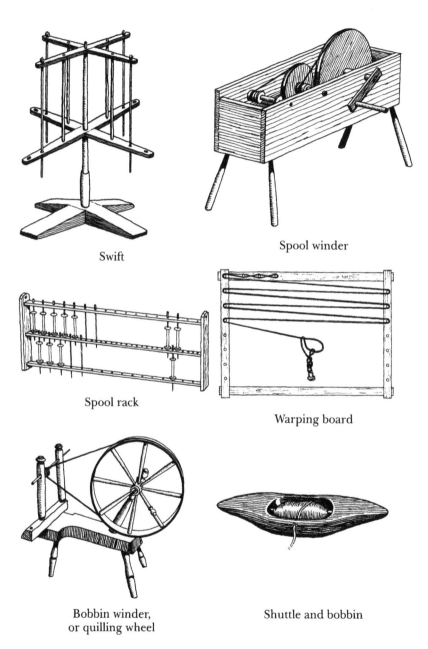

Swift

Spool winder

Spool rack

Warping board

Bobbin winder,
or quilling wheel

Shuttle and bobbin

Figure 14. Weavers required more than just a loom to practice their craft. The weaving accessories shown here represent the essential additional equipment required to produce cloth. From Marion L. Channing, *Textile Tools of Colonial Homes* (Marion, Mass., 1969), 31, 36–37, 41.

length of yarn, were placed on a spool rack (or scarne) that held the threads as they were wound onto a warping board (also called warping bars or frames)—a wooden frame with pegs at measured intervals to hold the warp ends in sequence that either leaned against a wall or was built into it. A labor-saving, revolving warping mill could be substituted for a frame. Some warp yarn, especially linen or cotton, had to be strengthened by sizing, a process that involved boiling the yarn in a mixture of flour and water in large pots or tubs. When the warp was fully prepared, it was ready for the loom.

The size of a loom and its construction depended on the kind of textile made on it—tapes and ribbons could be woven on smaller, specialized equipment, while household linens or clothing fabric needed larger looms. Most of the looms used by the rural Pennsylvania weavers in this study had wooden frames and were about six feet high, five and a half feet deep, and four and a half feet wide (Fig. 16).[10] The breadth of these tools usually was restricted by the weaver's reach—he threw the shuttle containing the weft yarn with his right hand and caught it with his left. As a result, a large proportion of the handwoven cloth was made in widths of twenty-seven, thirty-six, or forty-five inches, and was seamed together if it needed to be wider.

When the warp was finally ready, the weaver placed groupings of ends in a wooden raddle (raith) that consisted of pegs locked into a frame at measured distances to keep the warp spread out over the desired width. Then, aided by an assistant, the two wound the warp onto the warp beam of the loom, taking care to ensure an even tension. Once on the loom, each end was threaded through the eye of a string heddle (made with a wooden heddle maker) that was held top and bottom on rods; the entire unit was called a shaft. The shafts (there had to be at least two) were attached to foot treadles that moved them up and down with a pulley mechanism. This whole section of the loom—shafts, pulleys, cords, and heddles—was often simply called "tackling." Any pattern in the cloth was determined by the sequence in which the warp ends were threaded through the heddles, the number of shafts used, and the order in which the treadles were depressed. The simplest textile required only two shafts with alternate ends threaded on each; when one shaft was raised it created a space, or shed, for the weft to pass through; when the other was raised it locked the first weft in place and created a new shed for the next weft to go through. Patterns that were more complicated required a larger number of shafts and an irregular threading. To keep track of what could amount to over 1,000 warp ends in a required sequence, the weaver used a draft—a design drawn on paper. Once threaded through its heddle eye, each warp end was drawn through a slit (dent)

Detail showing spool being wound using a spool wheel

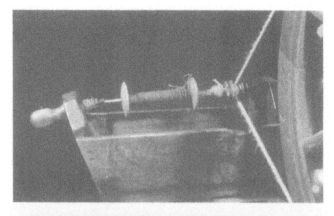

Spools with linen thread ready to be made into a warp

Figure 15. A weaver needed a lot of equipment in addition to a loom in order to operate on a commercial basis. (Top) A detail of a spool-winding wheel that was used exclusively to wind the spools that held the threads to make a warp. (Bottom) Fourteen spools containing linen thread for a textile that could contain fourteen warp ends per inch or a multiple of that. In this case, the finished fabric (used to make the author's wedding ensemble) contained fifty-six ends per inch. Photographs by author.

in a reed (sley)—slivers of reed bound together with cord and pitch—that maintained the density of the cloth (a blanket with twenty ends per inch might be woven with a ten dent reed with two ends per slot) (Fig. 17).

British-style loom

German-style loom

Figure 16. Although all looms require similar components to make cloth, there were stylistic differences. German-style looms were often of heavier construction and with a different frame than those used by British weavers. This may reflect the fact that many German cloth workers emigrated from linen producing areas that would require sturdier looms than those used mostly for the wool weaving practiced by so many British artisans. Acc. # 1959.1.7.1 and # 64.40.1. Permission of the American Textile History Museum, Lowell, Massachusetts.

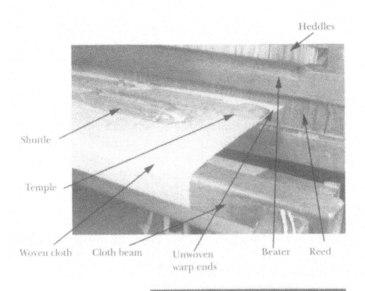

Heddles

Shuttle

Temple

Woven cloth   Cloth beam   Unwoven   Beater   Reed
                            warp ends

Details of reeds: top for finer cloth and bottom for coarser cloth

Figure 17. (Top) A detail of cloth in the loom as it is being woven. (Bottom) Details of two reeds used to determine the degree of fineness of a textile. The fabric was woven by the author and made into a jacket that is presently in the collection of the Royal Ontario Museum, Toronto. The reeds were probably made by a professional in the eighteenth or early nineteenth century, using reed cane, pitch, tar, and twine and a gauge to ensure the exact spacing between each slit. The numbers on the ends indicate the spacing of the reed. Photographs by author.

Weavers usually owned a number of reeds to make cloth of varying degrees of fineness; a linen tablecloth might have forty ends per inch, whereas coarse tow bagging might have eight. The reed was set into a beater that the weaver pushed back while inserting a weft and pulled forward to beat or lock it into place, an action that required strength and stamina (linen, which was less elastic than wool, generated the most work). After the threading was completed, the warp was tied onto the cloth beam at the front of the loom where the finished textile was rolled for storage; the width of the cloth might have been restricted by the weaver's reach, but it could be almost infinitely long. A metal gear attached to the right side of the cloth beam maintained the tension needed to work on the warp.

For the weft, weavers also needed quilling wheels to wind the weft yarn onto quills (or bobbins), which were inserted into shuttles to carry it across the warp (Fig. 18). They also needed brushes to apply size to strengthen a warp already on the loom; a temple to maintain the desired width during weaving (usually made of two pieces of wood with metal prongs in each end that were inserted into the selvages of the cloth to keep them from pulling in), and smaller items like weaver's shears and needles to repair broken threads and to burl the cloth (remove knots) after they removed it from the loom.

All of these tools represented expenditure on the part of the owners in terms of money to buy them, time to make them, or both. The inventories I examined from Chester County, Pennsylvania, and Essex County, Massachusetts, showed that male artisan weavers who specialized in the craft owned many, if not all, of these tools if they were weaving both linen and wool cloth. In contrast, the female domestic weavers in New England generally did not possess all the implements, and either did without some or borrowed them from a neighbor. Weaving families often passed equipment down through the generations, but when a tool wore out it would have to be replaced. Unlike spinning wheels, however, which required skilled turning and joining in order to make the wheels and flyer mechanisms, the frame of a loom could be constructed with basic carpentry skills and tools.

Approximately 40 percent of Chester County loom owners had tools and materials with which they could have made much of their weaving equipment.[11] Some people, like Henry Brower of Coventry (d. 1784), had materials specially earmarked for loom making; Brower's inventory listed "Some Iron for a Loom." Others, such as Thomas Coldwell in 1736 and Nicholas Snider in 1823, not only had their own woodworking tools, but they also had anvils on which to forge such things as metal gears.[12] Artisans not able or willing to expend the time and labor to build their weaving equipment could buy it new from

Figure 18. In addition to spinning wheels for making yarn and spooling wheels for winding the spools for the warp, a professional weaver would have had yet another special wheel for winding the bobbins that held the weft yarn carried across the warp in a shuttle, like the hand-turned quilling wheel shown here. Often an apprentice or the child of a weaver would have been responsible for filling the many bobbins (or quills) needed by a weaver during the weaving process. Photograph by author.

someone who specialized in making it, or secondhand from neighbors, through newspaper ads or at auction.[13] In addition, from 1731 through the eighteenth and into the nineteenth century, many weavers, like Joseph Eldridge introduced at the beginning of this chapter, inherited their weaving equipment.[14]

Regardless of their ability to construct and repair much of their own equipment, some of it, like reeds and brushes, was just too specialized or time consuming for most weavers to make themselves. For example, in 1809, reed maker Thomas Bell owned "a Clockwork reedmakers Machine," "a bench of shaveing & gage tools for the reeds," two boxes of lashing yarn and pitch twine, and small knives, augers, gimlets, and cane splitters.[15] All of this reed-making equipment would represent a significant investment of time and skill in addition to that required for the other tools a weaver needed. Although Joseph Hobson (d. 1797) had both looms and "Cane for Reeds" in his inventory, the majority of weavers bought their reeds either from a local artisan or from a reed maker in Philadelphia.[16] Weavers' brushes, particularly needed by linen weavers, came from brush makers, most of whom worked in Philadelphia and sold their goods in rural areas through local storekeepers and peddlers.[17]

Whether a loom owner made or bought equipment, the tools represented a sizable investment. If a weaver was lucky, he inherited them at little or no cost, but if he wanted more looms or if he had none to start with, he needed to make a substantial outlay of time, money, or both, to establish himself in his craft. For single men whose inventories listed weaving equipment, tools and accessories were worth an average of 8.5 percent of the value of their entire estates, with some ranging as high as 22 percent. As loom owners aged and their wealth grew, the proportional value of the weaving equipment gradually diminished. Thus, implements belonging to elderly men averaged only about 2.1 percent of the value of their estates.[18] In Essex County, where with a few exceptions, the weaving was generally less specialized, the tools were worth a considerably smaller portion of one's wealth, regardless of age.[19] Indeed, Joseph Challis of Amesbury Township, who died in 1737, owned only "an intrist in a Loomb" valued at £1.[20]

As might be deduced from artisan weavers' investment in their equipment, their craft was more structured than fiber processing and spinning and necessitated more specialized training. Even the less formal female cloth economy of eighteenth-century New England required a mechanism by which people could learn the rudiments of weaving. Training was only the beginning, however. Hand textile manufacture was extremely labor intensive, and integrating commercial production with other agricultural work, as was the case in Pennsylvania, required some form of flexible work force.

It took time to acquire the knowledge needed to make cloth and even more time to make it suitable for sale.[21] In eighteenth-century Chester County, the two most common methods of learning weaving and cloth finishing were through a legally recognized apprenticeship and working with a skilled family member. Occasional indentures, court petitions and depositions, and will and inventory notations suggest that apprenticeships occurred regularly throughout the period.[22] A young man entered into a contract with a weaver to learn the skills and "mysteries" of the craft, usually for a period of seven years. If all went well and the master fulfilled his end of the obligation, once an apprentice had acquired the rudiments of weaving, he assisted his master until he had sufficient training to take over much of the work. At this point, the teacher could devote more time to agricultural pursuits or to expand his cloth output by working on another loom.[23]

Indentured servants provided another source of artisanal labor, especially in Pennsylvania, a popular destination for many. As discussed in Chapter 2, this type of bound labor was most prevalent prior to the last third of the eighteenth century, when there were fewer young, underemployed native-born craftsmen than later, and immigration was active (loom owners rarely had slaves, so African-Americans did not constitute an alternative labor force).[24] Servant workers required a cash investment that might include payment of the passage from Europe to America, the cost of upkeep during the period of indenture (usually about four years), and perhaps a fee for "freedom dues" upon completion of the contract.[25] This cost could be offset, however, by hiring one of the many men arriving in Pennsylvania who were fully trained weavers; such an individual would be immediately productive and able to assist with farming duties as well.[26] If advertisements for runaway indentured servants are representative, it appears that the peak decades for servant weavers were the 1730s, 1740s, and 1750s, and that they were almost exclusively Irish and English. There were about twice as many Irish as English, although the English were more numerous before 1740.[27] Among loom owners with servants or apprentices, married men with no offspring or whose children were minors had the most hired help. Because such males lacked the expanded work force of a larger, more mature family, especially sons who could learn their father's craft, they invested in the training of an apprentice or the purchase of an indentured servant to assist them in their work. Bound labor decreased as the population expanded in Chester

County, however, and was replaced by a growing number of property-less young people who were available to work as wage laborers on short-term contracts.[28]

An artisan weaver would teach his sons at least basic elements of the trade, although not all may have practiced the craft as adults. A young son might wind spools and bobbins, and, having mastered these easy chores, be allowed to throw the shuttle and weave plain cloth. When he was proficient and skilled enough, he would learn how to make a warp and dress the loom in order to produce a variety of patterned fabrics. At this stage, the young son became an important contributor to the family's cloth output and was allowed to retain some of his earnings. Until he reached the age of majority, he was legally obligated to provide his services to his father; after that, he could set up on his own.[29]

There was no hard and fast rule about which sons learned their fathers' trade or inherited his tools. In some instances, the oldest son received all the equipment; in others, the first two male offspring shared it.[30] If a father with young children died before training them in his craft, he might demand that an elder son teach the skills to his brothers, after which they would divide the weaving equipment among them. James Rogers of Goshen Township stipulated in his 1793 will that his son

David continue to live on the place with his mother and to have his diet as usual without expence to him for one year, he having the profits of his work in order that he may instruct his younger brother Mahlon in the Weaving business: and at the end of the year that he . . . shall have one loom, at his choice and one half the Gears, and . . . Mahlon to have the other Loom & the other half the Gears & to work with his mother till he is Twenty one.[31]

This custom was not unique to the male cloth workers in Chester County. John Dennison, a weaver in Ipswich, Massachusetts, left his son George "half my Shop One Loome and half the Tools to S^d Shop belonging," providing that George gave his brother John "the priviledg of having three Slays out of Georges half John Shall Choose."[32] Whether an American-born boy learned weaving from his father or elder brother, it was often a family affair, as it had been in England, with both the skills and equipment passed from generation to generation.[33] A weaver without children, like James Garrett, might take on a relative to train and to whom he could bequeath his tools and property, as he did with his sister's son Joseph Eldridge.

It is much easier to document weaving where it was a male occupation than where it was a female occupation. Men, who were regularly taxed for their trade, appeared far more frequently on tax lists than women. In addition, a larger number of males than females left wills disposing of their property, making it possible to trace equipment passed from generation to generation.[34] Finally, men kept account books recording their transactions, thereby shedding light on what they made, who bought their products, and how they were paid.

The paths of inherited looms, and apparently weaving knowledge, in the Garrett/Eldridge family suggest not only how the craft was organized in eighteenth-century Chester County but also how little it changed. When English "webster" (weaver) William Garrett and his family settled in Darby Township, Chester County, in 1684, he soon resumed his profession, passing it on to his son Samuel. A yeoman who owned a farm in Darby Township and had eight children who grew to adulthood, Samuel combined agriculture with his craft work of wool combing and weaving. Like his father, Samuel passed on his textile skills to his offspring (three of his four sons became weavers and his daughter Hannah married a weaver), and he trained an apprentice.[35] When he died in 1744, Samuel left his worsted combs to two of his sons, Thomas and Nathan.[36] The brothers who had learned the weaving craft—Samuel, Jr., of Willistown, Joseph of Goshen, and Thomas of Darby townships—all owned property and all had more than one loom, suggesting that they were producing cloth on a commercial basis during the middle decades of the eighteenth century.[37] Indeed, Samuel, Jr., and Thomas each had a servant to help them with their work, especially needed because none of Samuel's children seems to have followed their father's trade and Thomas died without offspring.[38] The other brother, Joseph, also had two looms, but because he had trained James (one of his seven children) in the craft of cloth manufacture, he had less need for the help of a servant. At his father's death in 1770, James inherited some property in Goshen and two looms.[39] None of James's siblings was a weaver, a change from the previous generation (see family tree, 86).

All the Garrett loom owners had large properties, which they farmed.[40] Despite the fact they had a lot of cloth-making equipment and that Thomas called himself "weaver" in his will, they practiced their craft seasonally when agricultural activities were minimal, like many artisans in Chester County and Europe. When they could not do all the weaving themselves, they had the help of a servant or, in one case, a son.[41]

James Garrett, working in the last half of the eighteenth century, represented the fourth generation of Garrett family weavers in Pennsylvania. As we have seen, he had land (150 acres) but never married: his ten-year-old nephew, Joseph Eldridge, came to live with him after Joseph's mother (James's sister) died and his father remarried. Having trained Joseph as a weaver, James left his entire estate to his twenty-nine-year-old nephew at his death in 1794. Over the years, Joseph's status had changed several times: in 1789, at the age of twenty-four, having completed his apprenticeship with his uncle, he was a fully trained weaver, an occupation for which he paid tax that year. Even though he was married and had a young family, Joseph continued to live on his uncle's farm, paying for his keep by weaving and assisting with agricultural work.[42] After inheriting James's estate and money from his grandparents, Joseph, a fifth-generation weaver, now had a trade, tools, property, and capital with which to expand his own growing household and become an independent farmer-weaver.

Joseph Eldridge's meticulous account books and ledgers provide insight into how he carried on his business, beginning in 1786.[43] Most remarkable is the variety of Eldridge's activities. According to numerous entries, not only did his neighbors and relatives pay him to weave for them, he also made money by harvesting; drawing wood; taking livestock and produce to market; lending cash; and selling meat, agricultural products, and fiber.[44]

The earliest entry in Joseph's account book is 1786 when he was still unmarried. Between 1786 and 1789, as a single, journeyman weaver, Eldridge produced more cloth (an average of 625 yards annually) than he did later. During this time, it seems he had little help with his weaving, the exception being some work done by his young cousin James, whom he paid for nine days of winding spools. He may also have trained James to weave.

By the late 1790s, however, as a propertied master weaver, Eldridge was doing less of the actual work himself, concentrating more energy on his farming. Increasingly, his customers paid him cash for the cloth they bought, and they traded a variety of services, including weaving, to buy the other goods in which he dealt.[45] In addition, young freemen living with him made much of the cloth Eldridge sold. On April 14, 1795, Isaac Yarnall began a year's boarding with Eldridge for which he earned £22, 10 shillings. Like the young, single female spinners who spent their earnings on personal items, Yarnall bought from his employer such things as a sheepskin apron, a silver brooch, yarn for stockings, tobacco, powder and shot, and candles. In return, the bachelor weaver wove for half pay and performed agricultural jobs for additional compensation. At the end of the year, Eldridge and Yarnall could renew their agreement, but if the younger man had saved sufficient money to marry or move on, Eldridge could find a replacement and enter into a similar arrangement.[46] With his paid help, Eldridge personally wove less than he had when he was single and propertyless. In 1794, for example, he made only 60 yards of cloth himself, while his paid worker produced 470 yards. By 1809, two of Eldridge's sons had joined their father in the cloth business. In that year, the output of the workshop, which continued to use contractual labor, was 1,499 yards, more than double what Eldridge had produced when he worked alone.

Eldridge's life as a farmer-weaver paralleled that of his weaving forebears, both English and American. He learned his trade from a relative with whom he worked until he acquired his own land. After weaving first for himself, and later supplementing his output with the assistance of young freemen and inmate weavers, Eldridge was able simultaneously to produce more cloth for sale and to expand his agricultural operations. Although while his family was young he hired contractual workers rather than the bound labor used by earlier generations, Eldridge continued the tradition of training his sons in his craft, which they practiced until well into the nineteenth century.[47] The artisanal-agricultural life cycle of the male members of the Garrett/Eldridge family remained remarkably unchanged throughout the eighteenth century and over five generations.

The most active stages of an artisan's life occurred during his younger years when he was either single or married with minor children or without offspring.[48] This is when the majority of people were identified by the craft they practiced (Table 1). Single men were most frequently called weavers, followed by married men with no children, which is not surprising given that many of them would not yet have had the responsibilities attendant on working a farm; according to tax assessments, 75 percent of people taxed as weavers were nonlandholders.[49] These artisans would have lived as either boarders or inmates in the household of a landholder, most likely one like Joseph Eldridge who worked in the weaving business.

In return for weaving (using their employer's equipment) and doing other work around the farm, freemen would be given wages, keeping some and using the rest to pay their living expenses. An inmate might have his own equipment and therefore be able to retain a larger percentage of the money he made. Moreover, a married inmate could augment his earnings through the labor of his wife, who could also work for their landlord. In addition, she could maintain her own garden, reducing expenses for food.[50] Thus, an inmate usually had more control over the disposition of his time and output and greater ability to accumulate capital than did a freeman weaver. If he did not have a farm when he married, a freeman could move into the inmate category. Some landholding weavers would have employed both types of contractual labor, thereby increasing their cloth output and expanding their agricultural operations.

TABLE 1
FROM LOOM OWNER TO EMPLOYER: CHANGES ACROSS LIFE STAGES (PERCENTAGES)

	Stage 1	Stage 2	Stage 3	Stage 4	Stage 5
Had apprentices or servants	0	31	25	21	10
Owned weaving shop	0	6	7	0	13
Was called "weaver"	40	25	13	21	15
Owned two or more looms	30	37	33	38	35
Had crops or farming implements	40	69	87	85	85

Notes: The life stages were based on those delineated by Mary McKinney Schweitzer, *Custom and Contract: Household, Government, and the Economy in Colonial Pennsylvania* (New York: Columbia University Press, 1987), 25–34. They are (1) a single youth beginning to acquire capital with which to set up his own farm; (2) a married youth with no offspring; (3) a young family with only minor children; (4) a household of people of mixed ages, including minors, adolescents, and young adults; and (5) a household with grown children who were dispersing to set up their own households. Percentages are rounded off. The categories are not mutually exclusive, as some people show up in more than one.

Source: Chester County Wills and Inventories, Chester County Archives, West Chester, Pennsylvania. Based on data obtained from 115 Chester County inventories with looms.

Not all young weavers could expect to become property owners. After the death of his parents in 1725, six-year-old Benjamin Simcock was bound as an apprentice to weaver John Lea, who died several years later.[51] Lea's executors sent the young boy to work for another weaver in East Marlborough, where he stayed "two winters & one summer," until his master moved to Philadelphia County and sold him to John Sketchely. Simcock served Sketchely "some more than four years, he then being about 20 years, & worked there a Journeyman Some more than three years." Simcock soon married and went to live as an inmate for the next thirteen years with Sketchely's stepson, to whom he "Paid ten Pounds a year . . . Paid all Taxes & Served Parish Offices." At the end of this time, Simcock made the step to which most artisans aspired when he bought a house and lot of his own in Darby Township, although he never lived there and sold it a year later. He was about thirty-three years old when he next moved to a plantation in Marion County, Pennsylvania and resumed inmate status for a rent of £15 a year. Beginning in his early forties, Simcock "broke up housekeeping and . . . worked about from Place to Place as a Journeyman Weaver and some time for himself" until, at age sixty-nine, he presented himself as a pauper to the overseers of the poor to be looked after in Ridley Township in Chester County, the place of his birth. Although Simcock experienced the traditional life cycle of apprentice, journeyman, inmate, and, briefly, homeowner, without the support of a propertied family or children to assist him, he never attained a stable livelihood.

Having responsibility for land, whether as owner or tenant, usually occurred later in life, and the attendant duties kept most weavers from devoting the majority of their time to their craft. Frequently, a change in nomenclature in legal documents signified a different stage in a cloth maker's life; many of the same men taxed as weavers or who were called weavers on a property deed and in court depositions were designated as "yeoman" or "farmer" in probate when they died.[52] This suggests both that their status rose as they acquired and worked more land and that as they aged they spent less time at their craft.[53] Although loom owners of all ages had crops or husbandry tools listed in their inventories, the highest number were among the men in the later stages of life who had families and their own farms. Once a weaver made the transition to landholder, therefore, his time was spent on a wider variety of tasks than previously; it was at this point that his craft ceased to be a full-time occupation. It may seem strange that after working so hard to acquire a skill an individual abandoned it. For many, however, the remuneration from weaving was a means to the end of acquiring property—a more promising scenario in Pennsylvania than in Europe. Farming, not the labor-intensive craft of weaving, was the route to wealth in this region. Benjamin Simcock, who ended life as a pauper, is a good example of the precarious living to be made from textile production alone. Moreover, it is unlikely that older farmer-artisans stopped weaving altogether, but rather devoted less time to craft work while obtaining the help of younger artisans (either family members or contract workers) (see Table 1).

Many Chester County weavers had people to assist them and had more than one loom, requiring appropriate working space. For some artisans, especially those who worked alone, a room in the house would be sufficient; James Shortledge (d. 1739) had two looms listed as "Goods in the house."[54] Weaving can be a noisy and dirty occupation, however; the friction of moving warp ends generates dust and lint, the loud crack of the beater as it pounds the weft in place creates a lot of clatter, and linen, tow and hemp cloth need be kept wet while weaving. With more than one person working, the dust, noise, and dampness would have been compounded. As a result, some weavers worked in outbuildings, and about 6 percent of the loom owners had separate structures identified as weavers' shops. These independent buildings would have been similar to that listed on the property of David Bailey of East Fallowfield in the 1796 tax assessment: "1 Log house for a Weaver Shop 16 Feet Square." Such a structure could house two and possibly three looms (Fig. 19).[55] The listing of some looms either immediately preceding or following tools of husbandry or livestock in inventories suggests that they were outside the main dwelling, as inventory-takers itemized articles they encountered while moving from the exterior of a home to the interior. For example, the loom of James Clark (d. 1808) was in the "spring house," where it may have been stored.[56] Men with weaver's shops had larger than average property holdings and were in the later stages of their lives.[57] Throughout the eighteenth century these older, propertied men were also most likely to hire younger weavers to work for them, conducting their weaving operations more along the lines of a small business than when they did the work themselves (see Table 1).[58]

The strong male bias in eighteenth-century records makes it difficult to know to what extent girls might have participated in learning the requisite cloth-making skills along with their brothers. Male artisans dominated the craft of weaving in eighteenth-century Chester County, but some evidence suggests that females also participated.

Although many Chester County women possessed their own spinning equipment, only five could be identified who had looms.[59] In each case, the implements originally belonged to their husbands or, in the instance of Rebecca Davis, her son, who predeceased her. Several

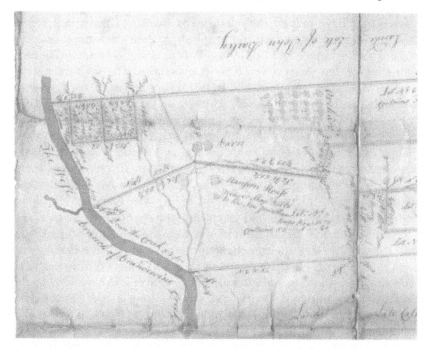

Figure 19. This 1792 Chester County property deed shows a weaver's shop that was situated closer to the house than the barn. The property, owned by Robert Chalfont, was divided among his sons, and he stated in his will that he bequeathed "unto my Son Jonathan . . . the Weavers' Shop that is now on my place for his own use." Chester County Archives, Will # 4224 and Estate Papers of Robert Chalfont, 1792, Orphan's Court. Permission of Chester County Archives, West Chester, Pennsylvania.

of the women inherited the tools only because their children were minors; indeed, Mary Willis's husband left her his estate in trust for their son John. Hannah Shortledge had no children and her husband bequeathed everything to her. John Davis willed his property to his brother, but only after the death of their mother; hence, the looms in Rebecca Davis's inventory had probably belonged to her son. When these women died, if they specified the disposition of the tools, it was to a male relative.[60]

It is almost impossible to know whether the women who owned weaving equipment actually used it. If not, it was probably because they had too many other responsibilities or were too old to weave. Daughters or wives of weavers were undoubtedly familiar with some if not all the tasks involved in making a piece of cloth. If they had time, they would have helped their fathers or husbands with their work. But weaving more than just the simplest patterns demanded concentration and uninterrupted time to follow drafts and create error-free fabric, which few women would have, especially those who were married or widowed and had children.[61] If looms were used after a weaver's death, probably a son, servant, or hired person carried on the work.[62] More likely, however, when a wife inherited her husband's equipment, if no one in the family could weave, she sold it.[63]

The male domination of cloth making in Chester County followed European traditions. As we have seen, in Britain at the time a variety of regulations excluded women from weaving. In his 1615 manual concerning the duties of an English housewife, Gervase Markham stated that once a woman had given her spun yarn to the weaver, she "hath finished her labour: for in the weaving, walking [shrinking], and dressing thereof she can challenge no property more than to entreat them severally to discharge their duties with a good conscience."[64] The one exception, as mentioned, was a weaver's widow, who could take over her husband's work and tools as long as she remained a widow. In Chester County, this practice continued throughout the eighteenth century.

Although the gender division of labor in seventeenth-century New England cloth making resembled closely the situation in Pennsylvania, by the middle of the eighteenth century it looked quite different. A changing economy and demographic structure meant that eighteenth-century New England women increasingly integrated weaving into their domestic routines, in the process bypassing the system of apprentice, journeyman, and artisan.[65] The more informal female practices that evolved in the north, of exchanging weaving skill and equipment to make cloth for individual households, had a large role in shaping the nature of industrialization in the region, as will be discussed in Chapter 7.[66] In contrast, the more conventional European textile craft structures persisted in Pennsylvania.

In Chester County, fiber production may have increased, as did the number of weavers, but the population was also growing. Moreover, the amount of equipment on which to make cloth did not proliferate in relation to the number of people in the county, and the gender division of labor remained in place. Only late in the eighteenth and early in the nineteenth centuries does one begin to witness alterations in the scale and organization of the craft of weaving in Pennsylvania's rural areas—much later and different than those in New England.

The final phase of textile production—finishing—also retained its traditional structure in Chester County. Cloth newly removed from the loom had to be further processed, or finished, before it could be used. Linen textiles required washing, bleaching, and possibly dyeing, while wool cloth needed to be washed and fulled, or shrunk, to make it denser and warmer, stretched to dry, brushed to raise a nap or pile, and sheared to give the brushed cloth an even texture. As discussed in Chapter 1, fulling was one of the earliest textile processes to be mechanized using waterpower to drive the hammers that pounded the wet cloth to condense it. During this last stage of production, therefore, the household ceased to be the primary location of the work as artisans operated out of water-powered fulling mills scattered around the countryside.[67] Like framework knitting and weaving, all of the finishing tasks, when performed by a specialist, took capital, training, and skill, and in North America, as in Europe, skilled male fullers, or clothiers, dominated the craft.[68]

The mill consisted of a building with a waterwheel on the side, driven by diverted river water that was stored in a millpond. When water was needed, the fuller directed it through a channel called a "mill race," thereby controlling its force and regulating the speed of the fulling hammers, activated by the waterwheel.[69] Usually built of stone and up to three stories high, a mill could have a footprint measuring as small as twenty feet square and as big as fifty by thirty-three feet; they were costly to build and maintain in terms of money and time.[70] Unlike the weaver, who could make some of his own equipment, the fulling-mill operator relied on the services of builders (stone masons, carpenters, and so on) to help construct the mill, and millwrights to design, install, and repair the gears and shafts that operated the fulling mechanisms.[71]

The building, equipment, and materials used in the finishing profession demanded even more capital outlay than cloth making. The mill structure housed a variety of equipment and facilities that varied, depending on the type of cloth being finished and whether it was dyed. A complete operation would consist of a mill to wash and shrink the fabric, a dye house where it was colored, tenter yards where it was stretched on frames to dry, a dress house where it was brushed and sheared, and a press shop where it was pressed and made ready to use.[72] The equipment contained within these working areas, most of which had to be purchased from local artisans or imported, would include hot and cold presses and weights, pressing (or fullers') papers, furnaces, vats and kettles, napping tools, cloth (or fullers') shears, and tenter hooks or bars.[73] A mill owner had to further invest in cleansing agents, dyestuffs (logwood, redwood, fustic, madder, and indigo), and mordants (chemicals used to set the dye or render the fiber more able to accept the color) such as alum, copperas, oil of vitriol, and blue vitriol. Dyers imported the majority of their dyestuffs and mordants.[74]

A comparison of the valuation of an individual's property (acreage and buildings) and fulling mills, as stated on the 1782 tax assessment, shows that the cloth-finishing operations were worth an average of just over 40 percent of the property values, representing a substantial investment on the part of a mill owner.[75] It is not surprising, therefore, that there were few mills in Chester County and that the number remained relatively constant from 1765 to the end of the century; in fact, during this time, more mills closed down than started up.[76] The expense of setting up and maintaining the fulling establishments was not the only reason for the lack of growth, however. A profitable cloth-finishing business required newly woven fabric to process, and the number of loom owners in eighteenth-century Chester County did not increase rapidly enough to support more such operations. Despite the many rivers and streams that etched Chester County, there was a tendency for a variety of mills (both textile and others) to cluster together, drawing on water from the same river

It was crucial for a miller to control the necessary water rights, and frequently an individual inherited water conveyances and conditions of use together with a building. For example, in 1802, Samuel Painter of East Bradford left his "son Joseph . . . the waters of Radley Run sufficient for his fulling Mill if there be so much the three winter months in each and every year and at all other times the said waters to be divided between my said sons Joseph and Samuel in proportion to their meadow grounds requiring water."[77] Different families might own the mills along a river, but the best way to ensure access to sufficient waterpower was for one man to control several milling operations housed either in individual structures or in one building that accommodated multiple functions. In 1799, Roger Kirk paid tax on a stone gristmill and a "fulling mill under the same roof."[78] During the last half of the eighteenth century in Chester County, an increasing number of people with fulling establishments also had saw, grist, boulting (flour-sifting), hemp, or paper mills. Only about one quarter of the fulling mill owners were identified as fullers; the others would have had to hire trained artisans to rent their space or to run their operations on shares.[79] Cloth fulling was a far more complex process than saw or flour milling because the fulling itself took knowledge and skill and the finishing required even more expertise.[80] Fullers had to understand the operation of a mill sufficiently to control the action of the hammers so they did not over shrink and ruin the cloth. Moreover, the further processing needed could destroy the cloth if not done properly. Many Chester County fullers also dyed yarn and cloth, though as mentioned, there were a few professional dyers in the region.[81] Specialists might do some of the jobs like shearing, but, for the most part, they were all elements of the fuller's work.[82]

As with the craft of weaving, fulling skills took time and special training to acquire, and not every mill owner had them. Because there were more weavers than there were fullers (approximately eight to one) in Chester County, and many of the fulling operations were family-run businesses, there were fewer apprenticeship opportunities for people outside of a fuller's family, although this did not entirely preclude formal training.[83] After his period of apprenticeship, a young, single man (whether he was a family member or an outsider) would work as a journeyman fuller, helping a mill owner until he wanted to marry. At this point, if he still lacked the capital needed to set up his own operation, he could continue to work as an inmate until he was able to buy or rent the needed facilities. Similarly, after the son of a fuller had learned his father's trade, he could work with him until able to purchase the mill, as did Calvin Cooper who assisted his father, William, until buying the operation in 1801.[84] If a young man was fortunate, he might inherit a business, because fathers left fulling mills, like weaving equipment, to their sons.[85]

Wherever it was practiced, cloth finishing was men's work. The entire operation was physically removed from the household, thereby making it more difficult for women to learn by observing or assisting in the work. In Chester County, only two women, Martha Harvey and Margaret Filson, both of whom were widows, had fulling mills, according to the 1782 and 1799 tax assessments, respectively, and in each case, the mills had belonged to their husbands before they died. A woman who found herself owner of a fulling mill likely sold the facilities, rented them out, or ran the business with a hired fuller doing the actual work. Martha Harvey's husband, Samuel, died intestate, leaving her with seven small children to raise and no son old enough to take over the business. Martha maintained the mill for fourteen years after her husband's death in 1770, but ultimately had to sell it to pay debts in 1784.[86] Thus, although a widow, like her husband, may have run a cloth-finishing business using hired labor or renting out the facilities, she would not have done the manual labor associated with it, even if her husband had done so.

Like many artisans in Chester County, cloth finishers did not work full-time at their craft. Some had other milling operations they combined with fulling.[87] Of the consolidated mills owned by fullers, sawmills comprised the majority, followed by gristmills and one papermill and one boulting mill.[88] Moreover, most fulling mill owners (94 percent) also had an average of 121.5 acres that they farmed in conjunction with their other occupations.[89] The peak periods for farming and mill-work often overlapped, because the best times for milling were spring and fall when the waters were running in full force.[90] One of the ways fuller-farmers overcame this conflict was to hire short-term workers to assist in agriculture (planting, harvesting, threshing), business (working in the shop or mill, repairing the mill, wagon driving), and the household (chopping wood, doing house repairs, and educating the children).[91] In addition, many fullers had some form of specialized assistance such as apprentices, journeymen, and inmate workers. Like weavers, they also had the option of buying an indentured servant, many of whom came to Pennsylvania as fully trained cloth finishers.[92] Fullers, then, like many of the craftsmen in Chester County, were farmers as well as artisans, and in their different capacities, they employed a variety of laborers on whom they relied to do their work.

About three-quarters of fulling-mill owners were not fullers, so from the earliest decades of the eighteenth century, qualified fullers and dyers would either rent a complete cloth finishing operation or work for the owners for wages or on shares. Job Harvey of Darby Township, for example, advertised to let or sell a fulling mill with a "Tenter-Yard, Press-Shop, and a good Stone Dye-House, with two large Furnaces one Led blue vat, all fixed, with very good Conveniences for carrying on the Trades of Fulling, Dying, Shearing and Pressing."[93] Indeed, a few owners like Francis Townsend built mills on speculation in the hopes of finding a suitable tenant who understood the fulling business. In 1765, Townsend advertised a "small plantation" for rent in East Bradford Township in Chester County, where he was building a fulling mill.[94] He clearly viewed this entrepreneurial venture as a potentially profitable investment. In the townships in which men were taxed for having fulling mills but not an occupation, the fullers from the same township who were taxed for their trade but did not have a mill would have assisted with the business of the mill owner or handled it completely.[95]

Whether one was in business, operating a cloth-finishing service with hired help, or self-employed, fulling needed to be profitable to justify the set-up and maintenance expenses. The fact that many people had multiple milling operations and almost all mill owners had good-sized farms suggests that while there was not enough work to keep a cloth finisher occupied full-time, he could make money with the right combination of other pursuits.

Most of the people in Chester County who needed them had access to the services of local weavers and fullers. Even in the early years when there seem to have been fewer cloth workers in the area, distances were not large and the artisans distributed around the county reflect the demand for their services; for example, Joseph Eldridge's customers all lived within an eight-mile radius of his farm. The expansion of the number of cloth-making artisans between 1765 and 1799 mirrors the increase in young, propertyless craftsmen in the general population, many without their own equipment, who could use existing tools of more established weaver-farmers.[96] Although the percentage of looms within the population did not keep up with the numbers of artisans available, what previously had been only a seasonal occupation could now be pursued full-time. Cloth finishing followed a similar pattern, with the result that as the population grew, local production kept pace with a demand that remained surprisingly stable, limited by fiber production and the availability of imported cloth, as discussed in the next chapter.

In eighteenth-century Chester County, skilled male artisans, not housewives, made some of the cloth used by the local residents. These men were professionals who, like Joseph Eldridge and his relatives, invested time and money to learn the requisite skills and obtain the appropriate equipment with which to execute their craft. Many weavers expanded their individual production capacity by purchasing bound servants trained as weavers in Europe, taking on native-born apprentices, and/or training their own sons to follow in their footsteps. In addition, young men living as boarders or inmates in the household of an older weaver provided a flexible system of unbound labor without the long-term obligations inherent in using indentured workers. Cloth making, however, was not organized on a large scale; the men who wove did so either in their own households, perhaps in a shop, using their own equipment, or in the households of someone who hired them, but in both cases they did it for sale, not just for their own use. Nevertheless, despite the existence of a commercial weaving economy in Pennsylvania, or the more extensive household textile production of New England women, local manufacture could not begin to satisfy the American demand for fabrics in either quantity or variety. The labor-intensive nature of the work; the fact that farming was generally more profitable than weaving, especially in Pennsylvania; and the abundance and relative cheapness of imported cloth all combined to limit the expansion of textile manufacture in early North America.

Chapter 6
From Loom to Market: Meeting Consumer Demand

Early immigrants to Pennsylvania not only brought European craft skills and traditions to their new home; they also expected to produce for and participate in a growing marketplace. The variety of textiles people owned, and the profusion of imported fabric coming into the province, together with the limited output of Chester County weavers, indicates that while local production provided some of the cloth used in the region, a great deal of it also came from outside individual households and from outside the immediate community. In 1728, a merchant in Philadelphia advertised for sale "Oznabrigs, Garlicks, Calicoes, Duroys, Shalloons . . . , Strouds, Duffels, Stripe Blanketing, Blankets, Hats, and sundry other sorts of Linnens, Woollens . . . , lately imported from London," which he promised could "be paid for next Spring in Country Produce."[1] The acceptance of "Country Produce" as payment meant that the targeted market was as much rural as it was urban.

As we have seen, throughout the eighteenth century, most Chester County farm families did not live at a subsistence level and were sufficiently prosperous to engage in the Atlantic trading network. The result was an economy well enough developed to allow the inhabitants to purchase their textiles from either local artisans or import merchants. But if country people had access to locally made textiles, why did they purchase the imported cloth? How did the availability of an ever-increasing variety of British-made and exotic Eastern fabrics affect eighteenth-century rural cloth producers and consumers? Did British goods cut into the weavers' markets, or did they provide a source of cloth that was unavailable locally? Finally, were local textile producers and suppliers of imported fabric complementary or competitive in rural Pennsylvania?

Eighteenth-century Chester County homes contained a wide variety of cloth items such as sheets, pillow and bolster cases, bed ticking, bed and window curtains, blankets, coverlets, bed rugs, tablecloths, napkins, and towels; personal items such as handkerchiefs and clothing; and farm-related textiles like bags, sacks, winnowing cloths, and wagon covers. Because many inhabitants did not have the skill or equipment to produce a piece of cloth from start to finish, they either paid for the processing they could not do themselves or purchased imported goods. Those buying fabric from a neighboring craftsman could help lower the cost by providing fiber and yarn, which also freed weavers to concentrate on making cloth without having to generate large quantities of raw materials.

Although loom owners in Chester County had more flax (12.1 percent) and wool (6.6 percent) fiber and linen (2.4 percent) and wool (5 percent) yarn among their inventoried goods than did the general population, the difference was not significant enough to suggest that weavers invested time or money to acquire quantities of raw materials for large-scale fabric manufacture. Similarly, loom owners also had more spinning equipment than did the general population (Table 2). However, given that six to ten spinning wheels were needed to provide yarn for one loom (as discussed in Chapter 5), no loom owner had more than five wheels, and only 7.2 percent of them had more than three, weavers apparently were not engaged in extensive yarn production for their cloth making (Table 3). Rather, they operated on a custom-order basis, using raw materials provided by their customers, perhaps supplemented by yarn produced in their own households or that they obtained in payment for their services.

The account book of farmer William Smedley for the years 1751 through 1800 provides a glimpse of how weaving fit into the local economy. Smedley, a yeoman/cabinet-maker from Middletown, kept between ten and twenty sheep and planted flax and hemp.[2] He paid a series of men and women to assist him with the flax harvesting and processing and hired three women to help the family spin tow, flax, and woolen yarn; he bought prepared worsted wool fiber for the women of the household to spin. Smedley gave the yarn spun in his household, along with some that he purchased, to Thomas Taylor, whom he paid to make tow, linen, woolen, linsey, flannel, drugget, serge cloth, bagging, and blanketing. Taylor was a smallholder, not a cottager, who leased a shop from Smedley and wove for him on and off for twenty years, in addition to helping with farm work and performing other small services.[3]

Most people who patronized a local weaver would have, like Smedley, taken yarn spun from fiber they grew or purchased to an artisan and instructed him to make whatever they needed. Some inventoried decedents had yarn earmarked for a variety of items, including linen for bags, flax for eighty yards of linen, woolen and linen for coverlets, woolen for flannel and blankets, and tow for checked fabric.[4] Because fiber processing and spinning was not a full-time occupation for most

TABLE 2
OWNERSHIP OF SPINNING WHEELS IN CHESTER COUNTY

Years	Percentage of Spinning Wheels Owned by Loom Owners*				Percentage of Spinning Wheels Owned by General Population (Decedents)			
	None	1	2	3 or more	None	1	2	3 or more
1715–1718	75	25	0	0	72	6	16	6
1734–1737	43	14	43	0	51	15	24	9
1754–1757	13	13	33	45	42	16	21	18
1773–1776	16	11	16	53	33	19	19	26
1792–1795	25	21	25	31	35	23	21	18
1810–1813	46	0	18	36	42	26	17	15
1828–1831	31	19	6	44	53	17	19	9
Total	28	15	21	36	44	19	19	16

* Where no number was specified but the quantity was clearly more than one the value "2" was assigned.

Note: Percentages have been rounded.

Source: Chester County Wills and Inventories, Chester County Archives, West Chester, Pennsylvania. Based on data taken from a sampling of 1,272 inventories.

TABLE 3
FIBER AND YARN OWNERSHIP IN CHESTER COUNTY (PERCENTAGE)

| | Loom Owners | | | | General Population (Decedents) | | | |
| | Fiber[a] | | Yarn | | Fiber | | Yarn | |
	Flax	Wool	Linen	Wool	Flax	Wool	Linen	Wool
1715–1718	25	0	0	25	9	6	2	2
1734–1737	29	14	14	14	19	22	11	9
1754–1757	47	27	33	33	26	21	13	12
1773–1776	48	37	24	12	36	24	15	13
1792–1795	42	25	0	8	37	18	12	12
1810–1813	46	27	9	0	31	11	8	6
1828–1831	38	19	6	6	17	9	5	3
Total[b]	42	25	13	13	27	16	10	9

[a]Represents those households with fiber present. The quantities were specified on such an irregular basis that it is difficult to draw conclusions from anything other than the presence or absence of fiber. These categories are not mutually exclusive.

[b]Total = Percentage of population with fiber or yarn 1715–1831. Total number of loom owners is 96. Total number of general population is 1,272.

Note: Percentages have been rounded.

Source: Chester County Wills and Inventories, Chester County Archives, West Chester, Pennsylvania. Based on data taken from a sampling of 1,272 inventories.

rural inhabitants, it could take several months or perhaps even years to accumulate sufficient material for a project. Thus for many, the services of the weaver were required only on an irregular basis.

The more preparation a person could do before the yarn went to the weaver, the less the finished product would cost. For example, if the cloth was to be striped or checked using colored yarns, some customers would dye small amounts themselves.[5] However, as dyeing was a highly skilled job, requiring knowledge of chemicals and specialized materials to produce a good, fast color, most people took their yarn to a fuller/dyer.[6] A weaver with several orders for colored cloth might advise his customers to bring him white yarn that he would incorporate with material belonging to others before taking all of it to the dyer; he included the expense of this process in the price of the finished fabric.[7] Some people further defrayed costs by winding their yarn onto spools from which the weaver made the warp, saving the artisan the time-consuming job of spooling.[8] Although a few customers even made their own warps to cut costs, such interventions were rare as these tasks required extensive skill, time, and equipment. For many people, it was more efficient to pay the weaver for the work. He, in turn, based his cost on custom as well as the market.[9]

Throughout most of the eighteenth century, the nature of the demand for locally made cloth meant that, unlike their European counterparts, the majority of rural Chester County weavers did not specialize in making a single product. In contrast, some artisans hoped that a city like Philadelphia, with access to both urban and rural markets might be able to support a more specialized business where they could make only linen cloth, for example, or woolen cloth, or broadcloth, or plush (wool velvet), or tapes (thin strips of cloth used as a binding).[10] Rural Pennsylvanians could buy such specialty fabrics from urban artisans or local retailers if they needed them. Their demand for an array of functional linen and wool fabrics, however, meant that weavers working in farm communities had to be more versatile. Using their clients' yarn, Chester County cloth workers wove several different types of linen and wool fabrics—generally more linen than wool cloth. Joseph Eldridge (see Chapter 5) wove three and a half times more linen than wool between 1786 and 1789 (1,374 yards of linen, 386 yards of wool).[11] Caleb Wickersham, working slightly later, made about three times more linen than wool (2,983 yards of linen to 988 yards of wool).[12] Linen outpaced woolen production because of the importance of flaxseed to the local economy, the wide variety of household furnishings and clothing made of this durable textile, and the ready availability of imported woolen cloth.[13]

Eldridge and Wickersham made coarse and fine linen; plain, checked, and striped tow (a low-grade linen cloth); plain and striped linsey (wool and linen cloth) with up to four colors in it; bagging; bedticking; blankets; flannel; drugget (a coarse cloth of linen or cotton warp and wool weft); camlet (probably a fine wool fabric); shirting; carpet; handkerchiefs; and coverlets. Although working with different fibers, Eldridge's and Wickersham's textiles are similar to those produced by Thomas Taylor. None of the weavers specialized in one particular item, and, despite the different skills and tools needed to weave linen and wool, all wove with both fibers.

The equipment owned by weavers throughout the eighteenth century reflects this lack of product specialization. In 1726, John Lea, who called himself a weaver, had three looms, at least one of them a broad loom on which he could make wool broadcloth. He also owned sixteen sets of sleys (reeds with slits set at intervals to maintain the density of the cloth), which indicate that he wove linen cloth as coarse as sixteen threads per inch (perhaps tow bagging or sacks) and as fine as forty threads per inch (perhaps sheets or shirting) (Fig. 20). He had three sleys designated for wool products, five for weaving broadcloth, and numerous related pieces of equipment.[14] In his 1741 will, George Garrett left one son "that Loom that he usually worketh in with the Twelve Shaft Gear" capable of producing complex patterns; his two others were suitable for simpler materials.[15] In 1783, Andrew Snider had one broad and one narrow weaver's loom, and when he died in 1805, Samuel Sellers had two looms, one of them a "Coverlid Loom" for weaving coverlets, or bed hangings, the other with "huckaback geers" (the heddles—through which the warp ends were threaded in a pattern to produce the huckaback pattern—and the shafts to which they were attached) for making toweling and table linens.[16] (see Fig. 23). Inventories alone cannot reveal what types of weaving the majority of loom owners did because the entries regarding cloth-making tools were very general, usually only specifying "a loom and tacklings," or "two looms and appurtenances," for example. The more detailed notations combined with account-book entries indicate that many weavers did not specialize in a single product and that there were Chester County artisans capable of weaving a variety of plain and complex fabrics.

Historians have argued that most textiles made in the American colonies were plain, of simple construction, and often coarse, and that fine woolen materials like broadcloth were never produced.[17] The equipment documented here belies these suggestions, proving that from the early decades of the eighteenth century Chester County weavers could weave a wide range of goods, including patterned linens and broadcloth. In fact, according to his own definition, Joseph

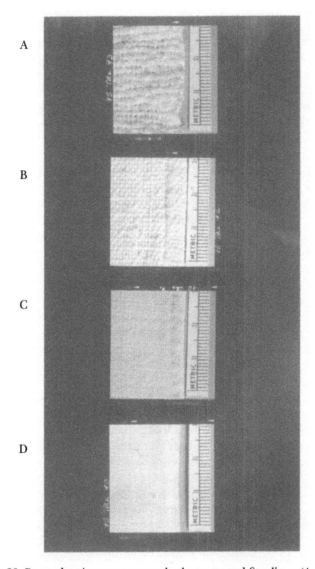

Figure 20. Pennsylvania weavers wove both coarse and fine linen (A through C), but none as fine as the cloth imported from Europe (D). Weavers John Lea and Joseph Eldridge, both of Chester County, would have woven coarse tow cloth for such things as sacking or wagon covers, like that shown in A, with seventeen warp ends per inch or for toweling or sheeting, as in B, at twenty-seven ends per inch; or finer cloth suitable for shirts or table linens, as in C, at fifty ends per inch. The finest cloth woven by John Lea was forty threads per inch, while the textile shown in D had more than double that, at ninety threads per inch. Fabric of the quality shown in D was invariably imported in the eighteenth century, often from Ireland. Photographs by Brian Boyle, Permission of the Royal Ontario Museum, Toronto.

Eldridge wove almost two and a half times more fine linen cloth than coarse tow cloth. Although this linen was a comparatively refined product, it was not equal to the elaborate linen damask or exquisite shirting materials produced by European cottage industries.[18] One could purchase such fabrics only as imports (see Fig. 20). Some weavers may have combined general textile manufacture and specialized production with the exact nature of the business determined by the weaver's training and skill, the demand for a certain product, or a combination of these two factors. By the end of the eighteenth century, a few weavers were becoming more specialized; coverlet and hairsieve (an open-weave cloth made of horsehair and used for sifting) weavers were listed for the first time on the 1799 tax returns.[19] The presence of such specialists suggests that there was an increasing market for finer or more specialized textiles.

For the most part, weavers made cloth only for custom orders.[20] From time to time, they received payment for their services with extra fiber or spun yarn, especially from female customers.[21] Although a weaver might in turn sell some of this, he could also use it to supplement the yarn produced in his own household and make fabric to sell to clients who could not supply the raw materials.[22] Joseph Eldridge sometimes kept a few yards from a larger piece of cloth he wove, either to use himself, or to sell to a person who required only a small amount of fabric but who did not need or could not afford anything larger. Such transactions were not the majority of a weaver's business, and people who did not want custom-made fabric could buy it from a local merchant.

Although Chester County weavers had the skills and equipment needed to manufacture a wide variety of plain, patterned, coarse, and fine textiles, their output met only part of local consumer demand. The cloth requirements of their community can be determined by estimating what a rural population might need and the quantities of fabric the weavers produced. Because wearing apparel accounted for the most fundamental use of cloth, the amount required by a household for a basic wardrobe serves as a good yardstick, although estimating it can be tricky.[23] Newspaper ads for runaways are full of information about clothes worn by the laboring and dependent classes.[24] Probate inventories give a glimpse of the garments of their social superiors.[25] Both these sources, however, grant only snapshots in time. For quantitative purposes, we need to know the types of clothing a person might have owned over the course of a year, and what items he or she would have replaced and how often. One could possess the requisite cloth or skin clothing and bedding for basic warmth, but what about issues of

conspicuous consumption, comfort, status, and the varying commit-
ment to fashion?[26]

The recorded quantities of apparel given to male paupers yearly, or
the wardrobe an urban laborer could afford, can supplement newspaper and inventory data by serving as indicators of some basic clothing items and the frequency of their replacement. Such information is
not abundant, however, and does not exist at all for Chester County,
so examples must be extrapolated from other Pennsylvania contexts.
Between 1770 and 1816, the Mennonite Church in neighboring
Montgomery County, Pennsylvania, provided pauper Isaac Gross with
a pair of long pants and a shirt annually, a waistcoat every four to five
years, and one great coat in sixteen years, during the forty-six years in
which it cared for him. The church had these items made for Gross;
not included are unrecorded donations of secondhand clothing.[27]
Also at the lower end of the social scale were Philadelphia laborers. According to Billy G. Smith, such men made enough money annually to
buy a pair of coarse laborer's shoes, a pair of cloth breeches, a cloth
coat, two shirts, and a felt hat, but these made only a minimal
wardrobe, apparently not even equal to clothing given to almshouse
inmates every year in the early nineteenth century. The estimate does
not account for clothing acquired secondhand, stolen, or made at
home.[28]

Further up the social ladder, David Henry, a Chester County miller,
owned a new broadcloth coat, a double-breasted velvet jacket, a pair
of velvet breeches, a pair of jean breeches and jacket, a blue cloth coat,
a double-breasted cloth jacket, a second cloth coat, three pairs of
trousers, three partly worn shirts, a new barcelona handkerchief, and
a partly worn cotton and silk handkerchief when he died in 1788.[29]
Generally, though, over the course of the century, most of the few inventoried men with lists of clothing possessed at least one great coat
(Fig. 21) and approximately three other coats, three jackets, three pairs
of breeches, three pairs of trousers, three shirts, and a handkerchief.[30]

Using this information as a rough guide and thinking only in terms
of the cloth required to make the bare necessities, we may calculate
some yardages for a man's clothing. At the very least, he would need
one good suit (seven yards), two good shirts (seven yards), three
coarse shirts (ten and a half yards), two pairs of work trousers (eight
yards), two pairs of drawers or lining for breeches (eight yards); one
waistcoat (two and a quarter yards), and one coat (four yards), totaling
forty-six and three-quarters yards (see Table 4 for the yardage needed
to make some clothing and household textiles). If an individual replaced everything but the good suit and shirts every two years, the basic amount of cloth needed annually would have been sixteen and

Figure 21. This fawn-colored woolen great coat shown from the back was a staple item of a man's wardrobe in the second half of the eighteenth century. Dating from the 1780s, the tightly woven and well-fulled outer fabric could have been made locally or imported. Great coats were outer garments worn in winter. The cape would have provided extra warmth and protection from moisture, while the full cut of the skirt made it practical for riding horses. Acc. # 1991.7. Permission of Chester County Historical Society, West Chester, Pennsylvania.

TABLE 4
YARDAGE NEEDED FOR TEXTILE ITEMS

	Yardage[a]
Clothing	
Petticoat	4
Shift	3.5
Apron	1
Gown	7
Cloak	4 (1.5 yards of broadcloth)[b]
Breeches	3
Shirt	3.5
Great coat	5
Household	
Blanket	6
Sheet	6
Tablecloth	1
Napkin	1[c]
Towel	0.5
Bedtick (double)	10
Farm	
Large bag	2
Winnowing cloth	8

Note: All measurements are approximate and are based on cloth that is thirty-six inches wide.

[a]According to Linda Baumgarten, curator of costume and textiles, Colonial Williamsburg, personal communication.
[b]A cloak made of broadcloth needed less length because it was wider (fifty-four to sixty-three inches wide) than other cloth (thirty-six inches wide). The broadcloth quantity of 1.5 yards listed here is obtained from a list of goods claimed for compensation because of having been destroyed or stolen during the American Revolution. Depredation Claims, Chester County Papers, #115a, Historical Society of Pennsylvania, Philadelphia.
[c]Linda Baumgarten, personal communication, notes that all eighteenth-century napkins were a yard square.

Source: Estimates are derived from information contained in Ellen J. Gehret, *Rural Pennsylvania Clothing* (York, Pa.: Liberty Cap Books, 1976), and Adrienne D. Hood, "Reproducing Nineteenth-Century Handwoven Fabrics: A Weaver's Guide to Accurate Reproductions" (unpublished, 1981).

two-fifths yards (Table 4). According to advertisements describing runaway female servants and slaves between 1750 and 1800, their clothing usually consisted of shifts and petticoats, covered by a gown or short gown, and an apron (Fig. 22).[31] The clothing of better-off, inventoried women is more difficult to assess because, as for their male counterparts, detailed lists are scarce.[32] Probate records recording apparel for seven women between 1750 and 1793, suggest that their basic wardrobe would have consisted of two to nine petticoats and gowns, three to fourteen shifts, three or four bodices or short gowns, one to seven cloaks, three to thirteen aprons, three to six handkerchiefs, and other miscellaneous items such as bed gowns, coats, wrappers, bonnet covers, stays, hoods, and sleeves.[33]

A woman's basic wardrobe and the minimum amount of cloth needed to make it might thus consist of one good gown, one petticoat, one good cloak, two bodices or short gowns, two aprons, two shifts, and a coarse cloak, requiring thirty-seven yards of fabric (Table 4). Again, if all but the good clothing was replaced every two years, the amount of cloth needed annually would have been thirteen yards. It is almost impossible to make estimates for children because they could wear hand-me-downs or otherwise recycled clothes. A rough estimate is about three yards per child annually.[34]

Population figures suggest that in the last quarter of the eighteenth century the average Chester County household had six people, consisting of two adults and four children.[35] If men annually needed at least sixteen and a half yards of fabric for clothing, women about thirteen, and each child about three, a household of six would require about forty-two yards of cloth or almost seven yards per person, just to replace essential apparel that had worn out. These figures are minimums and do not consider the clothing people may have bought for display and adornment.

In addition to clothing, Chester County inventories contained listings of a wide variety of household textiles. Linens included sheets, pillow and bolster cases, bed ticking, bed and window curtains, tablecloths, napkins, and towels. Blankets, coverlets, and bed rugs were made of wool or wool and linen combined. For farm use, bags, sacks, winnowing cloths, and wagon covers were made of coarse tow linen or hemp.[36] Most of these items would have lasted longer than clothing; the frequency with which such things as bags, towels, sheets, table linens, and bed ticks required replacement depended on how many of each item a family possessed, which was determined by the size and wealth of the household, the number of beds, and how much they were used. "Bed furniture" (the term used to denote both the bed and its textiles) used a lot of cloth—as much as fifty yards for a set consisting of bed curtains, valances, covers, and window curtains—in addition to blankets, and coverlets; these items were replaced less frequently because of wear than other household textiles (Fig 23).[37] Chester County residents, therefore, required a wide array of functional cloth and clothing, but even this rural population participated in the growing consumerism of the eighteenth-century Atlantic world, acquiring textiles for reasons other than need.

Figure 22. Made and worn in the late eighteenth century, this printed cotton short gown and petticoat (there was likely an overskirt that would have allowed the printed border of the petticoat to be seen) was made from imported cloth. The fact that this clothing was for everyday use demonstrates the broad range of imported textiles available and used by the colonists—from simple and inexpensive, to costly and elaborate. Acc. # 00/76, CLF 186. Permission of Chester County Historical Society, West Chester, Pennsylvania.

Detail of doublecloth bed hanging handwoven in natural and indigo-dyed linen. Chester County, last half of the eighteenth century.

Handwoven woolen blanket, plain weave, seamed up the middle, Chester County, dated 1792 (detail).

Handwoven linen napkin, huckaback weave, Chester County, late eighteenth century (detail).

Figure 23. The all-linen bed hanging, woolen blanket, and linen napkin shown here represent a range of locally made household textiles with a variety of patterns and weave structures that one might expect to find in an eighteenth-century Chester County home. Acc. #1997.792 (bed hanging), Acc. #2000.1202 (blanket), Acc. #1999.618 (napkin). Permission of Chester County Historical Society, West Chester, Pennsylvania.

Functionality was not the only reason to purchase cloth; it was also a visible status symbol. In addition, as Susan Prendergast Schoelwer has argued, for many eighteenth-century Pennsylvanians, textiles, especially fabric furnishings, functioned on psychological and physical levels beyond mere necessity. In terms of comfort, they "softened, warmed, secluded and cleansed man's living spaces, making them thereby more suitable for his higher social, intellectual, and spiritual activities." Socially, they ensured privacy (window and bed curtains) and indicated social or economic status (quantities and types of fabrics).[38] Gradually, according to Schoelwer, the psychological and social need for fabric use overtook the original physical needs. Thus, as Neil McKendrick and colleagues observed, " 'luxuries' came to be seen as mere 'decencies,' and 'decencies' came to be seen as 'necessities.' "[39] As this occurred, the bed, with an obviously central role in the household, and the table, as the focus of social activities and hence a visible indicator of status, were the prime locations for textile furnishings. Window coverings were further indicators of wealth (in addition to providing privacy and insulation), as were floor coverings. Schoelwer found that in eighteenth-century Philadelphia, bedding and table linens were among the most frequently owned household textiles. This was also true in Chester County: bedding comprised 188 of 266 textile items (71 percent) from a sampling of 100 inventories during the period, while table linens were found 49 times (18 percent).

Sheets and blankets were the most frequently inventoried household textiles, with tablecloths not far behind. Napkins and towels were also listed in the sampled inventories throughout the eighteenth century.[40] Not surprisingly, the range of household textiles increased over the century, although some items like bed rugs listed in 1715, had disappeared by 1795, while others, like wagon covers, appeared for the first time, perhaps indicating changes in fashion and mobility, respectively.[41]

An even more immediately perceivable indicator of social and economic status than furnishing fabrics, however, was the clothing people wore. Many of the garments worn by rural inhabitants were made of simple and durable wool, worsted, linen, or mixed fabrics. People in the country would have less need than their urban counterparts to make an impression of wealth and status, but the proximity of Chester County to Philadelphia undoubtedly influenced rural fashion.[42] Throughout the eighteenth century, in addition to their more simple apparel, women also owned garments of various types of silk, chintz, calico, fine broadcloth, cambric, and muslin, while men had clothing of velvet, fine linen, marsails (white quilted cotton), and silk

(Fig. 24).[43] All these clothing materials were costly imports, but nonetheless they were seen beyond urban areas in early America. Chester County was, however, a region inhabited by many Quakers who believed in simplicity of dress, thus it is important to bear in mind that religion, length of time in the New World, ethnicity, and race would affect regional variations in degrees of finery.[44]

The wider array of clothing and furnishing textiles in American household inventories in the 1790s than earlier in the century suggests that, like their British counterparts, Americans were developing a taste for items that went beyond necessity.[45] Consumer goods were increasing in both quantity and variety, and inhabitants had more disposable income to channel into expensive merchandise, which were in turn important to their comfort, in addition to communicating social and economic status.[46] Pennsylvanians could find status and luxury only in goods manufactured outside the province, however. No matter how much local weavers expanded their capacity, they could not provide the silks, chintzes, and increasingly elaborate printed fabrics available from abroad. In that regard, they faced a similar challenge to that of British weavers and dyers, who struggled to equal the vibrant and diverse patterns found in Asian silks, chintzes, and calicoes. Moreover, the mechanical cotton-spinning equipment used in Britain in the last decades of the eighteenth century lowered the cost of imported functional fabrics manufactured there, making it even more difficult for American production to compete. Until that time, however, locally made and imported fabrics had a stable and complementary coexistence in rural Pennsylvania.[47]

Armed with basic annual clothing requirements and the number and variety of woven household items, we can evaluate the ability of local producers to meet the textile needs of Chester County's farm families by going back to their capacity for fiber production. The average number of sheep per household was six to seven, enough to provide a family of six with only about three pounds of wool per person annually.[48] This would make about three yards of wool cloth, or half a blanket, a man's shirt, a woman's linsey petticoat, or a pair of mittens and stockings, for one individual each year (see Table 4). Fiber production and spinning, however, were supplemental to the agrarian livelihood of the rural residents, comprising only some of their daily activities. In addition, almost half the probated population did not own sheep, and weavers did not produce enough fiber to make quantities of cloth to sell on speculation, making it necessary for some people to obtain wool elsewhere if they were to buy locally made cloth.[49] Wool was not imported to the province and, as there were very few large sheep

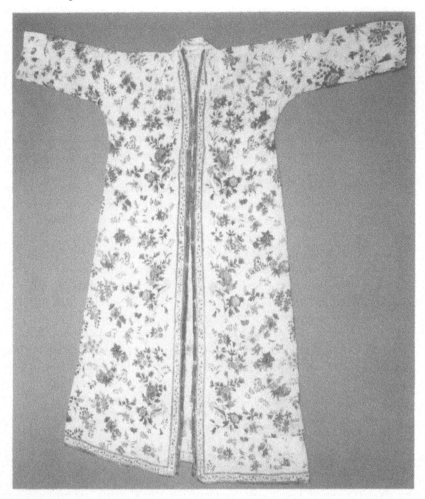

Figure 24. This man's loose coat, or banyan, was worn for leisure or informal occasions over a shirt and breeches. The lightweight, colorfully printed, imported Indian cotton chintz banyan belonged to William Buckley of Chester County (1745–1816). It would have been suitable to wear during the hot days of summer, in addition to being easy to wash. Acc. #1990.500 (CLM 208). Permission of Chester County Historical Society, West Chester, Pennsylvania.

farmers, many inhabitants who could not acquire the requisite raw materials had to obtain their textiles by means other than local production, usually as imports. Linen, too, although more extensively available than wool, was far from ubiquitous. More than 80 percent of the decedent households did not have flax (linen or tow) yarn, and

40 percent lacked any means to spin yarn. Moreover, as we have seen, some people used the fiber and yarn they produced to pay for a variety of goods and services.[50] In general, the population of Chester County, including textile workers, lacked the quantities of yarn or spinning equipment to indicate large-scale manufacturing. Even those who did make yarn did not make enough to rely on a neighboring artisan to provide all their cloth needs.

William Smedley recorded the quantity and types of fabric Thomas Taylor wove for him between 1758 and 1766. Taylor's total yardage of 286 can be broken down as follows: forty-nine yards of woolen (suitable for breeches, coats, shirts, cloaks, or gowns), thirty-one yards of linsey (breeches, petticoats, gowns, blankets), seventy-nine yards of tow (shirts, breeches, tablecloths, sheets, ticking, towels, winnowing cloths), forty-three yards of linen (breeches, aprons, tablecloths, napkins, sheets), fifteen yards of flannel (coats), twenty-one yards of blanketing, sixteen yards of bagging, seventeen yards of drugget (petticoats and gowns), and fifteen yards of serge (gowns) (Table 5). In a nine-year period the locally made cloth could have produced two bedticks, five coarse and four fine bed sheets, four blankets, four tablecloths, six napkins, eight coarse towels, eight large bags, one winnowing cloth, five petticoats, four gowns, two aprons, five shirts, ten pairs of breeches, five coats, and two cloaks. These items would have used about thirty yards a year or, in an average-size household of six, about five yards of fabric per person.[51] If minimal apparel for a family of six required forty-two yards of cloth annually and cloth goods (especially clothing) are extremely susceptible to wear and require frequent replacement, this amount would not have begun to meet even the basic textile needs of the family. Moreover, Smedley had more sheep than the average household and grew and processed flax as well. If a rural family like this, with fiber and the equipment to spin it, did not produce sufficient raw materials to supply their textile requirements through local production, then it is unlikely that many other families did.

The account book of Joseph Eldridge further corroborates the limited scale of local cloth manufacture. Textile production relied on more than the ability of the rural residents to provide the fiber; it also depended on how weavers chose to divide their time between agriculture and craftwork. Between 1786 and 1789, Eldridge produced 2,498 yards of cloth, ranging from an annual high of 950 yards in 1788 to a low of 275 yards in 1789; his average yearly output was 625 yards.[52] Factors such as illness, childbirth (his first child was born in July 1789 and died a year later), customer demand, the type of cloth (finer fabric took more time to weave), and the profitability of directing his energies to agricultural work accounted for Eldridge's fluctuating output. His lowest production was in 1789, only three years before the death of his uncle James with whom he lived. Given James's poor health during this time and the fact that he had a 150-acre farm to take care of, Eldridge probably had to devote more energy to agricultural work than to his weaving.[53] These responsibilities would have claimed even more of Eldridge's time when he inherited the farm after his uncle's death in 1793. His total cloth production for 1794 was a mere 60.5 yards. He did hire James Allcorn, however, to weave for half pay between February 19 and August 9, 1794, during which time Allcorn wove a total of 470 yards for Eldridge's customers in addition to working nineteen days doing a variety of agricultural jobs. The combined output of Eldridge and Allcorn for 1794 was 531 yards of cloth—substantially less than Eldridge had produced before he had the responsibilities attendant on running a large farm.

Between 1794 and 1809, Eldridge hired a number of journeymen weavers to work for him on one of his looms while he used the other when time permitted. In 1809, he employed Thomas Nicholson to work on shares (share his earnings with his employer) between March 17 and October 13, during which time the hired man produced more than 700 yards of cloth. By this time, however, Eldridge's two eldest sons, Joseph and Enos—seventeen and fourteen years old, respectively— were learning their father's craft. Joseph Jr. was fully trained and Enos would have been advanced enough to warrant the acquisition of another loom and accessories that his father bought from John Townsend in 1809. That year, the Eldridge family wove nearly 800 yards. As a result of the expansion of the familial labor force to include Nicholson, Eldridge, and his sons, the Eldridge workshop in 1809 wove just under 1,500 yards, almost three times as much as in 1794.

The ability of a weaver to produce cloth depended on more than just his own labor or the availability of raw materials. In Eldridge's case, even when his sons worked for him he continued to hire a journeyman weaver, thereby substantially increasing the output of his operation. A key to the higher production levels was the newly obtainable machine-spun yarn that freed weavers from their reliance on local wool and flax. A notation in the back of Eldridge's second account book shows that in 1810 he received "A Packet of Cotton yarn from Providence R.I. Manufacturing Company."[54] Provided that he could find trained artisans to work for him, Eldridge could move into what, according to John Commons, is the second stage of production, shop work—a combination of custom or bespoke work and standard items kept in stock for sale.[55] With the establishment of a fulling mill run by

TABLE 5
ESTIMATED QUANTITIES OF LOCALLY MADE TEXTILE GOODS
FOR ONE HOUSEHOLD:
FABRIC WOVEN FOR WILLIAM SMEDLEY, 1758–1766[a]

Fabric	Yardage	Annual Production (yards)	Goods Produced[b]			
Woolen	49	5.4	Breeches = 2 pr	Cloaks	= 2	
			Coats =	2 Gown	= 2	
			Shirts =	2		
Linsey	31	3.4	Breeches = 2 pr	Gown	= 1	
			Petticoat =	2 Blanket	= 2	
Tow	79	8.7	Tablecloths = 2	Sheets	= 5	
			Towels =	8 Shirts	= 3	
			Winnowing	Ticking	= 2	
			cloth =	1		
			Breeches = 4 pr			
Linen	43	4.7	Napkins =	6 Sheets	= 4	
			Breeches =	2 Aprons	= 2	
			Tablecloths = 2			
Flannel	15	1.6	Coats =	3		
Blanketing	21	2.3	Blankets =	4		
Bagging	16	1.7	Bags =	8		
Drugget	17	1.8	Petticoat =	3 Gown	= 2	
Serge	15	1.6	Gown =	1		
Total	286	31.2				

[a]Based on quantities recorded between 1758 and 1766 in William Smedley, Account Book, 1751–1800, ms. #77049, Chester County Historical Society, West Chester, Pennsylvania.
[b]These represent the types of goods that Smedley might have had made from the cloth. Based on articles found in inventories during the period in which Smedley lived.

his son Joseph in 1813, Eldridge had transformed his workshop operation into a small manufacturing business capable of making quantities of finished cloth.[56] Until machine-spun cotton was obtainable in the early nineteenth century, however, Eldridge's output depended on the availability of locally handspun yarn, the amount of time he could devote to his craft, and his ability to hire someone to help.

In 1787, working without assistance, Eldridge wove 661.5 yards of cloth for twenty-three customers (28.8 yards per household or 4.7 yards per person annually).[57] This is very close to the 5.2 yards of cloth woven yearly for the members of William Smedley's household several decades earlier. In 1794, Eldridge produced 531 yards for thirteen households, averaging 6.7 yards per person. These figures suggest that for much of the eighteenth century in Chester County, weavers were producing about 5.5 yards per person annually. If 7 yards of fabric were required for minimum annual clothing needs without including household textiles in this estimate, it is clear that even the people who patronized local weavers did not obtain all their cloth from them.

In 1809, although Eldridge's workshop produced three times the cloth it had earlier because he now employed three artisans, his customer base was not expanding; he did make more cloth for each household, however.[58] Instead of weaving 5.5 yards of fabric per person, he now was making 10.2 yards for each, or almost double his eighteenth-century output. The availability of inexpensive machine-spun cotton yarn to weavers like Joseph Eldridge was critical to their shift into the second stage of craft production where they stocked goods for sale, as it freed them from reliance on locally grown raw materials provided by their customers—especially flax for which cotton could be substituted (discussed in Chapter 3). But the beginnings of industrialization began to permeate the countryside. In 1794, Tench Coxe observed that

[t]he manufactures of Pennsylvania have increased exceedingly within a few years. . . . The hand-machines, for carding and spinning cotton, have been introduced by foreigners, and improved, but we have obtained the water mill for spinning cotton, and a water mill for flax, which is applicable also to spinning hemp and wool. These machines promise us an early increase of the cotton, linen, and hempen branches, and must be of very great service in the woolen branch. Additional employment for weavers, dyers, bleachers, and other manufacturers must be the consequence.[59]

Clearly, this prediction was accurate in the case of weaver Joseph Eldridge. The hand machines and water mills described by Coxe would have initially increased household production of yarn by transferring the onerous and time-consuming work of flax breaking and scutching, and wool carding away from the family to a mill, allowing people to spend more time spinning (see Chapter 3). As they were able to make increasing quantities of yarn, the rural populace could buy more of their cloth from neighboring artisans. Once spinning was mechanized, local weavers no longer had to rely on their customers for raw materials and residents did not have to produce it. Larger quantities of raw material from within the province supplemented with yarn imported from elsewhere allowed local weavers to expand their output by employing more artisans to work it up. The growing number of landless weavers in the county reflects this fact.

Most of Eldridge's clients lived close to him (within a radius of five to eight miles) and many were relatives, but he was not weaving for everyone who lived in the area.[60] Whether the cloth he wove was for a neighbor or a family member, Eldridge charged everyone for his work and kept careful account of his transactions. He based the cost of a yard of fabric on the time involved in making the warp, dressing the loom, and weaving (thus a striped cloth that was made with more than one shuttle and was more time-consuming to weave cost more than a plain fabric). When he sold his products on credit, the estimated interest would be included in the final price.[61] In some cases, people paid him with a variety of goods and services such as meat, drink, agricultural products, work on the farm, or spinning and knitting, but by far the majority of Eldridge's customers used cash to settle their accounts.[62] Even artisans working in the early eighteenth century received more cash payments than goods and services, although the difference was not as great.[63]

The practice of paying cash for cloth made in Chester County must be stressed. Scholars have thought that local textile manufacture existed because inhabitants lacked money to buy imported fabrics and could exchange commodities or services for locally made cloth, allowing the colonists to be as self-sufficient as possible.[64] The fact that less than 10 percent of Chester County households had looms and that cloth workers were usually paid for their services in cash suggests that this was not the case. Moreover, merchants selling imported textiles also accepted "Country Goods" in payment.[65] Textile production in eighteenth-century Chester County obviously did not owe its existence to a lack of money with which to pay for imported material. By providing their own yarn to a local artisan, individuals could reduce the cost of finished goods, leaving them more to spend on other commodities, imported textiles among them.

Although structured differently, New England fabric production had a similar economic function. Laurel Ulrich describes the scene of young women at home weaving woolen shirting while their parents were in Boston buying luxurious imported silks and satins: "The shirting the girls were weaving helped pay for the satin, though it never appeared in the credit column under their father's name at the store."[66] By making some of their own more functional clothing and textiles, the girls saved the cost of buying them, freeing up money for more elaborate acquisitions. Weaving in New England, like fiber and yarn production in Pennsylvania, was part of the hidden work that

Ulrich argues contributed to a family's ability to participate in wider markets. For early Americans, items made from cloth were necessary and desirable commodities that they obtained in several ways in addition to what they got from local weavers.

The stream of immigrants moving to Pennsylvania throughout much of the eighteenth century brought quantities of clothing and fabric with them as some of the essential goods they needed to begin their new life. Writing in 1725, Robert Parke urged his sister in Ireland to join him in Pennsylvania, advising her to clothe herself "very well with woolen & Linnen, Shoes & Stockings, & hats, for Such things are dear hear, yet a man will Sooner Earn a Suit of Cloths here than in Ireland, by Reason workmens Labour is So dear." He also suggested that if his friend Samuel Thompson chose to emigrate, he should "Cloath his family as well as his Small Ability will allow." In addition to his advice for the future immigrants, Parke asked his sister to bring several yards of silk with her to Pennsylvania so that "Sister Raichell" could make two hoods.[67] Thus, many of the first-generation immigrants who arrived in Pennsylvania brought most of the fabric items they needed with them from Europe.[68] Enough cloth was damaged by the ocean crossing, in fact, that some artisans set up businesses to remove mildew and stains from textiles.[69] The continued communication of recent arrivals with family members who had remained at home made it possible to ask for luxury goods like silk to be sent over with later émigrés. For new Pennsylvanians who had provided themselves amply with such items, it could be some time before they had to replace them. When they did, they had several options, in addition to a local weaver.

Fulling-mill operators and local storekeepers in Chester County often sold fabric, as did nearby Philadelphia merchants. Given the labor intensity of textile manufacture, regardless of whether cloth was made by Pennsylvania artisans or imported, it was an expensive and valued commodity. For example, wealthy eighteenth-century Philadelphians' fabric was worth more than their wrought silver.[70] Because of their value, textiles were often used as payment for goods or services, resold at a profit, or used as promissory notes.[71] Historian Beverly Lemire has noted that in Britain at this time "a wardrobe could be the equivalent to a savings account," as it could also be used as currency. No doubt immigrants continued this practice and refined it to suit their new circumstances.[72]

Many mill owners, in particular those who ran fulling mills, were also storekeepers who sold a variety of goods.[73] As early as 1710, Chester County miller Richard Hayes sold Martha Taylor imported muslin, some of which she paid for "by the weavinge 24 yards of Cloth by her husband." Hayes could in turn sell this cloth.[74] During the 1770s and 1780s numerous people paid fuller Roger Kirk for his services by weaving a variety of cloth which he finished and sold at a profit.[75] Despite the purchase of quantities of fabric made by his customers, Kirk obviously had a larger market for his finished textiles, especially during the War for Independence. Several times in 1780, 1781, and 1783 he bought cloth from Maryland through agents, transactions that were profitable even after he had paid freight and commission.[76] A few fullers, like Thomas Marshall of Darby and William Kirk of East Nottingham, also had looms that weavers could work on for wages or on shares. The fullers would finish and sell the cloth produced by these artisans.[77] These fulling and weaving operations were perhaps the closest thing to a cloth manufactory in existence in eighteenth-century Chester County.

In addition to purchasing newly woven cloth to sell, fullers also recycled old materials. Because fabric was such an expensive commodity, it is not surprising that it was used and reused. The fuller, with his dyeing, washing, and pressing facilities was the ideal person to revive old clothing and textiles. In 1746, David Davis, who ran a fulling mill in Darby Township, advertised in the May 15 edition of the *Pennsylvania Gazette* that he would dye, scour, and press old garments.[78] In 1780, Roger Kirk scoured and pressed an "old Cloke" for Dinah Churchman; three years earlier, he had dyed and dressed "Old Blankets for Sadlecloth"; in 1776, he "Mill Scoured Old blankets to sell."[79] The service of revitalizing old fabric was a valuable asset during the American Revolution when textiles in the country were scarce because of trade interruptions with Britain. In Pennsylvania, the shortage of clothing and bedding for the Continental Army was somewhat alleviated by the collection of old blankets and linens that were sent to fullers to be cleaned before shipping them out for military use.[80] Fulling-mill owners who bought locally woven items, produced finished cloth manufactured within their own establishments, and cleaned and revitalized old textiles, were a major source of new and used fabric goods for rural residents. An extensive secondhand trading network flourished throughout Europe, and North America also recycled its old cloth goods.[81] New or used, textiles of all sorts retained their economic value.

Local fabric production, supplemented by cloth brought over by immigrants and the constant reuse of old textiles, furnished some of the fabric needs of local inhabitants, but imported cloth provided even more. The exact quantities of imported textiles that reached the rural residents, however, are difficult to determine.[82] One major problem in this undertaking is lack of consistent and clear terms for fabrics in sources from the period.[83] Words like "homespun," "homemade," or "country cloth," used so often in newspaper descriptions of clothing worn by runaways, seem to indicate fabric woven at home or in the American countryside. Indeed, these descriptions, coupled with fragmentary government reports, have been instrumental in forming our vision of homespun cloth made and worn by rural, colonial Americans.[84] The homespun attire of runaway servants and slaves, however, appears much more frequently than in Chester County household inventories, where it is almost nonexistent (less than 1 percent).[85] Moreover, local weavers and fullers rarely used the term in conjunction with the cloth they manufactured. What did "homemade" mean, if it did not refer to cloth made by Americans at home?

During the eighteenth century in North America and in much of Europe, as we have seen, almost all the yarn and fabric produced was manufactured within the household.[86] Technically, therefore, all cloth was homemade.[87] If the terms "homespun," "homemade," or "country cloth" referred solely to material made at home, why were they applied to only some types of fabrics? Textile historian Arthur Cole has argued that chief among wool products in the colonies "was that called 'homespun.' This was an all-wool fabric, well fulled, worn without artificial coloring or piece-dyed, and more rarely dyed in the wool, but ever distinctly rough in character."[88] A closer look at the descriptions of runaway clothing shows that, in contrast to Cole's definition, "homespun" fabrics included linen, fine linen, worsted, kersey (a cheap, coarse, but warm, woolen fabric), linsey-woolsey, flannel, tow, drugget, and stuff (a catchall term for a variety of worsted fabrics).[89]

To confuse the issue further, imported "homemade" cloth was sold in the colonies. For example, the April 12, 1764, *Pennsylvania Gazette* recorded "housewifes or home made checks and stripes" among the textiles imported from England.[90] Rather than designating locally made products, "homespun" generally referred to coarse, irregular goods that lacked the even quality of professionally manufactured items. Thus, the proficiency of the weavers or the quality of the fiber was a major factor in determining the use of the term.[91] In Chester County, because the artisans were skilled, one would not expect to find great quantities of this fabric, and the inventories bear this out. In contrast, in eighteenth-century Essex County, Massachusetts, where the growing number of female weavers received more informal instruction, there was a substantially greater quantity and variety of homespun items listed among the inventoried population.[92]

Not only is the term "homespun" difficult to pinpoint in eighteenth-century use, many locally made fabrics had the same names as imports. One would expect the large quantities of textiles arriving in North America from places like England, Ireland, Scotland, France, Germany, Russia, Italy, Spain, Holland, and the "Orient" to be identifiable.[93] Cargo lists and newspaper advertisements show such geographically designated fabrics as "Russia sheeting"; a variety of plain and striped "Hollands"; "Irish Linen"; "British sail cloth"; "Oznaburgs"; "Barcelona Handkerchiefs"; "Scots linen"; and "German serge." Closer examination reveals that, although these labels may have originally denoted country or region of manufacture, they had become generic by the eighteenth century.[94] The examples of "Irish Hollands" and "British Oznaburg," or "Dutch Linsey" woven in New Jersey, shows that such terms cannot reliably identify the place of origin.[95] In addition, adjectives used to identify an item for sale like "Russia Sheeting" usually disappeared in lists of household goods, becoming instead "coarse linen sheeting" or simply "sheets." Geographic identification from the name alone is therefore difficult, as is determining the type of cloth. The problem of deciphering terms is not new, for, in 1760, the English agents of the Beekman family of New York wrote from Bristol, England: "You will Observe in the Long Ells (which we take to be what you mean by Serges folded up as Shalloons) we are afraid the Maker has not been exact in Colours."[96] In addition, a word like "dimity" denoted a wide variety of textiles, from corded fabrics to those embellished with large flower patterns. Without a description or a fabric sample, it is often impossible to know what was meant.[97]

Confusing labels notwithstanding, the products made by Chester County weavers can be compared with those advertised for sale by Philadelphia merchants, sold by local shopkeepers, and owned by rural residents, in order to make some generalizations. Many imported textiles were of high to medium quality and included Indian chintz, nankeen (cloth made from yellow cotton), oriental silks, and calicoes.[98] These fabrics were purchased in the East by factors working for Philadelphia merchants or through the East India Company, which shipped large quantities of exotic material to England. After 1721, much of the East India Company cargoes were directed to the colonial markets, as all Indian cottons were banned in Britain in attempts to protect the British textile industry. Not only were these foreign textiles sold in cities like Philadelphia, Boston, and Salem, Massachusetts, but many also reached the rural residents who purchased them from urban merchants or through local storekeepers.[99]

Printed and painted fabrics and silks comprised only a part of the trade, however. Much of the imported cloth was functional and replicated some of the material made by Pennsylvania weavers, including druggets, blankets, bedticks, checked linen, tammy (a multipurpose, lightweight, openweave, worsted fabric), huckabacks, coarse linen, shirting cloth, coverlets, and, as already mentioned, "homemade" cloth.[100] This duplication is not surprising given the labor-intensity of textile manufacture and that Chester County weavers were only a small percentage of the population. Thus many rural inhabitants bought both luxury and utilitarian imported cloth to satisfy their needs.

There was even more motivation to buy foreign goods when they were cheap. According to Thomas Doerflinger, "from 1749 to 1790 the constant cry in Philadelphia, broken only by a few brief pauses, was that the city was glutted with dry goods, that cloth was cheaper in Philadelphia than in Manchester, and that dozens of importers were about to go broke. There is no question that these complaints, though exaggerated, had a real basis in fact."[101] Easy availability of inexpensive, imported cloth goods, therefore, would definitely slow the impetus for establishing local textile manufacture, and residents of eighteenth-century Chester County lived within easy access of Philadelphia merchants.

It was not necessary to travel to Philadelphia to buy imported textiles, however, because Chester County shopkeepers also sold them. The fabric stock of five retailers from 1729 to 1773 demonstrates that for the most part these men sold goods that were not obtainable through local manufacture. Storekeepers imported almost 80 percent of the material sold. Less than 20 percent was made by weavers in the area or was imported yet resembled local production; only 1 to 2 percent was actually called "homespun."[102] Given this breakdown, it is unlikely that retailers were competing with neighboring cloth makers for a market. Rather, imported and locally made fabrics were more complementary than competitive in this era, serving different needs within the colonial community. The people who needed inexpensive, coarse goods but did not produce fiber to supply to the weaver, would have been able to buy the equivalent from among the lower end of the shopkeeper's merchandise. Access to cheap, foreign cloth, combined with the labor intensity of weaving, made this imported material attractive to many rural consumers.

Although many eighteenth-century Chester County residents participated in various aspects of cloth production, most did not assemble fabric from start to finish; they expected to pay for some stage of local manufacture in addition to buying imported fabrics. The economic success of the region meant that individual households did not need to make their own furnishing and clothing fabric in order to eke out a living.[103] As long as they continued to engage in profitable mixed farming, the inhabitants could afford to buy both the luxury and functional imported fabrics that were arriving in the colony in large variety and quantity throughout the eighteenth century. The small scale of the craft and its dependency on locally grown fiber, however, meant that cloth production would remain relatively static until there was an increase in available raw materials. Most important, imported textiles did not compete with local manufacture or vice versa. The intense labor of production in a primarily agricultural community ensured the two were complementary. As the eighteenth century ended, however, new technology began an industrial transformation that would change forever a long-established craft tradition.

Chapter 7

Weaving Moves into the Mills

"The short period between 1810 and 1830 saw the center of gravity of textiles shift from the fireside to the factory," observed business historian Victor S. Clark in 1929. "The transfer of spinning and weaving in America from homes to factories was a greater change than their transfer from workshops to factories in Great Britain. No other industrial arts were so universally practiced by our people and no other were so suddenly taken from their hands."[1] Clark's conclusions about the timing of the transfer from domestic to factory production in the early decades of the nineteenth century are relatively accurate, but, as we have seen, his claims about the universality of spinning and weaving are not. If we compare how local textile manufacture operated in Chester County, Pennsylvania, with the better-studied region of New England, it is clear that even without technological change, there were regional variations.

In New England, what ultimately became massive textile factories and mill towns originated in the countryside, close to waterpower and a native-born, rural female labor force, many of whom were hand weavers. The large-scale industrialization of cloth manufacture in Pennsylvania, although less well known, was an urban phenomenon that drew on a large pool of skilled, immigrant textile workers. Outside Philadelphia, the tradition of bespoke, or custom ordered, weaving continued as small rural mills extended the operations of the male hand weavers. Until now, scholars have failed to recognize why industrialization evolved so differently in New England and Pennsylvania given their similarities. Closer examination of the differences between the two regions, however, combined with the deeper understanding of eighteenth-century cloth production provided by this look at Chester County, helps to explain more broadly the industrial process in the United States. A summary of the New England experience, therefore, will provide the basis of contrast for that of Pennsylvania.

The agricultural base of the Massachusetts economy was in general decline over the eighteenth century. Inhabitants of Essex County, just north of Boston, found it increasingly difficult to grow enough wheat to feed themselves and had to import it from the middle colonies and the Chesapeake. Rather than the extensive market agriculture practiced in Chester County, this region engaged in small-scale mixed farming. Even so, more than half the households had to buy much of the farm produce they consumed.[2] Agricultural change in the region was a major factor in determining how textile making fit into the local economy.

In the seventeenth century, New England cloth making was surprisingly similar to that of Chester County in the eighteenth century. Daniel Vickers argues that the goal of early New England Puritans was to obtain a "competency," that is, to clear land and establish farms with which to feed themselves and generate enough surplus to buy imported manufactured goods, cloth in particular.[3] But they had also come from East Anglia, where most people derived income from the wool trade, so it is not surprising that some artisans continued to produce textiles in their new home. By the late seventeenth century there was a small group of cloth makers in the province who carried on much as in Pennsylvania, with women spinning the yarn and skilled male weavers making the cloth.[4] A further indication of how closely the textile trade in Massachusetts paralleled that in Chester County can be found in equipment ownership: between 1650 and 1699, 7 percent of decedents in Essex County owned looms, and about a third owned spinning wheels.[5] Moreover, account books from that period reveal that weavers charged people for the cloth they wove, as did fullers, who received a separate fee to finish the cloth. Like their later Pennsylvania counterparts, early New England weavers used an extended labor force in the form of journeymen or family members. Essex County weaver John Gould's account book from the 1690s looks very much like that of Chester County weaver Joseph Eldridge a century later, the single exception being that Gould's daughters wove.[6] At the same time, other women in the region also began to take over the cloth-making work that had always been done by men, foreshadowing a trend that became more pervasive as the eighteenth century progressed.[7]

By the third and fourth generations of settlement in Massachusetts, farm formation took up less energy and rural properties were diminishing in size. With this transition gradually came the time and the need to extend household manufacturing. As Laurel Thatcher Ulrich observes, "In families where field labor was thought unseemly and wage labor a sign of declining fortunes, household manufacturing allowed men to employ their girls without appearing to do so."[8] The commercial workshop production that was such a stable component of the rural Pennsylvania economy, however, receded over time in New England. Granted, a few skilled male textile artisans continued to work out of their shops, especially in towns like Ipswich, which seems to have been a center for making specialized fabrics throughout the eighteenth century.[9] As more rural women began to weave for themselves, however, the number of looms proliferated. The seventeenth-century extent of loom ownership in Essex County had doubled by 1714 to 14 percent and, by the last third of the century, more than 20 percent of all households had weaving equipment, which is more than twice the ownership in Chester County.[10] Furthermore, unlike the many commercial weavers of Chester County who had more than one loom and whose inventories often went into detail about the ancillary equipment associated with a weaving business, the notation for Essex County looms was usually just "loom and tackling" or "a loom and gears," suggesting that they were the tools of people trained and working informally.[11]

Not only was household cloth making becoming more prevalent over the eighteenth century in New England, but, by the last third of the century, it was clearly women's work and functioned quite differently than the domestic industry of Pennsylvania and seventeenth-century New England. Although some New England female weavers sold their cloth and others exchanged various stages of textile work with their neighbors, for most the work was episodic and had to fit around the many other female household responsibilities.[12] Nevertheless, these rural women were pivotal for the first phases of New England's industrialization, in contrast to Chester County farm women, who generally did not weave.

The well-documented transition to industrial textile production in New England began in Rhode Island with the late eighteenth-century establishment of spinning mills. These early factories required an unskilled work force and found it by bringing families to the new factory towns of Slatersville and Webster, which consisted of single-family dwellings with gardens. The children provided a tractable group of mill workers, while some of their fathers were managers. As the first spinning mills opened, married women and widows remained in their traditional spheres at home and rarely entered the factories, although some may have woven on their own looms, as they would have done anyway.[13] Once yarn production was well under way, however, it became clear that an even larger labor force was needed to weave it.

In the beginning, a trickle of immigrant British hand-loom weavers arriving in Providence either worked in the weave sheds of Almy and Brown or bought yarn from them and wove it on their own equipment. But the mills produced more yarn than the male weavers could work up.[14] The industrialists solved the problem by persuading the many rural women who already owned looms to substitute weaving on commission for the cloth they made for their households.[15] This out-work system was a distinctly New England pattern and would not have worked in rural Pennsylvania, where there were fewer weavers and cloth production was already commercial.

New England farm women who did outwork weaving were young and single and glad to earn money for the kind of work to which they were accustomed. They were not prepared to alter their life-styles to do it, however, much to the frustration of the merchants and manufac-turers who were increasingly dependent on the weavers. As Almy and Brown noted when they were first attempting to put out yarn to rural women weavers, they "do not in general follow the occupation regu-larly; it is done during their leisure hours, and at the dull times of the year."[16] According to Thomas Dublin, "workers were members of rural, property-owning families who engaged in outwork in slack pe-riods when it suited their purposes. They might weave a piece of cloth in a week or keep the yarn for three months before completing their task."[17] To increase production under this system, more weavers had to be brought into the network by expanding the geographical base. There was still the problem of controlling the quality of finished pieces and having the fabric returned in a timely manner. These diffi-culties resulted in yet another stage of industrialization that was unique to New England—boarding-house mills.

Although the Rhode Island factories concentrated on carding and spinning, by 1814, a group of Boston merchants had established an integrated textile mill at Waltham, Massachusetts. Larger and better financed than earlier ventures, the Waltham Company used the first power looms (developed by Francis Cabot Lowell and Paul Moody) and brought all the textile processes efficiently together under one roof, ultimately cornering the market for cheap cloth goods. As their enterprise expanded, the Boston Associates (as the partners came to be called) needed a new location for another mill. The site that they found north of Boston on the banks of the Merrimack River grew into the town of Lowell (incorporated in 1826), which was dominated by several textile corporations: Hamilton; Appleton and Lowell; and Suf-folk, Tremont, and Lawrence. With their large mill buildings and workers' boarding houses, these corporations transformed the region from a small farm community with a population of 200 in 1820 to a bustling city of 6,000 in 1830. Rural women weavers played a major role in this transformation.[18]

Industrialization that began in Rhode Island soon moved well be-yond its borders. Because it was impossible to increase the output of individual weavers, a growing number of workers who lived further from the mill had to be employed. Combined with the expansion of new spinning firms, by the 1820s, women all over New England were part of a large weaving network.[19] With the establishment of the Lowell mills, these young, single women easily moved into the recently built boarding houses to become mill operatives on the new power looms. Enticed by the corporate paternalism of the company owners, who provided housing, moral supervision, and entertainment, the girls, most of whom were between fifteen and thirty years old, generally worked only for a period until they married.[20]

Thus was born the factory system we know so well and that has become synonymous with American industrialization—large-scale, water-powered textile mills churning out quantities of cotton cloth using locally recruited female labor. With the move of the women weavers from their homes to the factory boarding houses, the mill owners finally had the beginnings of a compliant work force that allowed them to implement quality standards and control the output. This entire system rested on the pervasive presence of looms in eighteenth-century rural New England households, and on the numerous women who used them. Not surprisingly, at the peak of the outwork system in 1811, 20 percent of Essex County households had hand looms. Once the women moved into the factories to work on power looms, domestic production disappeared quickly. By 1830, there were half as many loom-owning households.[21]

The situation in Pennsylvania was quite different. In 1775, the *Pennsylvania Gazette* carried a notice asking for public support of "The United Company of Philadelphia for Promoting American Manufactures," which intended to employ the poor to manufacture woolens, cottons, and linens.[22] Despite the fact that the owners had installed a spinning jenny with twenty-four spindles—self-declared to be the first in North America—they also intended to allow spinning to be done "outside the house." Spinning jennies, like spinning wheels, were hand operated, but, instead of a single spindle, they had from sixteen to one hundred mounted in a frame. Invented by James Hargreaves in 1764 and patented in 1770, the jennies were still operated by a single individual and did not require water power. Jennies (or their facsimiles) could be used almost anywhere (smaller ones in a home and larger ones in factories), increasing yarn output while saving labor—an important consideration in North America, which had a smaller work force than did Europe (Fig. 25).[23] By 1776, the United Company publicly boasted that it had managed to make coarse cloths, mostly used to dress the poor, but that the spinning and selling of thread and

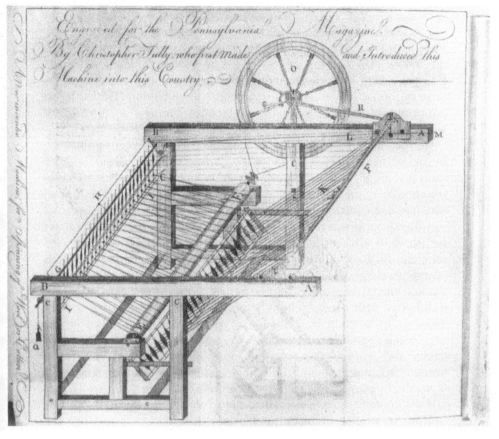

Figure 25. Because textiles required so much time and labor to produce by hand, there were constant attempts to speed up the process on both sides of the Atlantic. The implement pictured here resembles a spinning jenny and claims to be "A New invented Machine, for Spinning of Wool or Cotton." Instead of the single spindle found on the spinning wheel, the twenty-three spindles on this device would have represented a tremendous expansion of the output of a single operator. The caption claims that Christopher Tully "first made and Introduced this Machine into this Country," in addition to making the engraving. From Thomas Paine, ed., *Pennsylvania Magazine*, April 1775. Permission of the Library Company of Philadelphia.

yarn was the most successful branch of the operation.[24] Unlike similar, unsuccessful schemes to employ the poor in other American cities, Philadelphia's venture looked like it might work, but it ended when the British occupied the city two years later. Nonetheless, the United Company, with its spinning jenny, represented a first step toward industrialization that would continue after the revolution, shaped by an important factor present in the eighteenth century—an immigrant work force that made specialty textiles.

In Philadelphia and its suburbs, because of its relative insignificance in the eighteenth century, the textile industry went through a more radical change and was more dynamic than in the Pennsylvania countryside in the late 1700s and early 1800s. Colonial cloth manufacture had been most vigorous in the rural areas; the key to the later urban turnaround was massive immigration comprised of thousands of British cloth workers and their families. In the early nineteenth century, almost three-quarters of the textile operatives coming to North America were hand-loom weavers displaced by the success of new textile machinery. Very few, at least initially, brought the new industrial technology with them, although that began to change after 1820.[25] They set up a traditional European gender division of labor in the city: females produced wheel-spun yarn, and males wove on their own looms and worked the spinning mules (heavy frames that were pushed back and forth and could hold hundreds of spindles; see Fig. 9) that were beginning to appear in factories. The large numbers of new arrivals in the first decades of the nineteenth century meant that it was cheaper to employ them in hand production than to mechanize the work, as did their New England counterparts.[26] In 1810, according to contemporary observer Tench Coxe, these immigrant weavers produced almost all of Pennsylvania's fringes, floor cloths, lace, and carpets, and more than half the stockings.[27] This production by the Philadelphia hand-loom weavers, in conjunction with some of the newly established mills in the city, complemented the New England industry that produced quantities of plain, functional fabric. The early power looms in use at Lowell could not yet handle the more complex cloths; only skilled craftsmen would weave these textiles.

Moreover, Philadelphia's hand-loom weaving industry developed in conjunction with the new cotton mills, which provided necessary yarn. Sixteen of the seventeen textile firms located in the city manufactured cottons, with adult males constituting about half the work force. The urban mills made both yarn and cloth, but they sold their excess yarn to weavers who owned their own looms and thus the material they produced. This was not simply a transitional phase. Philip Scranton has shown that the ongoing immigration of British artisans reinforced the hand weaving that was still an important component of the city's cloth production in 1850, although the products changed over time from handwoven cotton specialty goods to "wools, knitted specialties, and finally carpets, both rag and ingrain."[28]

Not all hand weavers operated in small shops, however; many worked in large factories in North Philadelphia until a glut of post-war (of 1812) English goods flooded the market between 1816 and 1820, causing piece rates to fall. As a result, some mills cut back their operations in order to survive, but many of the hand weavers went out of business. With economic recovery in the 1820s, the bigger factories began to expand, investing in power looms and spinning frames, largely replacing the hand-loom weavers, although immigrants continued to form the majority of the labor force. In Philadelphia, as elsewhere, industrialization occurred incrementally, resulting from local conditions. Compared to New England, the mechanization process was late in coming. But the eighteenth-century presence of a few hand-loom weavers left an indelible mark on the nature of textile manufacture in the city, and fancy goods continued to be a Philadelphia specialty.[29] The effect of industrialization on Philadelphia was profound, for an extensive industry grew up where there had been almost nothing in the past. This period of transition also affected the countryside, although not as radically.

Artisan production in rural Pennsylvania was steady throughout the eighteenth century, but growing population, decreasing farm sizes, and an increase in landless laborers in the first decade of the nineteenth century would soon bring change.[30] Textile production nevertheless retained many of the characteristics that kept it stable during the eighteenth century.

The number of looms in Chester County, never a large percentage of household equipment, declined slightly between 1795 and 1810 and leveled off for the next twenty years; only about 20 percent of households with looms possessed more than two.[31] The owners of this equipment operated it much as they had in the eighteenth century, and workshop production continued on a bespoke basis.[32] Country people still produced fiber that they were accustomed to taking to a weaver and paying him to make into household textiles. Although many textile artisans continued to farm, they maintained an adequate base of customers for their cloth products, much as they always had. When compared to New England, there were few looms and fewer weavers, with the result that there was not a large enough pool of underemployed rural workers for spinning-mill owners to engage in weaving for them. Chester County was not untouched by industrialization, however, as it adapted some of the new tools and processes to complement a well-entrenched system of cloth production.

By 1820, six of Chester County's fourteen textile mills were cotton-spinning factories that produced only yarn and no cloth. In contrast to more urban Philadelphia County, where there were only four spinning mills out of twenty-nine total mills, there was clearly a greater market for yarn in the country than the city.[33] The persistence of traditional cloth making in Chester County is underscored by the fact that these spinning mills were established almost a quarter of a century after those in New England. By 1796, Almy and Brown in Rhode Island produced enough machine-spun yarn to have developed a network of rural hand weavers to make cloth.[34] In addition, they marketed their product outside of New England; Pennsylvania weavers like Joseph Eldridge were buying yarn from Rhode Island by 1810. This ability to import New England yarn partly explains why Chester County still had no spinning factories and only two carding mills at that late date. During the next decade, this region finally began to industrialize, and, by 1820, the county could boast three carding mills, four cotton mills/factories, two woolen mills (at least one of which had been a fulling mill in 1782), and one hemp mill.[35] Interestingly, these enterprises did not have a major impact on rural cloth production for at least the first third of the nineteenth century.

Two of the largest operating cotton mills in Chester County, each with almost one thousand spindles, employed twelve men and forty-four children between them. When business was good, they sold their yarn to Philadelphia factories, to merchant houses who took goods on commission, and to rural buyers.[36] They also produced sturdy and useful cotton fabric that could be used for a variety of clothing and household textiles. The Hopewell Cotton Mill in Oxford Township is an excellent example of the local entrepreneurial spirit during the early decades of the nineteenth century. In 1809, a well-to-do farmer, Samuel Dickey, caught up in the nationalistic fervor to create an American manufacturing base, built a small horse-powered cotton-spinning mill. He later built a larger water-powered mill, with three of his brothers as partners, several miles from the original, on Hopewell Creek. The three-hundred-pound bales of raw cotton needed for spinning could be transported from the ports of Philadelphia or Wilmington, Delaware, to the new location relatively easily. By the 1820s, the mill was manufacturing more than one hundred varieties of mostly cotton cloth, with checks and stripes predominating (Fig. 26). The specialty of the mill was a blue-and-white checked fabric (Fig. 27) that, according to Samuel's nephew, created a distinctive dress for

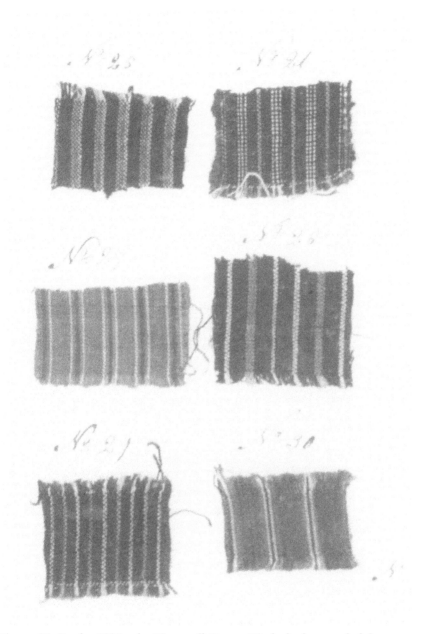

Figure 26. By the 1820s, the Hopewell Cotton Works had expanded from a small horse-powered operation, established in 1809, to a large water-driven mill capable of weaving more than one hundred varieties of checked and striped cotton cloth. This page of a sample book illustrates a few of the striped patterns in red, white, and blue. Sample Book, Hopewell Cotton Works, 1828, Chester County Historical Society. Photograph by author; reprinted with permission of the Chester County Historical Society, West Chester, Pennsylvania.

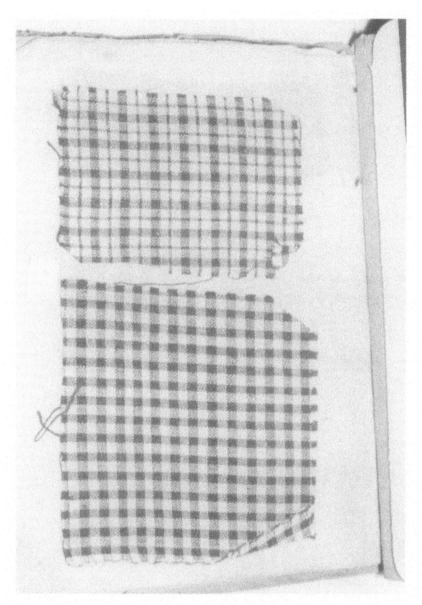

Figure 27. Schoolchildren in Oxford Township in Chester County proudly wore coats and pantaloons of blue and white checked fabric (like that shown here) made locally at the Hopewell Cotton Works. To them, it appeared "more modern" than the handwoven cloth worn by children who lived too far away from the factory to buy its goods. Sample Book, Hopewell Cotton Works, 1828, Chester County Historical Society. Photograph by author; reprinted with permission of the Chester County Historical Society, West Chester, Pennsylvania.

local schoolchildren: "[Our] usual school dress was rather different in summer from that of other neighborhoods as we boasted the Hopewell cotton works, and the blue and white cotton, striped and crossbarred, for coat and pantaloons, gave us a rather more modern appearance than those who depended upon the spinning wheel with the flax and wool manufactured at home."[37] There was clearly a strong local market for the fabrics of the mill, which would have been cheaper and appeared "more modern" than the hand weaving of the previous century.

The glut of British textiles on the American market after the War of 1812 depressed the local cloth market, and smaller cotton-spinning mills either went out of business or added a loom to enable them to produce a finished product.[38] Hopewell Mill survived the depression. An advertisement to sell it in 1832 provides some insight into its operation and potential output.[39] (Newspapers provided an important medium through which to advertise the products and fortunes of new business endeavors and to try to entice people to use their services.) The building was "70 X 40 feet, built of stone, 3 stories high, with a head and fall of 20 feet," and at full power, it could drive from fifteen hundred to two thousand spindles (Fig. 28). There were also eleven stone tenant houses for the workers. The manufacturing equipment consisted of spinning mules and throstles (a machine that combined the processes of drawing, twisting, and winding to produce fine yarn at a faster rate than the mule), and twelve power looms.

Cotton mills were larger than woolen mills and more technologically and organizationally advanced. The two woolen mills in Chester County operated more like the earlier weaving workshops, only now they manufactured cloth from start to finish, like some of the fulling operations of the eighteenth century (one of the new woolen mills had, in fact, originally been a fulling mill). Each had carding and spinning machinery, approximately two hand looms, and finishing equipment. Between them, the two mills employed five men, one woman, eight boys, and one girl. Factory or workshop labor at this time and in this region was not a major work option for women given that they always had a clearly defined but limited role in cloth production and that many could earn extra money by dairying.[40]

A closer look at the fortunes of the Charlestown woolen mill between 1813 and 1822 illustrates the precarious nature of early factory production in Chester County. Moreover, it demonstrates how these pioneering mills supported the system of domestic industry established in the eighteenth century. In May 1813, the first ad appeared in a local paper that a mill on Pickering Creek in Charlestown Township had new carding and spinning machinery to transform local wool into

Figure 28. The Hopewell Cotton Mill, built in the early nineteenth century, was located on Hopewell Creek in Oxford Township, Chester County, where it manufactured a variety of striped, checked, and plaid cottons that quickly replaced the locally grown, handspun and woven linen clothing and furnishing fabrics used in the region. Photograph by Patricia A. Maley, courtesy of John Bradley.

yarn. The proprietors noted that they also had looms and could weave the yarn into cloth if desired. A year later, the mill owners offered to card and spin only yarn that they also wove into cloth. This is a variation of the old bespoke system where the customer took the raw materials to the hand weaver. Over the course of the next six years, the mill operated under various owners, as old partnerships dissolved and new ones formed, often with British-trained individuals. By 1817, the mill had a surplus of cloth on hand to sell, so customers could buy material for which they need not provide the usual raw materials. At the same time, the new proprietors reverted to offering carding and spinning services without demanding that they weave the yarn, suggesting they were having difficulty competing with the easy availability and low cost of British cloth. The saga continued until 1819 when the mill burned. It reopened two years later under its original owner, but provided only carding and spinning services, as it had early on.[41]

Industrialization had had a major impact on rural New England by this time, but its effect in rural Pennsylvania was limited. Entre-preneurial weavers and fullers altered their production mode, and well-to-do business-minded farmers invested in new manufacturing opportunities. The presence of spinning mills permitted textile arti-sans to expand their output beyond bespoke production. Without de-pending on their customers for yarn, they could weave stocks of cloth that they could sell. They found a ready market, as fewer people pro-duced fiber because of the increasing cost of land and labor.[42] For those who continued to produce their own materials, the carding and spinning mills took over the processing, potentially increasing the quantity of yarn they could take to a weaver. The craftsman, in turn, could expand his output for these clients. Some weavers could even work out of the new mills, but the most enterprising artisans could transform their weaving workshops into the small woolen factories that frequently advertised their wares in local papers. Weaver Joseph Eldridge did exactly that in 1813 when he bought a fulling mill, where he and his sons carded fiber, spun yarn, and wove and fulled cloth un-til Joseph's death in 1845. One son took it over and continued to op-erate it with little change until 1851.[43] For at least the first third of the nineteenth century, then, hand-weaving workshops in Chester County functioned much as they had in the 1700s, but they operated in con-junction with the early factories. The mills may have caused hand pro-duction to decrease, but they did not immediately replace it, and local weaving products continued to coexist with textiles manufactured outside the community as foreign imports or American-made in New England or Philadelphia.

Industrial growth in America followed distinctive regional paths. Soil and settlement patterns assured considerable variation in colonial agriculture and manufacturing. The different circumstances of New England and Pennsylvania determined the manner in which industri-alization took hold in each place, demonstrating for the United States what British historians are recognizing on their side of the Atlantic. According to Pat Hudson,

No longer are those wishing to analyse the mainsprings of industrial growth in a region [of Britain] satisfied merely to explore a shopping list of locational factors. It is now necessary to consider how manufacturing meshed in with agriculture through the seasons, how systems of landholding, inheritance and wealth distribution conditioned the nature, organization and finance of indus-trial activities in an area, how urban production functioned in relation to rural manufacturing, how the family, household and personal life adapted to changes in work regimes and market opportunities, how these were reflected in demographic behaviour and how all these variables related to one another.[44]

This study of early American cloth making, the touchstone of the industrializing process, shows that while the American and British experiences were different, local conditions determined industrialization in each place.

In both New England and Pennsylvania, the organization and extent of nonmechanized textile manufacture demanded that early industrialists work within the existing local systems. It is not surprising that the biggest mills congregated in New England, where they churned out large volumes of plain, functional fabrics. The work force was already in place, as was the waterpower. Over time, entrepreneurs persuaded young farm women to move into the mills, first by paying them to weave on their own looms and later by hiring them to work in the new textile factories while living in the nearby boarding houses. Pennsylvania did not have an equivalent rural source of labor because of its successful market agriculture, but it did have a dynamic port city with a history of making specialty fabrics. The displaced, trained hand-loom weavers on the other side of the Atlantic were naturally attracted to Philadelphia, where they established an industry that made use of their skill. Despite the urban focus of Pennsylvania's large-scale nineteenth-century textile industry, the new technology did not bypass the rural areas of the state. The new spinning mills meant there were more raw materials for weavers to use, and the small factories extended rather than replaced the workshop production of the previous century.

Tracing a line from seventeenth-century Europe, through the establishment of the English North American colonies, past their independence, and into the first decades of nationhood, we can see that despite changing environments and technologies, fabric production followed a continuum that has been little understood until now. There is no question that it evolved in response to regional social and economic realities, most obviously during the early national period when the implementation of technological innovation accelerated change. But this study of the nonmechanized cloth-making traditions that preceded the use of the new textile machinery demonstrates that in North America industrialization was not the wrenching transition that scholars like Victor Clark believed it to be.

There are two keys to understanding the flow of industrial change. The first lies in knowing that the colonists were never self-sufficient. Even more important was the fact that in the rural economies of Pennsylvania and Massachusetts, the two regions of the United States where industrialization had the earliest and most significant impact, manufacturing and agriculture were collaborative enterprises, each affecting the other and setting the terms for indigenous textile production. Moreover, early American craft production did not compete with imported goods; rather, they were complementary. The money saved or generated by local cloth manufacture allowed people to participate in the expanding world of international consumer goods. During the nineteenth century, as the national spirit demanded a country that could provide for itself without depending on foreigners, new modes of manufacturing drew on local human resources without displacing them, as was often the case in England. Indeed, American manufacturing even absorbed many of the cloth workers from abroad whose skills had become obsolete.

Despite the many similarities between early modern English and American textile production and consumption patterns, differences were apparent as soon as the colonists established their new farms. For artisans who remained in Europe over the eighteenth century, the relationship between agriculture and craft changed dramatically as populations expanded and fewer people were able to farm. The general shrinking of agricultural opportunities over the eighteenth century resulted in an intensification of craft production and a rise in the number of workers who were increasingly dependent for survival on their manufacturing wages. A rural English artisan, for example, might become a smallholder, if he was lucky, whereas in Pennsylvania and even in New England people with a skill could often become landholders and farmers of substance. In the eighteenth century, as the nature of agricultural resources and opportunities molded manufacturing patterns in colonial America, they also generated demand that was met from both local and foreign sources. The growth of English industries and the affordable goods they provided to the colonists, combined with the availability of land in North America and the money with which to acquire it, created a stable pattern of production and consumption throughout the colonial period.

British and European textile workers were prominent among the people who immigrated to North America, in Pennsylvania more than in New England. Many of these artisans replicated Old World work routines by combining agriculture and cloth manufacture and dividing the work along gender lines. In Pennsylvania, the dynamic economy and steady stream of immigrants supported the ongoing existence of the textile sector. Because economic opportunity continued to flourish throughout the eighteenth century, textile artisans had a constant local market for fabric ordered and paid for by their customers. At the same time in New England, however, agricultural productivity and the size of land holdings were declining, with the result that women took over the formerly male work of weaving and began producing mostly for their own households.

Yet local cloth manufacture in early America could not meet the community's textile needs for several reasons. In Chester County, weavers operated on a custom-order basis using yarn provided by their customers, but raw materials were always in limited supply and often of mediocre quality. In New England, young women wove cloth to provide items for their dowries and other functional household furnishings, thereby freeing up money to buy a variety of goods they wanted or needed, among them assorted imported fabrics available to all the colonists. Finally, rural residents in both regions, like their urban counterparts, wanted to own imported luxurious clothing and fabric furnishings to enhance their comfort and have visible indicators of their prosperity. Therefore, even if local weavers had increased their output, they could never have met the demand for the exotic and fashionable fabrics available only through international trade.

The stable agricultural orientation of Chester County, the seasonal nature of craftwork, and the availability of imported cloth were all factors restraining the growth of textile manufacture in the region. Never during the eighteenth century did this community begin to approach self-sufficiency, nor did it want to. Not until the 1790s do we see change in a system that remained relatively unaltered for over a hundred years. By that time, weavers began to have access to greater quantities and better qualities of raw materials because of more efficient agriculture, better hand tools, a proliferation of carding mills, and yarn imported from the newly established spinning mills in New England. The growing number of young, landless artisans available for employment by established, propertied weavers and the building of early textile mills finally changed what had been a stable situation.

Although comparative stability characterized rural Pennsylvania cloth production, Philadelphia was more dynamic during the early industrial period, as was New England. Less productive agriculture, smaller farms, war, fewer immigrants, and demographic change were responsible for a shift in the gender division of labor in textile production in the northern region. As women took over the weaving that had been men's work, it became less commercial and more of an extension of their domestic tasks. Even with this change, cloth production and consumption of imported textiles remained complementary. But the large number of female weavers in the region would provide the necessary work force to work up the yarn manufactured in the spinning mills built in the late eighteenth century.

The story of weaving in Chester County compels us to revise traditional and sometimes entrenched views of agriculture, craft, and industry. The long sweep of almost a century and a half of regional differences reveals that technology alone did not determine the structure of industrialization; the more significant factor was people responding to opportunities and change. In Massachusetts, women took over weaving, whereas in Pennsylvania, men held on to this work. Both were responses to different immigration patterns and agricultural economies. We must recognize the subtle cultural and economic forces that created remarkably different communities, even those with as much in common as Pennsylvania and New England, if we are to understand the evolution of North American society in all its diversity.

Glossary

Definitions are from Florence M. Montgomery, *Textiles in America, 1650–1870* (New York, 1984); Linda R. Baumgarten, "The Textile Trade in Boston, 1650–1700," in *Arts of the Anglo-American Community in the Seventeenth Century*, Ian M. G. Quimby, ed. (Charlottesville, Va., 1975), 219–73; Dorothy K. Burnham, *Warp and Weft: A Textile Terminology* (Toronto, 1980); and the *Oxford English Dictionary*, second edition, online version *http://www.chass.utoronto.ca/oed/oed.html*. Textile terms are not always clear or consistent in their meaning. This book reinforces Florence Montgomery's observation that "even in the eighteenth century cloth names were not always precisely understood by merchants and their English factors" (p. 345). Moreover, terminology often changed meaning over time and from place to place. The following definitions represent what is generally understood to be the meaning of a term.

Alapeen (allopeen): A cloth made of mixed fibers, usually silk and wool, used for men's clothing and upholstery.

Bast fibers: Fibers that come from the stems of dicotyledonous plants, a flowering plant with two seed lobes. To extract the fiber from the stalk, the woody outer bark must be removed, a process that involves using moisture to rot it, after which it is pounded to break it up further; the remaining fiber is then combed to ensure it is tangle-free and ready for spinning. Flax and hemp are bast fibers.

Broadcloth: A woolen cloth woven in a plain weave on a wide loom (fixed by a statute of 1465 as twenty-four yards long by two yards wide). After weaving, the cloth was fulled or shrunk to make it warmer and denser.

Calico: Cloth made from cotton that first came from India and was later made in Europe. It came in many qualities and varieties and was used for both men's and women's clothing. It was also a popular good for the North American Indian trade.

Cambric: A fine white linen cloth originally made in Cambray in Flanders; by the mid-eighteenth century, it was being made in Ireland and, by the nineteenth century, it was made from cotton. It was used for shirt ruffles or trimming.

Camlet: The characteristic feature of a camlet was its plain weave structure. Otherwise, it came in many lengths and widths and could be made from all wool or a variety of fibers, including goat hair, silk, or linen. Quality and color also varied and it was suitable for clothing, household textiles, and upholstery.

Cassimere: Patented in 1766 by Frances Yerbury, cassimere was a woven twill made with a fine yarn and, unlike broadcloth, did not need to be fulled (although some was). It was thinner and lighter than broadcloth and had a smoother finish:

Chintz: According to Montgomery, the word "derived from *chitta,* meaning spotted cloth. . . . In seventeenth-century India, the word referred to a specially designed painted or printed cotton which was sometimes glazed" (p. 200). By the middle of the eighteenth century, British textile printers used woodblocks to create attractive facsimiles of the Indian cloth and American colonists used it for both clothing and furnishing fabric.

Corded dimity: *Dimity* is a broad term that refers to a variety of fabrics patterned during weaving. They are generally all white, usually made of cotton or linen and many have stripes created with a heavy cord during weaving. According to a 1739 commentator, "The striped [or corded] dimities are the most common, as they require less labour in weaving than the others, and the mounting of the looms being more simple, and consequently less expensive, they can be sold at much lower rates" (quoted in Montgomery, p. 219).

Diaper: Usually an all-linen fabric (sometimes cotton) woven with a small diamond-shaped pattern. The weave structure created an absorbent textile that was suitable for household furnishings such as towels and table linens, especially napkins. It was also used for bed hangings.

Drugget: Generally, a fairly coarse cloth woven in plain weave with a wool weft and linen or cotton warp. It could be undyed or colored, and was used for clothing (petticoats, coats) and, later, floor rugs. Drugget was both made in America and imported from Britain.

Duffel(s): A heavy woolen cloth that was brushed to bring up a nap. It came in a variety of colors (usually blue, green, or red), and its weight and texture made it a suitable for overcoats; duffel(s) was also used as a trade good.

Duroy: A fabric made of worsted (combed) wool that was lightweight and suitable for men's suits. Depending on where it was woven, it could be a plain weave, a solid color and glazed (London), or striped (Exeter).

Flannel: Made of loosely twisted woolen yarn and woven to create a soft white cloth that could also be dyed.

Flocks: Usually consisting of low-quality wool or cotton that was unsuitable for spinning, or strips of cloth torn from worn-out fabric, flocks were used as stuffing for quilts, beds, cushions, and mattresses.

Fustian: A variety of coarse fabrics made of linen and cotton and used for household textiles and clothing. In the nineteenth century, *fustian* was a thick twilled cotton cloth, usually dyed an olive or gray color.

Garlick (garlits, garlix, gulick, gulix): An all-linen cloth that could be completely or partly bleached. Originally from the linen-producing region of Görlitz in Prussian Silesia (now in southeastern East Germany), it was suitable for a variety of household textiles and imported to America in large quantities.

Haircloth: Woven on a special loom, haircloth used the long hairs from a horse's tail as the weft with wool, cotton, or linen as the warp. It produced a sturdy textile that could be used for sieves, as stiffening for clothing, or for upholstery.

Holland: A fine quality linen cloth originally made in Holland and later elsewhere. When bleached, it was called "Holland cloth"; when unbleached it was called "brown Holland."

Huckaback: A linen cloth with a small repeating raised pattern. The raised pattern provides greater absorbency so this was usually used for toweling.

Kersey: A coarse, twill-woven, inexpensive woolen cloth, originally made in the East Anglian town of Kersey. Its weight and structure made it good for repelling wet and cold, and its low price made it a product in great demand throughout Europe and North America where it was used for overcoats and military clothing.

Lawn: A fine linen used for handkerchiefs, shirts, ruffles, and aprons. Lawn resembled cambric.

Linsey (linsey-woolsey): Woven in a plain weave using a linen warp (later, cotton) and wool weft, this coarse fabric was made in quantity by North American weavers. It was also imported from Europe and could be plain or striped in many colors. Linsey was often used for aprons and petticoats.

Madder: A climbing, leafy plant known as *Rubia tinctorum* that was cultivated for the red dye it produced. Native to Asia Minor, it was being grown extensively in Holland and France by the eighteenth century and was regularly imported to the American colonies.

Nankeen: Originally from Nankin in China, this plain-woven, cotton cloth was known for its yellow color, derived from cotton plants that produced yellow fiber. By the mid-eighteenth century, textile manufacturers in Manchester, England, produced a facsimile with the same name, but the color was obtained by dyeing white cotton.

Osnaburg (oznabrig): Initially made in Osnabrück, Germany, and later elsewhere in Europe, this coarse, unbleached cloth made of linen or hemp was imported extensively to the American colonies where it was used for work trousers, sacks, and bags. By the nineteenth century in the United States, the term designated a variety of checked, striped, or solid-colored cottons used for work clothing in the United States.

Plush: Made of wool with a pile or nap, this was wool velvet. Plush came in all colors and was used for breeches, waistcoats, and winter jackets, as well as for furnishing upholstery.

Sailcloth: A heavy canvas-like material used for making sails.

Serge: Woven in twill weave using a worsted (combed) wool warp and a woolen (carded) weft, it was a light cloth narrower than broadcloth and finer than kersey. It came in a range of qualities and a variety of types and was durable and hardwearing, making it popular for clothing among the lower classes even though it was not especially cheap.

Shalloon: An inexpensive worsted fabric woven in tight twill weave that was chiefly used as a lining material. Imported shalloons were in high demand in the American colonies.

Stroud: A woolen cloth made in Stroud, Gloucestershire. It was usually dyed red and made into blankets for the North American Indian trade.

Stuff: A general term used variously to describe any woven fabric or, more specifically, a fabric woven of worsted (combed yarn) without a nap or pile.

Taffeta (taffety): A glossy silk fabric woven in plain weave.

Tammy: A worsted cloth woven in an open-textured plain weave with a glazed finish. It was strong and light and came in a variety of colors. Quantities of tammies were imported into the North American colonies where they had many uses; for example, as linings for men's coats, petticoats and dresses for women, bed hangings and window coverings, and strainers and sieves.

Tape: A narrow strip of woven cloth with a variety of uses such as tie closures, garters, and apron strings.

Tow: Consists of the short fibers that remain after flax has been processed. When spun, tow produces a coarse linen yarn that can be used for such items as sacks, bags, work clothing, and coarse bedding.

Warp: All the lengthwise threads of a woven cloth. A single warp thread is called an *end*.

Weft: All the crosswise threads of a woven cloth. A single weft is called a *pick*. Each weft passes through a warp *shed* (the opening caused by a sequential raising of some warp ends and the lowering of others that allows a shuttle to carry the weft thread through).

Woolen (woollen): A yarn or cloth made from wool that is carded (brushed and rolled so that the fibers are aligned at a right angle for spinning).

Worsted: A term used to describe both a yarn and the cloth made from it. The yarn is made from long-staple wool that is combed to align the fibers parallel to each other. Worsted cloth is generally lightweight with a smooth finish.

Notes

Introduction

1. *Holland* was a fine linen cloth originally made in Holland; *cambric* was a fine linen used for trimming and ruffles; *broadcloth* was a woolen cloth approximately two yards wide made on a broadloom; *taffety (taffeta)* was a glossy silk fabric woven in plain weave; *alopeen* was usually made of silk and wool and used for men's clothing and upholstery; *fustian* was a coarse fabric made of linen and cotton used for household textiles and clothing; *calico* was a cotton cloth of varied design and color used in men's and women's clothing; *lawn* was a fine linen that resembled cambric (see Glossary).

2. Philadelphia was not so different from England in having markets for secondhand and stolen clothing. For the English situation, see Beverly Lemire, "Consumerism in Preindustrial and Early Industrial England: The Trade in Secondhand Clothes," *Journal of British Studies*, 27 (1988): 1–24, and Lemire, "The Theft of Clothes and Popular Consumerism in Early Modern England," *Journal of Social History*, 24, no. 2 (1989): 255–76.

3. For example, Cary Carson argues that the life-style changes that occurred during the eighteenth century, when people increasingly took their identity from material goods, resulted in a cultural revolution in values, attitudes, and needs that governed consumption. Cary Carson, "The Consumer Revolution in Colonial British America: Why Demand?" in *Of Consuming Interests: The Style of Life in the Eighteenth Century*, Cary Carson, Ronald Hoffman, and Peter J. Albert, eds. (Charlottesville, Va., 1994), 483–697.

4. Adrienne D. Hood, "Reproducing Nineteenth-Century Handwoven Fabrics: A Weaver's Technical Guide to Accurate Reproductions," Royal Ontario Museum, Toronto; Canadian Museum of Civilization, Ottawa; Winterthur Museum, Delaware; Nova Scotia Museum, Halifax; Parks Canada, Ottawa (unpublished).

5. Peter Stallybrass, "Worn Worlds: Clothes, Mourning, and the Life of Things," in *Cultural Memory and the Construction of Identity*, Dan Ben-Amos and Liliane Weissberg, eds. (Detroit, 1999), 30.

6. Gail Fowler Mohanty, "From Craft to Industry: Textile Production in the United States," *Material History Review*, 31 (1990): 23–31, provides a review of the American scholarship on textile production. Jack P. Greene, *Pursuits of Happiness: The Social Development of Early Modern British Colonies and the Formation*

of American Culture (Chapel Hill, N.C., 1988), 28, comments on the problems with New England–centered interpretation of American history.

7. Philip Scranton, *Proprietary Capitalism: The Textile Manufacture at Philadelphia, 1800–1885* (Cambridge, 1983), 7.

8. Laurel Thatcher Ulrich, *The Age of Homespun: Objects and Stories in the Creation of an American Myth* (New York, 2001), 12–40.

9. Ulrich, *The Age of Homespun*, 32–36; Christopher Monkhouse, "The Spinning Wheel as Artifact, Symbol, and Source of Design," in *Victorian Furniture: Essays From a Victorian Society Symposium*, Kenneth L. Ames, ed. (Philadelphia, 1982), 157, 159, 167; Rodris Roth, "The New England, or 'Olde Tyme,' Kitchen Exhibit at Nineteenth-Century Fairs," in *The Colonial Revival in America*, Alan Axelrod, ed. (New York, 1985), 159–83; William B. Rhoads, *The Colonial Revival* (New York, 1977), 390–400; and Celia Betsky, "Inside the Past: The Interior and the Colonial Revival in American Art and Literature, 1860–1914," also in *The Colonial Revival in America*, 264.

10. Alice Morse Earle, *Home Life in Colonial Days* (1898; Stockbridge, Mass., 1974); Elizabeth Cynthia Barney Buel, *The Tale of the Spinning Wheel* (Litchfield, Conn., 1903); and Carl Holliday, *Woman's Life in Colonial Days* (Detroit, 1970). Ulrich, *The Age of Homespun*, 32–36, provides useful background information on Elizabeth Buel.

11. See Mary Beth Norton, "The Myth of the Golden Age," in *Women of America: A History*, Carol Ruth Berkin and Mary Beth Norton, eds. (Boston, 1979), 37–48, for a full discussion of this idea.

12. Mary Beth Norton, *Liberty's Daughters: The Revolutionary Experience of American Women, 1750–1800* (Boston, 1980), xiii–xiv, and Claudia Goldin, "The Economic Status of Women in the Early Republic," *Journal of Interdisciplinary History* 16 (1986): 379–380.

13. William R. Bagnall, *The Textile Industries of the United States, Including Sketches and Notices of Cotton, Woolen, Silk and Linen Manufactures in the Colonial Period* (New York, 1971); Perry Walton, *The Story of Textiles: A Bird's Eye View of the History of the Beginning and the Growth of the Industry by Which Mankind Is Clothed* (Boston, 1912); Arthur Harrison Cole, *The American Wool Manufacture*, volumes 1, 2 (Cambridge, Mass., 1926); Rolla Milton Tryon, *Household Manufactures in the United States, 1640–1860* (New York, 1966); and Victor S. Clark, *History of Manufactures in the United States*, volume I, 1607–1860 (New York, 1949).

14. Cole, *The American Wool Manufacture*, I:4, argues that there was no marked difference in American wool manufacture between the earlier and later colonial periods. He accordingly fixes on the years around 1760 for his analysis.

15. Thomas Dublin, *Women at Work: The Transformation of Work and Community in Lowell, Massachusetts, 1826–1860* (New York, 1979); Elizabeth Hitz, "A Technical and Business Revolution: American Woolens to 1832" (Ph.D. diss., New York University, 1978); David J. Jeremy, *Transatlantic Industrial Revolution: The Diffusion of Textile Technologies Between Britain and America, 1790–1830s* (North Andover, Mass., 1981); Gail Fowler Mohanty, "Experimentation in Textile Technology, 1788–1790, and Its Impact on Handloom Weaving and Weavers in Rhode Island," *Technology and Culture*, 29 (1988): 1–31; Gail Fowler Mohanty, "Putting up With Putting-Out: Power-Loom Diffusion and Outwork for Rhode Island Mills, 1821–1829," *Journal of the Early Republic*, 9 (1989): 191–216; Scranton, *Proprietary Capitalism*; Philip Scranton "Varieties of Pater-

nalism: Industrial Structures and the Social Relations of Production in American Textiles," *American Quarterly*, 36 (1984): 235–57; Cynthia J. Shelton, *The Mills of Manayunk: Industrialization and Social Conflict in the Philadelphia Region, 1787–1837* (Baltimore, 1986); Barbara M. Tucker, *Samuel Slater and the Origins of the American Textile Industry, 1790–1860* (Ithaca, N.Y., 1984); and Anthony F. C. Wallace, *Rockdale: The Growth of an American Village in the Early Industrial Revolution* (New York, 1972).

16. Joan M. Jensen, *Loosening the Bonds: Mid-Atlantic Farm Women, 1750–1850* (New Haven, Conn., 1986); James A. Henretta, "The War for Independence and American Economic Development," in *The Economy of Early America, The Revolutionary Period, 1763–1790,* Ronald Hoffman, John J. McCusker, and Russell R. Menard, eds. (Charlottesville, Va., 1988), 45–87; and Allan Kulikoff, "The Transition to Capitalism in Rural America," *William and Mary Quarterly*, 3rd series, 66 (1989): 120–44.

17. A good summary of this literature is in Allan Kulikoff, *The Agrarian Origins of American Capitalism* (Charlottesville, Va., 1992), 13-33.

18. Early works include Clark, *History of Manufactures in the United States*, volume I, 1607–1860; Cole, *The American Wool Manufacture*, volume 1; Carl Bridenbaugh, *The Colonial Craftsman* (Chicago, 1950); and Richard B. Morris, *Government and Labor in Early America* (New York, 1946). More recent studies include Mary Blewett, "Work, Gender and the Artisan Tradition in New England Shoemaking, 1780–1860," *Journal of Social History*, 17 (1984): 221–48; Edward S. Cooke, Jr., *Making Furniture in Preindustrial America: The Social Economy of Newtown and Woodbury, Connecticut* (Baltimore, 1996); Robert Blair St. George, "Fathers, Sons and Identity: Woodworking Artisans in Southeastern New England, 1620–1700," in *The Craftsman in Early America*, Ian M. G. Quimby, ed. (New York, 1984), 89–125; and Barbara McLean Ward, "Boston Goldsmiths, 1690–1730," also in *The Craftsman in Early America*, 125–57. For an overview of the literature on craftsmen, see Edward S. Cooke Jr., "Craftsmen," in *Decorative Arts and Household Furnishings in America, 1660–1920: An Annotated Bibliography*, Kenneth L. Ames and Gerald W. R. Ward, eds. (Winterthur, Del., 1989), 333–42.

19. See, for example, Marla R. Miller, " 'My Daily Bread Depends upon My Labor': Craftswomen, Community, and the Marketplace in Rural Massachusetts, 1740–1820" (Ph.D. diss., University of North Carolina, 1997); Marla R. Miller, " 'My Part Alone': The World of Rebecca Dickinson, 1787–1802," *New England Quarterly*, 71 (1998): 341–77; Laurel Thatcher Ulrich, "Wheels, Looms, and the Gender Division of Labor in Eighteenth-Century New England," *William and Mary Quarterly*, 3rd series, 55 (1998): 3–38; Ulrich, *The Age of Homespun;* James E. McWilliams, "Work, Family, and Economic Improvement in Late-Seventeenth-Century Massachusetts Bay: The Case of Joshua Buffum," *New England Quarterly*, 74 (2001): 355–84; and Adrienne D. Hood, "The Gender Division of Labor in the Production of Textiles in Eighteenth-Century, Rural Pennsylvania (Rethinking the New England Model)," *Journal of Social History*, 27 (1994): 537–61.

20. T. H. Breen, "An Empire of Goods: The Anglicization of Colonial America, 1690–1776," *Journal of British Studies*, 25 (1986): 477–84, and T. H. Breen, "The Meaning of Things: Interpreting the Consumer Economy in the Eighteenth Century," in *Consumption and the World of Goods*, John Brewer and Roy Porter, eds. (London, 1993), 250.

21. Two recent compilations of essays are John Brewer and Roy Porter,

eds., *Consumption and the World of Goods* (London, 1993), and Carson, Hoffman, and Albert, *Of Consuming Interests*. For a good historiographical overview, see Ann Smart Martin, "Makers, Buyers, and Users: Consumerism as a Material Culture Framework," *Winterthur Portfolio*, 28 (1993): 141–57, and Peter N. Stearns, "Stages of Consumerism: Recent Work on the Issues of Periodization," *Journal of Modern History*, 69 (1997): 102–17.

22. Two excellent works that combine production and consumption are Cooke, *Making Furniture in Preindustrial America*, and Ulrich *The Age of Homespun*.

23. Harold B. Burnham and Dorothy K. Burnham, *Keep Me Warm One Night: Early Handweaving in Eastern Canada* (Toronto, 1972), and Adrienne D. Hood and David-Thiery Ruddel, "Artifacts and Documents in the History of Quebec Textiles," in *Living in a Material World: Canadian and American Approaches to Material Culture*, Gerald L. Pocius, ed. (St. John's, Newfoundland, 1991), 55–91.

24. The *Pennsylvania Gazette* advertised "ready money for clean linen [or cotton] rags," or some variation thereof throughout the eighteenth century. See April 11, 1734; April 30, 1741; and August 6, 1752.

25. *Pennsylvania Gazette*, July 19, 1775.

26. Letter of James Meese to Council, 1777, in *Pennsylvania Archives*, Samuel Hazard, ed. (Philadelphia, 1853), 193.

27. Letter from General Washington to President Wharton, 1778, in *Pennsylvania Archives*, Hazard, ed., 6: 189.

28. *Pennsylvania Gazette*, April 17, 1776. Sarah Logan Fisher Diaries PAHV91-97, Historical Society of Pennsylvania, volume 1, Nov 7, 1776: Fisher comments that she "heard that the English had Possession of Newark, afternoon went up to Mammy's, 8 Men by order of the Committee of Safety came for Blankets they took two by force, afterwards 2 men came to us, but they took none."

29. Jan de Vries, "The Industrial Revolution and the Industrious Revolution," *Journal of Economic History*, 54 (1994): 255.

30. Using database software (Dbase, SAS, Excel), I created a record for each inventory containing thirty-three fields that permitted quantification of such things as the tools, fiber, and cloth for each household. I also created separate databases for tax lists and account books to calculate things like occupation, livestock, property, and quantities and varieties of cloth woven.

31. For the eighteenth century, I analyzed all the records in a four-year period, spaced at approximately fifteen-year intervals: 1715–1718 (68); 1734–1737 (102); 1754–1757 (160); 1773–1776 (242); 1792–1795 (253). I sampled two periods in the nineteenth century and used every second record because of the increase in population: 1810–1813 (179) and 1828–1831 (268).

32. For discussions of the strengths and weaknesses of probate data, see Holly V. Izard, "Random or Systematic? An Evaluation of the Probate Process," *Winterthur Portfolio*, 32 (1997): 147–67; Peter Benes, ed., *Early American Probate Inventories* (Boston, 1989); Rachel P. Garrard, "English Probate Inventories and Their Use in Studying the Significance of the Domestic Interior, 1570–1700," *Probate Inventories: A New Source for the Historical Study of Wealth, Material Culture and Agricultural Development*, Ad Van der Woude and Anton Schuurman, eds. (Utrecht, Netherlands, 1980), 55–81; Peter H. Lindert, "An Algorithm for Probate Sampling," *Journal of Interdisciplinary History*, 11 (1981): 649–68; and Winifred B. Rothenberg, "Farm Account Books: Problems and Possibilities," *Agricultural History*, 58 (1984): 106–12.

33. Kevin M. Sweeney, "Using Tax Lists to Detect Biases in Probate Inventories," in *Early American Probate Inventories*, Benes, ed., 32–40. For occupations, I looked at all taxables in the county for the years 1765, 1781, and 1799, years that contained the most complete data at sufficient intervals to indicate any change. For the rest of my study, given that there were about 6,000 taxables per year, I selected the townships of Darby, East Fallowfield, Goshen, Nottingham, Pikeland, Thornbury, and Tredyffrin as being the most representative of Chester County's heterogeneous population.

34. Cooke, *Making Furniture in Preindustrial America*, 5. Interestingly, Cooke is talking about New England and the very male-dominated craft of woodworking.

Chapter 1. European Origins

1. For some of the more recent literature on the economic changes in seventeenth-century England, see Jan de Vries, "Between Purchasing Power and the World of Goods: Understanding the Household Economy in Early Modern Europe," in *Consumption and the World of Goods*, John Brewer and Roy Porter, eds. (London, 1993), 85–132; Beverly Lemire, *Dress, Culture, and Commerce: The English Clothing Trade Before the Factory, 1660–1800* (New York, 1997); Beverly Lemire, *Fashion's Favourite: The Cotton Trade and the Consumer in Britain, 1660–1800* (Oxford, 1991); Margaret Spufford, *The Great Reclothing of Rural England: Petty Chapmen and Their Wares in the Seventeenth Century* (London, 1984); and Lorna Weatherill, *Consumer Behaviour and Material Culture in Britain, 1660–1760* (London, 1988). Important, though less recent, are Joan Thirsk, "Industries in the Countryside," in *Essays in the Economic and Social History of Tudor and Stuart England in Honour of R. H. Tawney*, F. J. Fisher, ed. (Cambridge, 1961), 70–88, and Joan Thirsk, *Economic Policy and Projects: The Development of a Consumer Society in Early Modern England* (Oxford, 1988).

2. James T. Lemon, *The Best Poor Man's Country: A Geographical Study of Early Southeastern Pennsylvania* (New York, 1972), 13, 47, 79, table 14, and James T. Lemon, "The Agricultural Practices of National Groups in Eighteenth Century Southeastern Pennsylvania," *Geographical Review*, 56 (1966): 468, table 1.

3. Ned Landsman, "The Middle Colonies: New Opportunities for Settlement, 1660–1700," in *The Origins of Empire: British Overseas Enterprise to the Close of the Seventeenth Century*, Nicholas Canny, ed. (Oxford, 1998), 361.

4. My intention here is not to discuss the transformation of the British and European textile industry in detail but to highlight major changes that most clearly demonstrate relevant influences on the New World immigrants.

5. The pervasiveness of the English textile industry in 1700 is mapped out in P. D. Glennie, "Industry and Towns 1500–1730," in *A Historical Geography of England and Wales*, R. A. Dodgshon and R. A. Butlin, eds. (London, 1990), 206, figure 8.1.

6. D. C. Coleman, *The Economy of England, 1450–1750* (Oxford, 1977), 49.

7. Coleman, *The Economy of England, 1450–1750*, 78. J. de L. Mann, *The Cloth Industry in the West of England from 1640 to 1880* (Oxford, 1971), 280–307 and 316–21, Appendix IV, has a detailed breakdown of the numbers of people involved.

8. Charles Wilson, *England's Apprenticeship 1603–1763* (London, 1965), 64. If it took fifteen people to weave a piece of broadcloth, and they produced

one piece a week, and 127,000 pieces were exported in a year, approximately 37,000 people would be involved. For wage estimates and details on processing, see Mann, *The Cloth Industry in the West of England*, 322–29.

9. E. Lipson, *A Short History of Wool and Its Manufacture* (London, 1953), 64, and Coleman, *The Economy of England, 1450–1750*, 73–74.

10. Alice Clark, *Working Life of Women in the Seventeenth Century* (London, 1982), 103–04, outlines the various British regulations prohibiting women from weaving. Lorna Weatherill, "A Possession of One's Own: Women and Consumer Behavior in England, 1660–1740," *Journal of British Studies*, 25 (1986): 145, 148, corroborates that these regulations were effective. John Rule, "The Frontier of Skill: Artisan Defences in the Eighteenth Century," paper presented at "The Social World of Britain and America, 1600–1820: A Comparison from the Perspective of Social History," (Williamsburg, Va., September 5–9, 1985); 11, says that the weavers' union successfully made a concerted effort to keep women out of skilled crafts until 1825.

11. C. S. Whewell, "Milling and Milling Machinery," in *The Wool and Textile Industry in Great Britain*, J. Geraint Jenkins, ed. (London, 1972), 157–69. For nonmechanized methods of fulling, see Beverly Gordon, *The Final Steps: Traditional Methods and Contemporary Applications for Finishing Cloth by Hand* (Loveland, Colo., 1982).

12. Eric Kerridge, "Wool Growing and Wool Textiles in Medieval and Early Modern Times," in *The Wool and Textile Industry in Great Britain*, J. Geraint Jenkins, ed. (London, 1972), 23. Urban textile production did not disappear, but it lost its long-held dominance.

13. Coleman, *The Economy of England, 1450–1750*, 74.

14. D. C. Coleman, "Textile Growth," in *Textile History and Economic History*, N. B. Harte and K. G. Ponting, eds. (Manchester, 1973), 3. For a classic study of these processes, see also Ivy Pinchbeck, *Women Workers and the Industrial Revolution, 1750–1850* (London, 1930).

15. Joan Thirsk, "Seventeenth-Century Agriculture and Social Change," in *Society in an Age of Revolution*, Paul S. Seaver, ed. (New York, 1976), 97.

16. For a discussion on the informal training women received from their husbands, see Ilana Krausman Ben-Amos, *Adolescence and Youth in Early Modern England* (New Haven, 1994).

17. The following discussion is based on Ann Kussmaul, *Servants in Husbandry in Early Modern England* (Cambridge, 1981), 5, 3, 31, 49, 81.

18. Thirsk, "Industries in the Countryside," 86.

19. John Smail, "Manufacturer or Artisan? The Relationship Between Economic and Cultural Change in the Early Stages of the Eighteenth-Century Industrialization," *Journal of Social History*, 25 (1992): 797, 811 n. 21.

20. Several decades ago, scholars coined the term "proto-industry" in an effort to define more precisely the complex economic and social changes arising where new patterns of agriculture and industry took root. Subsequently, many historians applied and explored the theory with a view to determining the essential nature of proto-industry. The result is that few over-arching features have emerged from the many regions they studied. On the contrary, regional experience determined that proto-industrial characteristics, and the term itself, has become no more precise than older terminology arising from such classic studies as Thirsk's, "Industries in the Countryside." In a 1998 review, Frederick Marquardt suggested that "it may be time to quietly abandon

the term *proto-industrialization*, with the word's inherent developmental implications, and return, with a new appreciation and perspective, to the old terms, *rural industry* and *cottage industry.*" Frederick Marquardt, " 'Schaffe, Schaffe, Hausle Baue': Hans Medick, the Swabians, and Modernity," *Journal of Social History*, 32 (1998): 200. See also D. C. Coleman, "Proto-Industrialization: A Concept Too Many," *Economic History Review*, series 2, 36 (1983): 435–48. I have chosen, therefore, not to apply the term to this study.

21. Thirsk, "Industries in the Countryside," 84, and Joan Thirsk, "Tudor Enclosures," *Historical Association Pamphlets*, 41 (1958), 3–22. Thirsk argues that enclosure eventually took place all over England in one form or another. Its worst effects, however, were felt in the Midlands.

22. Pat Hudson, "From Manor to Mill: The West Riding in Transition," in *Manufacture in Town and Country Before the Factory*, Maxine Berg, Pat Hudson, and Michael Sonenscher, eds. (Cambridge, 1983), 130.

23. Hudson, "From Manor to Mill, 131–32.

24. Smail, "Manufacturer or Artisan?" 796.

25. Smail, "Manufacturer or Artisan?" 806. For Smail's most recent explanation of the importance of regional credit practices, see "Credit and Commerce in the Eighteenth Century Wool Textile Industry," paper presented at the Second EuroConference on Wool: Products and Markets, Schio, Italy, October 24–27, 2001.

26. Jan de Vries, "The Industrial Revolution and the Industrious Revolution,"*Journal of Economic History*, 54 (1994): 257.

27. Smail, "Manufacture or Artisan?" 806. See also John Smail, *Merchants, Markets, and Manufacture: The English Wool Textile Industry in the Eighteenth Century* (New York, 1999).

28. The following discussion is taken from Thirsk, *Economic Policy and Projects*, 133–37.

29. Thirsk, *Economic Policy and Projects*, 8. See also, Spufford, *The Great Reclothing of Rural England*.

30. We tend to think that the majority of people who migrated to North America from England were poor and downtrodden. Recent literature has changed that perception and we now know that artisans, yeoman, and lower gentry from the middle ranks of society made up a substantial proportion of immigrants. See, for example, T. H. Breen, "Creative Adaptations: Peoples and Cultures," in *Colonial British America: Essays in the New History of the Early Modern Era*, Jack P. Greene and J.R. Pole, eds. (Baltimore, 1984): 195–232; Virginia DeJohn Anderson, *New England's Generation: The Great Migration and the Formation of Society and Culture in the Seventeenth Century* (New York, 1991); David Cressy, *Coming Over: Migration and Communication Between England and New England in the Seventeenth Century* (Cambridge, 1987); James Horn, *Adapting to a New World: English Society in the Seventeenth-Century Chesapeake* (Chapel Hill, 1994); and David Hackett Fischer, *Albion's Seed: Four British Folkways in America* (New York, 1989).

31. Weatherill, *Consumer Behaviour and Material Culture in Britain, 1660–1760*, 193, argues that the growing consumer culture was a middle-class phenomenon and did not include the lower ranks of society as Joan Thirsk suggests in *Economic Policies and Projects*, 193, 178–81.

32. Lorna Weatherill, "Consumer Behaviour, Textiles and Dress in the Late Seventeenth and Early Eighteenth Centuries," *Textile History*, 22 (1991): 298, 306.

N. B. Harte, "The Economics of Clothing in the Late Seventeenth Century," *Textile History*, 22 (1991): 277–96, notes that for the late seventeenth century about one-quarter of national expenditure was on clothing, according to calculations made by Gregory King. See also Margaret Spufford, "The Cost of Apparel in Seventeenth-Century England and the Accuracy of Gregory King," *Economic History Review*, 52 (2000): 677–705.

33. Beverly Lemire, "Consumerism in Preindustrial and Early Industrial England: The Trade in Secondhand Clothes," *Journal of British Studies*, 27 (1988), 2. See also Beverly Lemire, "The Theft of Clothes and Popular Consumerism in Early Modern England," *Journal of Social History*, 24 (1989): 256; Beverly Lemire, "Second-Hand Beaux and 'Red-Armed Belles': Popular Fashion and Its Challenge to Hierarchy in England, C. 1600–1800," *Continuity and Change*, 15 (2000): 392–94; and Weatherill, "Consumer Behaviour, Textiles and Dress," 308.

34. John Styles, "Clothing the North: The Supply of Non-Elite Clothing in the Eighteenth-Century North of England," *Textile History*, 25 (1994): 156.

35. De Vries, "The Industrial Revolution and the Industrious Revolution," 256.

36. Ibid., 261.

37. Lemon, *The Best Poor Man's Country*, 10–12. J. Smith Futhey and Gilbert Cope, *History of Chester County Pennsylvania*, (Evansville, Ind., 1986), provide genealogical sketches of many of the families that settled Chester County. I extrapolated the place of origin for 153: English, 84 (54.9 percent); Irish/Scotch-Irish, 41 (26.8 percent); German (including Switzerland and the German states), 14 (9.6 percent); Wales, 8 (5.2 percent); Scotland, 6 (3.9 percent). There are problems with this kind of data, the most obvious being that a compiler's agenda can cause bias (in this case, both were Quakers so Quaker families are likely overrepresented). Still, the English originated from twenty-eight locales that show a clear concentration around the cloth-making regions of Yorkshire (approximately 25 percent) and Wiltshire (approximately 30 percent).

38. Lemon, *The Best Poor Man's Country*, 19.

39. Aaron S. Fogleman, *Hopeful Journeys: German Immigration, Settlement, and Political Culture in Colonial America, 1717–1775* (Philadelphia, 1996), 6.

40. Marianne Sophia Wokeck, *Trade in Strangers: The Beginnings of Mass Migration to North America* (University Park, Penn., 1999), 16–17.

41. Sheilagh C. Ogilvie, *State Corporatism and Proto-Industry: The Württemberg Black Forest, 1580–1797* (Cambridge, 1997), 413, argues that in places other than England, the Lowlands, Switzerland, and some parts of the Rhineland, urban guilds or regional guilds actually remained strong into the nineteenth century. Ogilvie also studies an area of Germany that specialized in worsted wool production, not linen. See Chapters 3, 4, and 5 for a comparison of the work and time involved to produce finished linen and wool cloths.

42. Jean H. Quataert, "The Shaping of Women's Work in Manufacturing: Guilds, Households and the State in Central Europe, 1648–1870," *American Historical Review*, 90 (1985):1131, 1133. Merry Wiesner, "Guilds, Male Bonding, and Women's Work in Early Modern Germany," *Gender and History*, 1 (1989): 128, says "not only were women excluded, but connections were explicitly established between men. . . ." She goes on to say that even the traditional rights of widows were being eroded, p. 131.

43. For an excellent discussion of inheritance strategies, especially partible inheritance, see, David Warren Sabean, *Property, Production, and Family in Neckarhausen, 1700–1870* (Cambridge, 1990), 15–17.

44. Rudolf Braun, *Industrialisation and Everyday Life* (Cambridge, 1990), 3, 37–40.

45. The commentator was Johann Heinrich Pestlozzi, writing in the late eighteenth century, quoted in Braun, *Industrialisation and Everyday Life*, 77.

46. Herbert Kisch, *From Domestic Manufacture to Industrial Revolution: The Case of the Rhineland Textile Districts* (New York, 1989), 15–16.

47. Kisch, *From Domestic Manufacture to Industrial Revolution*, 16–17, 97. Ogilvie, *State Corporatism and Proto-Industry*, 14, 73–74 cautions that the regions I am discussing might well be the exception than the rule. She finds a very different situation in Württemberg, where regional guilds controlled both urban and rural artisan production in the early modern period.

48. Kisch, *From Domestic Manufacture to Industrial Revolution*, 103, 106–7.

49. Wokeck, *Trade in Strangers*, 215, and Maldwyn A. Jones, "The Scotch-Irish in British America," in *Strangers Within the Realm: Cultural Margins of the First British Empire*, Bernard Bailyn and Philip D. Morgan, eds. (Chapel Hill, N.C., 1991), 293.

50. Nicholas Canny, "Fashioning 'British' Worlds in the Seventeenth Century," in *Empire, Society, and Labor: Essays in Honor of Richard S. Dunn*, Nicholas Canny, Joseph E. Illick, Gary B. Nash, and William Pencak, eds. (University Park, Penn., 1997), 31.

51. Jones, "The Scotch-Irish in British America," 292.

52. Jones, "The Scotch-Irish in British America," 287.

53. Wallace Clark, *Linen on the Green: An Irish Mill Village, 1730–1982* (Belfast, 1982), 5–6.

54. W. H. Crawford, *The Handloom Weavers and the Ulster Linen Industry* (Ulster, 1994), 1, 24.

55. Brenda Collins, "Proto-Industrialization and Pre-Famine Emigration," *Social History*, 7 (1982), 130–31.

56. Vivienne Pollock, "The Household Economy in Early Rural America and Ulster: The Question of Self-Sufficiency," in *Ulster and North America Transatlantic Perspectives on the Scotch-Irish*, Tyler Blethen and Curtis Wood, eds. (Tuscaloosa, Ala., 1997), 71, Collins, "Proto-Industrialization and Pre-Famine Emigration," 132–34.

57. Crawford, *The Handloom Weavers and the Ulster Linen Industry*, 24–25.

58. Collins, "Proto-Industrialization and Pre-Famine Emigration," 132, and Crawford, *The Handloom Weavers and the Ulster Linen Industry*, 30.

59. Pollock, "The Household Economy in Early Rural America and Ulster," 73.

60. Collins, "Proto-Industrialization and Pre-Famine Emigration," 135.

61. Wokeck, *Trade in Strangers*, 189–92. Patrick Griffin, "The People with No Name: Ulster's Migrants and Identity Formation in Eighteenth-Century Pennsylvania," *William and Mary Quarterly*, 3rd series, 58 (2001): 592, notes that three out of four migrants went to Pennsylvania between 1717 and 1730.

62. Landsman, "The Middle Colonies," 361–62.

63. Quataert, "The Shaping of Women's Work in Manufacturing," 1147, discusses this process in what she calls a "developing world economy."

Chapter 2. Landholding and Labor

1. Marianne Wokeck, "German Immigration of Colonial America: Prototype of a Transatlantic Mass Migration," in *America and the Germans: An Assessment of a Three-Hundred Year History,* Frank Trommler and Joseph McVeigh, eds. (Philadelphia, 1985), 6, and Marianne Sophia Wokeck, *Trade in Strangers: The Beginnings of Mass Migration to North America* (University Park, Pa., 1999), 178, 186. Lucy Simler, "Tenancy in Colonial Pennsylvania: The Case of Chester County," *William and Mary Quarterly,* 3rd series, 43 (1986): 549, notes that, in the first half century of settlement in Chester County, most people who could afford to set up a household could also buy land. T. H. Breen and Stephen Foster, "Moving to the New World: The Character of Early Massachusetts Immigration," *William and Mary Quarterly,* 3rd series, 30 (1973): 189–222, argue that even earlier in New England the majority of immigrants in the 1630s arrived as nuclear families.

2. For a discussion of the apparent similarities between the Old and New World societies, see David Grayson Allen, *In English Ways: The Movement of Societies and the Transferal of English Local Law and Custom to Massachusetts Bay in the Seventeenth Century* (Chapel Hill, N.C., 1981), and Sumner Chilton Powell, *Puritan Village: The Formation of a New England Town* (Middletown, Conn., 1963). James T. Lemon, "Communications on Bettye Hobbs Pruitt 'Self-Sufficiency and the Agricultural Economy of Eighteenth-Century Massachusetts'," *William and Mary Quarterly,* 3rd series, 42 (1985): 559, stated that new studies using court records will demonstrate that early rural American society is "less unlike England than the Turners of the turn of century imagined."

3. J. Smith Futhey and Gilbert Cope, *History of Chester County, Pennsylvania* (Evansville, Ind., 1986), 3.

4. A. G. Roeber, " 'The Origin of Whatever Is Not English Among Us': The Dutch-Speaking and German-Speaking Peoples of Colonial British America," in *Strangers Within the Realm: Cultural Margins of the First British Empire,* Bernard Bailyn and Philip D. Morgan, eds. (Chapel Hill, N.C., 1991), 283.

5. Joan M. Jensen, *Loosening the Bonds: Mid-Atlantic Farm Women, 1750–1850* (New Haven, Conn., 1986), 8.

6. Chester County tax lists and some account books show that there was a mixture of nationalities within the various townships. Aaron S. Fogleman, *Hopeful Journeys: German Immigration, Settlement, and Political Culture in Colonial America, 1717–1775* (Philadelphia, 1996), 73–74, says even Germans from the same village in the third phase of immigration (1717–1775) found it difficult to live in the same place and had to live in scattered townships.

7. James T. Lemon, *The Best Poor Man's Country: A Geographical Study of Early Southeastern Pennsylvania* (New York, 1972), 102–17. See, in particular, figures 33 through 35, maps showing the extent of urbanization in eighteenth-century southeastern Pennsylvania.

8. Lucy Simler, "The Township: The Community of the Rural Pennsylvanian," *Pennsylvania Magazine of History and Biography,* 106 (1982): 44, 51–53, 63–64.

9. Simler, "Tenancy in Colonial Pennsylvania," 554. Between 1765 and 1781 the number of people taxed who had land stayed at 57 percent, rising slightly in 1799 to 61 percent and declining in 1810 to 54 percent, based on a tax-list database that includes a tabulation of all taxables in Darby, East Fallowfield, Goshen, East Nottingham, Pikeland, Thornbury, and Tredyffrin town-

ships for 1765, 1781, 1799, and 1810 (with the exception of Darby for 1799 and 1810, which had been separated from Chester County by a boundary change in 1789). Chester County Tax Lists, Chester County Archives, West Chester, Pennsylvania (hereafter, tax-list database).

10. Without differentiating between cleared and uncleared land, the average acreage of landowners was 1765, 125; 1788, 125; 1799, 107; and 1810, 85, according to the tax-list database. Duane Ball and Gary Walton, "Agricultural Productivity Change in Eighteenth-Century Pennsylvania," *Journal of Economic History*, 36 (1976): 107, show that the average size of landholdings fell from a high of 500 acres in 1700 to slightly less than 130 acres by 1791, but these numbers do not represent usable, cleared land. An analysis of the ownership of arable lands demonstrates that most were approximately 100 acres, which, they argue, may be on the low side. Lemon, *The Best Poor Man's Country*, 89, has similar numbers to mine for the 1760s and 1780s.

11. Lemon, *The Best Poor Man's Country*, 92.

12. See Lemon, *The Best Poor Man's Country, 150–83*, for a description of mixed farming in southeastern Pennsylvania.

13. S.D. Smith, "The Market for Manufactures in the Thirteen Continental Colonies, 1698–1776," *Economic History Review*, 51 (1998): 679, 696–97.

14. Between 1715 and 1718, approximately 20 percent of the inventoried population had an occupation other than farming and 16 percent were clearly designated as artisans, Adrienne D. Hood, "Organization and Extent of Textile Manufacture in Eighteenth-Century, Rural Pennsylvania: A Case Study of Chester County" (Ph.D. diss., University of California, San Diego, 1988), 35–36, Table 1.1. See also Mary M. Schweitzer, *Custom and Contract: Household, Government, and the Economy in Colonial Pennsylvania* (New York, 1987), 67, 83–84, and Simler, "Tenancy in Colonial Pennsylvania," 550, 545–46. Robert W. Malcolmson, *Life and Labour in England, 1700–1780* (London, 1981), 23, suggests that an occupational designation such as weaver can obscure the fact that bi-occupationalism was pervasive in England. Ann Kussmaul, *Servants in Husbandry in Early Modern England* (Cambridge, 1981), 23–24, and Joan Thirsk, "Industries in the Countryside," in *Essays in the Economic and Social History of Tudor and Stuart England in Honour of R. H. Tawney*, F. J. Fisher, ed. (Cambridge, 1961), 78, 86, would agree.

15. Schweitzer, *Custom and Contract*, 120.

16. Schweitzer, *Custom and Contract*, 115–39, 223.

17. Wokeck, *Trade in Strangers*, 48–49, 143, and Maldwyn A. Jones, "The Scotch-Irish in British America," in *Strangers Within the Realm: Cultural Margins of the First British Empire*, Bernard Bailyn and Philip D. Morgan, eds. (Chapel Hill, N.C., 1991), 293.

18. Simler, "Tenancy in Colonial Pennsylvania"; Lucy Simler, "The Landless Worker: An Index of Economic and Social Change in Chester County, Pennsylvania, 1750–1820," *Pennsylvania Magazine of History and Biography*, 114 (1990): 172–73; and Paul G. E. Clemens and Lucy Simler, "Rural Labor and the Farm Household in Chester County, Pennsylvania, 1750–1820," in *Work and Labor in Early America*, Stephen Innes, ed. (Chapel Hill, N.C., 1988), 106–43, provide an increasingly detailed picture of large numbers of landless in Pennsylvania and their role in the local economy.

19. Fogleman, *Hopeful Journeys*, 85, 93.

20. In New Jersey, access to such a labor market permitted a landholder to move beyond subsistence, according to Paul G. E. Clemens, "Material Culture

and the Rural Economy: Burlington County, New Jersey, 1760–1820," in *Land Use in Early New Jersey: A Historical Geography*, Peter O. Wacker and Paul G. E. Clemens, eds. (Newark, N.J., 1995), 265–96.

21. Gary B. Nash, "Slaves and Slave-Owners in Colonial Philadelphia," *William and Mary Quarterly*, 3rd series, 30 (1973): 244, notes that in Chester County only 4.2 percent of taxpayers had slaves in 1759. According to Nash, slavery in Pennsylvania was largely an urban phenomenon based in Philadelphia.

22. Simler, "The Landless Worker," 172, and Simler, "Tenancy in Colonial Pennsylvania," 545, 562. An analysis of the tax lists for 1765, 1781, and 1799 shows that between 1765 and 1781 the number of artisans with property was roughly split between large landholders and smallholders. In 1799, although there was an increase in the former over the latter, the average size of the landholdings for those with more than twenty acres decreased: 1765, 78.3; 1781, 91.1; and 1799, 59.9.

23. Nash, "Slaves and Slave-Owners in Colonial Philadelphia," 255, and Farley Grubb, "Immigrant Servant Labor: Their Occupational and Geographic Distribution in the Late Eighteenth-Century Mid-Atlantic Economy," *Social Science History*, 9 (1985), 254, table 2.

24. Schweitzer, *Custom and Contract*, 53, and Sharon V. Salinger, *"To Serve Well and Faithfully:" Labor and Indentured Servants in Pennsylvania, 1682–1800* (Cambridge, 1987), 15, 22, 69. Salinger's analysis is more compelling when dealing with the urban situation. She equates the lack of rural dependence on bound labor with the fact that family members could satisfy most work requirements. She seems unaware that nonfamily labor systems other than bound workers more fully met the needs of rural householders.

25. Simler, "Tenancy in Colonial Pennsylvania," 562–63, and Clemens and Simler, "Rural Labor and the Farm Household," 112.

26. Clemens and Simler, "Rural Labor and the Farm Household," 112, 113, table 2, and Simler, "The Landless Worker," 175–77.

27. Simler, "Tenancy in Colonial Pennsylvania," 546–48.

28. Kussmaul, *Servants in Husbandry in Early Modern England*, 22–23, and Vivienne Pollock, "The Household Economy in Early Rural America and Ulster: The Question of Self-Sufficiency," in *Ulster and North America Transatlantic Perspectives on the Scotch-Irish*, Tyler Blethen and Curtis Wood, eds. (Tuscaloosa, Ala.,1997), 73.

29. Malcolmson, *Life and Labour in England, 1700–1780*, 35.

30. Schweitzer, *Custom and Contract*, 34–56.

31. Simler, "The Landless Worker," gives a more detailed discussion of the growth of landless laborers in the county during this period.

32. Although this concerns only the last third of the eighteenth century, it is helpful in intimating earlier trends.

33. Percentage (rounded off) of all artisans taxed for land: 1765, 41; 1781, 31; 1799, 27; and 1810, 13. Percentage of artisans without their own property (renters, inmates, freemen, or no land specified): 1765, 59; 1781, 69; 1799, 73; and 1810, 87. Total number of artisans for each period: 1765, 69; 1781, 90; 1799, 196; and 1810, 204. Tax-list database.

34. Percentage (rounded off) of weavers taxed for land: 1765, 25; 1781, 35; 1799, 18; and 1810, 4. Percentage of weavers without their own property: 1765, 75; 1781, 65; 1799, 81; and 1810, 96. Total number of weavers for each period: 1765, 12; 1781, 17; 1799, 27; and 1810, 26. Tax-list database.

35. In 1765, 50 percent of weavers without property were renters; in 1781,

47 percent were inmates; in 1799, inmates and freemen each made up 37 percent of this group, with 7 percent renters; in 1810, there were no renters, only inmates (nearly 54 percent) and freemen (42 percent). Tax list database.

36. The term *yeoman* is ambiguous. A yeoman has been defined as "a farmer above the status of husbandman and below the status of larger farmers," with the emphasis on status. Immanuel Maurice Wallerstein, *The Modern World System II: Mercantilism and the Consolidation of the European World-Economy, 1600–1750* (New York, 1980), 87, note 80. In contrast, a yeoman could be a person who relied mainly on the land for income, according to Gordon Batho, "Landlords in England," in *Agrarian History of England and Wales, 1500–1640,* Joan Thirsk, ed. (Cambridge, 1967), 301–2. In Chester County, the term probably implied both a designation of status and an indication of how one made one's living, but some individuals are designated as both yeomen and artisans. For example, James Garrett was taxed as a "weaver" on the 1783 Chester County tax assessment but was called a "yeoman" in probate when he died eleven years later; see Chester County Wills and Inventories #4344, Chester County Archives, West Chester, Pennsylvania (hereafter, CCWI). Thus, Garrett's identification as a weaver at a time when he also had a farm of 150 acres suggests that weaving was his primary occupation. He was elderly when he died and had probably stopped practicing his craft by then, which might account for the appellation "yeoman" in his will.

37. The best example of inventoried equipment indicating that a person practiced his craft is John Lea, who died in 1726, CCWI #241. Lea also called himself a weaver in his will. See also William Lewis (d. 1731), CCWI #401 and George Lea, who was identified as a weaver on a property deed (d. 1731), CCWI #388.

38. Increasing population and decreasing availability of land may have been among the factors that stimulated further diversification within the economy, as argued by Duane E. Ball, "Dynamics of Population and Wealth in Eighteenth-Century Chester County, Pennsylvania," *Journal of Interdisciplinary History,* 6 (1976): 621–44, but they alone were not responsible for it until the end of the century.

39. Percentage of households with looms: 1715–1718, 5.9; 1734–1737, 6.7; 1754–1757, 9.4; 1773–1776, 7.9; and 1792–1795, 9.9. Although there was some growth of the households with textile tools, it is relatively insignificant when compared with the traditional beliefs that most colonial households made their own cloth. Inventory database.

40. Number of looms present for every 100 households: 1715–1718, 6; 1734–1737, 11; 1754–1757, 13; 1773–1776, 11; and 1792–1795, 12. Inventory database.

41. Lemon, *The Best Poor Man's Country,* 30, argues that opportunities for land investment and the attraction of most people to agriculture, which had higher rates of returns than craft production were other factors in the lack of dynamism.

42. See Chapter 5 for more details on the employment of journeymen weavers.

43. In 1765, there were 28 propertied weavers and 27 nonpropertied weavers; in 1781, there were 36 propertied and 97 nonpropertied; in 1799, there were 54 propertied and 129 nonpropertied. Tax-list database.

44. Sharon V. Salinger, "Artisans, Journeymen, and the Transformation of Labor in Late Eighteenth-Century Philadelphia," *William and Mary Quarterly,*

3rd series, 40 (1983): 62–84. The transformation Salinger described in Philadelphia occurred much more slowly in rural Chester County. According to Gay L. Gullickson, *Spinners and Weavers of Auffay, Rural Industry and the Sexual Division of Labor in a French Village,* 1750–1850 (Cambridge, 1986), 65, a textile cottage industry grew up in the prosperous cereal-producing region of Auffay because the nature of its agriculture created a large seasonally unemployed labor force that worked at cloth production in the winter months. Chester County had a similar agricultural orientation.

45. Simler, "The Landless Worker," 188.

Chapter 3. Flax and Wool

1. George Brinton Account Book, 1781–1800, Box E-G Family File, Chester County Historical Society (hereafter cited as CCHS), West Chester, Pennsylvania. The events described here did not all take place in 1788, but within several years of it. For the sake of clarity, they are presented here as though they occurred chronologically. Any fact not obtained from Brinton's daybook is noted.

2. Letter from Thomas Cheyney, Chester County, to John Waldren, England, October 26, 1796, #123, folder 183, Historical Society of Pennsylvania, Philadelphia (hereafter, HSP).

3. Unless otherwise noted, monetary values are stated as given in the various account books, tax lists, inventories, etc. In some cases, for several decades following the War for Independence money was noted in a combination of Pennsylvania currency and dollar values.

4. Brinton's account book has no entries to indicate that he paid anyone to spin wool for him, but he paid several women to spin flax.

5. See Glossary for explanations of textile terms tow, woolen, linsey, and worsted.

6. Although there are no specific notations in Brinton's account book indicating that he took his wool cloth to the fuller or his linen to the dyer or bleacher, these were important steps in the manufacture of cloth. The existence of account books of dyers and fullers and the occupation taxes levied on individuals who specialized in these jobs in eighteenth-century Pennsylvania suggest that Brinton would have used their services. See Chapter 5 for a discussion of these processes.

7. Bast fibers are "obtained from the stalks of dicotyledonous plants." Dorothy K. Burnham, *Warp and Weft: A Textile Terminology* (Toronto, 1980), 3.

8. Percentage of households with flax fiber: 1715–1718, 8.8; 1734–1737, 18.6; 1754–1757, 25.6. Wool fiber: 1715–1718, 5.9; 1734–1737, 21.6; and 1754–1757, 20.6. Based on data extrapolated from a sampling of 1,275 Chester County household inventories (hereafter, Inventory database).

9. Number of looms per 100 households: 1715–1718, 6; 1734–1737, 11; 1754–1757, 13; 1773–1776, 11; and 1792–1795, 12. Inventory database.

10. Percentage of households with wool fiber: 1773–1776, 23.6; 1792–1795, 17.8; 1810–1813, 11.2; and 1828–1831, 9.3. Flax Fiber: 1773–1776, 36.4; 1792–1795, 36.8; 1810–1813, 31.3; and 1828–1831, 16.8. Inventory database.

11. Account Book of a Philadelphia Merchant [probably John Yeates], 1734–1746, acc. #823, vol. 1, Hagley Museum and Library, Wilmington, Delaware (hereafter, HML). Invoice dated December 6, 1744, shows two half

barrels of linseed oil going to Jamaica, and on February 12, 1745, one barrel of flaxseed to the same place.

12. Thomas M. Truxes, *Irish-American Trade, 1660–1783* (Cambridge, 1988), 193.

13. June 16, 1743, letter to England, quoted in Anne Bezanson, Robert Davis Gray, and Miriam Hussey, *Prices in Colonial Pennsylvania* (Philadelphia, 1935), 267.

14. Bezanson, Gray, and Hussey, *Prices in Colonial Pennsylvania*, 67.

15. Conrad Gill, *The Rise of the Irish Linen Industry* (Oxford, 1925, reprint, 1964), 35; Truxes, *Irish-American Trade, 1660–1783*, 193.

16. N. B. Harte, "The Rise of Protection and the English Linen Trade, 1690–1790," in *Textile History and Economic History: Essays in Honour of Miss Julia De Lacy Mann*, N. B. Harte and Kenneth G. Ponting, eds. (Manchester, 1973), 99.

17. Truxes, *Irish-American Trade, 1660–1783*, 170.

18. According to Marc Egnal, "The Pennsylvania Economy, 1748–1762: An Analysis of Short-Run Fluctuations in the Context of Long-Run Changes in the Atlantic Trading Community" (Ph.D. diss., University of Wisconsin, 1974), 63, in 1752, flour and bread comprised the major export commodities of Philadelphia, but flaxseed was third in value and worth more than wheat.

19. Despite the fact that some immigrants came from linen-weaving regions (Ulster and some areas of Germany), there was no obvious concentration of flaxseed production in Chester County. Of 106 people with flaxseed listed in their inventories, I could determine the ethnicity of 51 who were scattered throughout the county, suggesting no geographic or ethnic specialization.

20. Percentage of households with flaxseed: 1715–1718, 0; 1734–1737, 0.1; 1754–1757, 10; 1773–1776, 16.1; 1792–1795, 19.8; 1810–1813, 10.7; and 1828–1831, 2.3. Inventory database.

21. Victor S. Clark, *History of Manufactures in the United States, Volume I, 1607–1860* (New York, 1949), 84, provides the 1750s figure. Helen Louise Klopfer, "Statistics of Foreign Trade of Philadelphia 1700–1860" (Ph.D. diss. University of Pennsylvania, 1936), 179, gives the 1771 statistic. The 1791–1792 number was calculated from Tench Coxe, *A View of the United States of America, in a Series of Papers Written at Various Times, in the Years Between 1787 and 1794* (New York, 1965), 414, who stated that in that year 10,150 casks of flaxseed were exported from Pennsylvania. According to [James Mease], *The Picture of Philadelphia, Giving an Account of Its Origin, Manufactures, and Improvements in Arts, Sciences, Manufactures, Commerce, & Revenue* (Philadelphia, 1811), a cask contains seven bushels of seed. If this figure is applied to Coxe's statistics, then 71,050 bushels of flaxseed were exported in 1791–1792. It should be noted that these figures might not represent flaxseed grown only in Pennsylvania because Connecticut seed was also shipped through the port of Philadelphia.

22. *American Weekly Mercury*, July 27 through Aug. 3, 1732, 4, published an ad by Reese Meredith to buy flaxseed. In the same issue, there was a complaint from Ireland that some of the Pennsylvania flaxseed was not growing because of improper processing, thus people were advised how to correct this "for the Good of the Province." The *Pennsylvania Gazette* also had ads for flaxseed, for example, Oct. 18, 1752, and March 21, 1765, 2. In 1811, James Mease gave instructions on how to ship and pack seed for export.

23. The British textile industry was unable to grow all the flax and hemp fiber it needed locally. In a 1726 speech to the Philadelphia Council, Lieutenant Governor Patrick Gordon encouraged the colony to produce iron,

hemp, and silk, for "These three are commodities for which Britain pays dear to other Countries, and with which there can be no Danger of overstocking the Market, therefore, as nothing can be acceptable to Britain, than to receive from its own colonies what it purchases more disadvantageously from Foreigners." *Minutes of the Provincial Council of Pennsylvania,* vol. 3, 265.

24. *Pennsylvania Gazette,* March 21, 1765, 2.

25. Thomas M. Truxes, "Connecticut in the Irish-American Flaxseed Trade, 1750–1775," *Eire-Ireland,* 12 (1977): 35, 40, 58.

26. Percentage of Essex County households with flaxseed: 1715–1718, 0.5; 1734–1737, 1.0; 1754–1757, 0; 1773–1776, 1.5; 1792–1795, 0.5; 1810–1813, 1.5; and 1828–1831, 0. Based on a sampling of 408 Essex County Wills and Inventories, Essex County Courthouse, Salem, Massachusetts (hereafter, Essex County database).

27. Marianne Sophia Wokeck, *Trade in Strangers: The Beginnings of Mass Migration to North America* (University Park, Penn., 1999), 210. New England farms tended to be less oriented to commercial agriculture and relied on their nuclear families and neighborly exchange for most of their labor needs. As a result, colonial Boston was not as attractive a destination for Irish servants as Pennsylvania, according to Daniel Vickers, "Working the Fields in a Developing Economy: Essex County, Massachusetts, 1630–1675," in *Work and Labor in Early America,* Stephen Innes, ed. (Chapel Hill, N.C., 1988), 56, 59, 63.

28. Percentage of Chester County households with hemp fiber: 1715–1718, 2.9; 1734–1737, 1; 1754–1757, 0.6; 1773–1776, 7.9; 1792–1795, 3.2; 1810–1813, 0.6; and 1828–1831, 0.6. Inventory database.

29. Hemp production was encouraged throughout the eighteenth century. For example, numerous bills were presented and speeches given to the Provincial Council of Pennsylvania in the 1720s and 1730s, *Minutes of the Provincial Council of Pennsylvania,* vol. 3, (Philadelphia, 1852), 166, 265, 270, 375, 392. C. W. Carter to the Royal Society of Arts, London, 1760, acc. #444 reel 1, HML, talks about the need to offer bounties and encouragement for hemp growing; *Correspondence and Transactions of the Royal Society of Arts, 1755–1840,* 3, acc. 444, reel 1, HML, notes that bounties were offered, but never awarded, for hemp production from 1760 to 1766. Edmund Quincy, Esq., *A Treatise of Hemp-Husbandry* (Boston, 1765) and [John Beale Bordley] *Hemp,* 1799, were both written with the attempt to encourage hemp production. See Clark *History of Manufactures,* 33–34, for a detailed discussion of the various bounties for hemp production and the colonists' reaction to them.

30. Quincy, *A Treatise of Hemp-Husbandry,* and *An Abstract of The most useful Parts of a late Treatise on Hemp,* translated from the French of M. Marcandier (Boston: 1766).

31. Bordley, *Hemp,* and Miscellany Book, Thomas J. Aldred, "Directions for Raising Flax," West Chester Pennsylvania, Am. 9991 vol.1, HSP.

32. Account Book of a Merchant, Lancaster County, 1768–1774, acc. #823 vol. 5, HML; various entries show people buying flaxseed from him. Also, Account Book, George Brinton, 1781–1800, CCHS, shows that Brinton sold flaxseed to his neighbor, James Robertson; and Weaving Account Book, Joseph Eldridge, 1788–1795, CCHS, indicates that Moses Davis gave Eldridge a peck (2 gallons) of flaxseed on account for weaving Eldridge did for him.

33. Dyer's Journal, Bucks County, Penn., 1763–1805, Guide #186, HSP. Every year from 1767 to 1775, the owner of the journal "Soed flax" invariably between April 12, at the earliest, and May 5, at the latest. The dates were simi-

lar in New England, according to Howard S. Russell, *A Long Deep Furrow: Three Centuries of Farming in New England* (Hanover, 1982), 73.

34. Depredation Claims, Chester County Papers, HSP. Claims 95 and 171 had a half-acre of flax; claim 76a, one acre; and claim 187, one and a half acres. This is further substantiated by Chester County Wills and Inventories, Chester County Archives, West Chester, Pennsylvania (hereafter, CCWI) #1630, Edward Tarran, (d. 1756) had an acre of flax; and CCWI #4378, Michael Holderman (d. 1794) specified in his will that his wife have a quarter-acre of flax planted yearly. Finally, an indenture between Rachel Hamer, John Jacobs, and Mathias Pennebecker, Jacobs Papers, AM.08545 bound volume #3 p. 763, HSP, to rent a farm to Cadwallader Jones in 1784 in Charlestown Township allowed the tenant to plant an acre of flax, one-quarter of which was to be for the use of widow Hamer. James T. Lemon, *The Best Poor Man's Country: A Geographical Study of Early Southeastern Pennsylvania* (New York, 1972), 158, suggests that people planted one and a half to two acres. It is more difficult to get specific information about hemp than flax acreage. In the 1,275 inventories and wills examined for this study there was no mention of hemp acreage. One Depredation Claim, #187, 1777, asked for compensation for one and a half acres of flax and a quarter of an acre of hemp (Bordley, *Hemp*, 2).

35. Alexander Johnston Warden, *The Linen Trade, Ancient and Modern* (London, 1967), 16.

36. Bordley, *Hemp*, 5.

37. Dyer's Journal, 1763–1805, #186, HSP, has numerous entries such as "Soed my flax this Day." Account Book, George Brinton, 1781–1800, Box E–G Family File, CCHS, shows that Elizabeth Burrned worked for Brinton to pay him for "Sowing a Peck of flaxseed and finding the Seed."

38. L. Brown and Kirk, Mill Book, Family Miscellany, acc. 1429 film, reel 1, HML, 76, shows that Roger Kirk paid Simon Woodrow for plowing flax ground for one day in 1776, with two horses.

39. Although there is no direct evidence concerning whose job this might have been in America, the fact that women and children did it in Europe suggests that a similar situation might have existed in the colonies (Warden, *The Linen Trade*, 34).

40. According to Warden, *The Linen Trade*, 9, "When sown in order to produce a good crop of seed, it must be put into the ground thinly, so that the plant may grow up with a strong and full stem, fit to support the seed bolls, and bring them to a perfect maturity, and it must not be pulled until it is fully ripe. When sown sparingly the seeds produce stronger plants, with great branching tops loaded with the seed capsules, but the quality of the Flax is generally found to be deteriorated, and always coarser than when the seed is sown thick."

41. Account Book, William Smedley, 1751–1765, ms. #77049, West Bradford B.H., CCHS, has several entries for women named Jane and Prudence being paid for pulling flax. In a 1784 rental agreement, it was stipulated that the widow renting the land could have a quarter of the tenant's flax crop on condition that she pull her share, Indenture, Jacobs Papers, v. 3 p. 763, HSP. Other account books such as Eldridge and Brinton show men being paid to do this work. For a discussion of the strength involved in pulling flax, see Martha Coons and Katherine Koob, *All Sorts of Good Sufficient Cloth: Linen-Making in New England, 1640–1860* (North Andover, Mass., 1980), 38.

42. A farmer could make a wooden rippling comb, but if the teeth were

iron, he probably either imported it or had it made by a local blacksmith. See Warden, *Linen Trade*, 35. An ad in the March 5, 1751, edition of the *Pennsylvania Gazette* advertised "flax screens" for sale. Some local weavers wove winnowing cloths for their customers; see Joseph Eldridge, Account Book.

43. *American Weekly Mercury*, August 3, 1732.

44. Aldred, Miscellany Book; Warden, *Linen Trade*, 37; John Wiley, *A Treatise on the Propagation of Sheep, the Manufacture of Wool, and the Cultivation and Manufacture of Flax* (Williamsburg, 1765), 36, quoted in Coons and Koob, *All Sorts of Good Sufficient Cloth*, 42; Quincy, *Hemp-Husbandry*, 18.

45. Evidence from several Chester County Wills and Inventories suggests that the practice in that area was to dew ret the flax. In particular, CCWI #1689 filed in 1757 noted that the decedent, John Worral had "flax on the ground Retting," and CCWI #4248 filed in 1792 showed that Benjamin Allen had "A quantity of flax Spred to rot" when he died. According to "Reports from the Navy Department . . . on American Water-Rotted Hemp," Doc. 68, House of Representatives, 20th Congress, Washington, 1828, 4, 8, 27, 30, 32, 33, cited in Carter Litchfield, "Early Pennsylvania Hemp Mills" (Delaware, about 1982 [no publication data]), HML, hemp, too, was most often dew retted.

46. Aldred, Miscellany Book.

47. Quincy, *Hemp-Husbandry*, 17.

48. Bordley, *Hemp*, 6. William Smedley, Account Book, 1770s, shows people worked flax in November, December, January, and February; Roger Kirk, Mill Book, L. Brown, and Kirk Family Miscellany, 1780s, acc. 1429, film reel 1, HML, paid for flax work in November and May; George Brinton, paid for flax work in December, January, and February; and Joseph Eldridge, 1790s, hired men for flax work in January, February, and March.

49. Most of the account books show that people doing this type of labor did so to pay for goods received from the employer. Sometimes they paid their accounts in cash or goods, but usually it was a combination of cash, goods, and services. This was true throughout the century. See, for example, account books of Jonas Ingham, Fuller, Hunterdon County, New Jersey, 1724–1748, acc. 890 III, HML; William Smedley, Cabinetmaker, 1751–1765; Joseph Eldridge, Weaver, 1788–1795.

50. Account book, William Smedley, 1751–1800. Smedley, a cabinetmaker and farmer made a flax break for Isaac Taylor in 1778, 96.

51. Quincy, *Hemp-Husbandry*, 19.

52. In 1765, Ully Rinhart, a man of German descent who lived in Coventry Township in the north of the county, owned the only hemp mill noted on that year's tax list; in 1781–1782, two mills were listed, one in East Caln, which was owned by several men of English heritage, and one in Uwchlan, which was owned by Robert Alison who was Irish.

53. Based on a sampling of 1,275 household inventories, thirty-one had hemp fiber and they were distributed throughout Chester County. Prior to 1774, Caln, Darby, and Westtown in 1717 were the only other townships in the sample to contain households with hemp fiber.

54. According to the Chester County tax lists, in 1765 there was one hemp mill in Coventry Township; in 1781, there were two hemp mills, one in East Caln and one in Uwchlan Township; and, in 1799, there was one hemp and oil mill in Tredyffrin Township.

55. Inventories CCWI #2842, of John Regester, a man of German descent

who died in 1774, had a flax mill and CCWI #4432, of John Waggoner, also German, who died in 1795, had a swingling mill.

56. Patricia Baines, *Spinning Wheels: Spinners and Spinning* (London, 1977), 23, describes these mills.

57. Sometimes the material of which hackles were made was specifically noted in the inventories; for example CCWI #1583, Samuel Painter had one made of brass and one of iron.

58. CCWI #2746.

59. Although merchants imported many types of metal goods to Pennsylvania for purchase, a survey of ads in the *American Weekly Mercury* and the *Pennsylvania Gazette*, shows that no hackles were advertised for sale despite the presence of other fiber-processing tools. According to the 1781 state tax assessment, Richard Jones of Thornbury Township had a wire mill that would also have been a local source of hackle material. In the same year, Nathaniel Keetch was taxed as a "Hackle Maker" in East Marlborough.

60. There are several ads in the *Pennsylvania Gazette* selling imported tow cards, see July 22, 1742, and June 14, 1753.

61. Baines, *Spinning Wheels: Spinners and Spinning*, 21. The *American Weekly Mercury*, July 24–31, 1735, has an ad for a runaway Irish servant who was a flax dresser, and the *Pennsylvania Gazette*, June 29, 1774, Supp. p. 1, has an ad to sell servants and redemptioners who had just arrived from London, including some "hemp and flax dressers."

62. Joshua Proctor, of Kennett Township, was taxed in 1766 and 1768 as a "hemp worker" and in his will, CCWI #5324, proved in 1806, he called himself a "Flax Hatcheler." In 1781, Valentine Feal of Uwchlan Township was taxed as a "hemp heckler" and James Bedford of East Caln, as a "Hemp dresser."

63. In each of the townships (East Caln and Coventry) that had hemp mills, according to the 1781 tax list, there were inmates who were full-time hemp workers.

64. Inventory database. Percentage of households with flax fiber but without flax breaks, hackles, or tow combs: 1715–1718, 83.3; 1734–1737, 78.9; and 1754–1757, 61. Some people earned money by "hawling flax," which could mean it was simply moved from the fields to the barn, or taken further afield to a mill or to the facilities of someone who had the equipment with which to process it. For example, Account Book, Zechariah Robins, Northumberland County, Pennsylvania, 1771–1808, p. 32, in. #7896, man.# 78x241, Winterthur, Rare Book Room (hereafter, WRBR). Chester County State Tax, 1781, Valentine Feal, a "hemp-heckler" owned 83 acres of his own land with buildings and improvements and might have dressed fiber that his neighbors brought to him.

65. Bordley, *Hemp*, 6.

66. Percentage of households with flax fiber that did have flax breaks, hackles, or tow combs with which to work it up: 1715–1718, 16.7; 1734–1737, 21.1; 1754–1757, 39.0; 1773–1776, 60.2; and 1792–1795, 51.6.

67. Paul G. E. Clemens, "Material Culture and the Rural Economy: Burlington County, New Jersey, 1760–1820," in *Land Use in Early New Jersey: A Historical Geography*, Peter O. Wacker and Paul G. E. Clemens, eds. (Newark, 1995), 269.

68. According to the author of "An abstract . . . of a late Treatise on Hemp," 18, "This work . . . [was] hard on account of the strength it required,

and dangerous on account of the fatal dust the workman drew in with his breath," making it clear that this was not an easy job. In Europe, women sometimes did scutching, but the evidence suggests that mostly men in eighteenth-century Chester County did flax and hemp dressing.

69. Account Book, William Smedley, CCHS: Smedley, a cabinetmaker and farmer, hired at least four different people to dress flax, break it, and swingle it in the 1750s. Account Book, Joseph Eldridge, CCHS: Eldridge, a weaver, hired numerous men to work up his flax in the 1790s. Mill Book, Roger Kirk, HML: Kirk paid people to lash (tie bundles of plants together), break, and scutch flax in the 1780s. Account Book, George Brinton, CCHS: Brinton hired several men to break and dress flax in the 1780s. In 1776, Richard Barnard of Bradford township paid Mary Bakes to dress eleven pounds of flax for him, cited in Joan M. Jensen, *Loosening the Bonds: Mid-Atlantic Farm Women, 1750–1850* (New Haven, 1986), 45.

70. Notations in the account books of William Smedley, Joseph Eldridge, and Roger Kirk.

71. Clemens, "Material Culture and the Rural Economy: Burlington County, New Jersey, 1760–1820," 24, describes a similar situation for New Jersey.

72. Peter J. Bowden, *The Wool Trade in Tudor and Stuart England* (London, 1962), 12, notes that in the mixed farming areas of Wiltshire and Norfolk, England, "sheep came to be kept as much for their fertility as for their wool. . . . In an age when there were no artificial fertilizers, sheep were essential to tillage if the best possible corn yield was to be obtained." See Lemon, *The Best Poor Man's Country*, 173–74, for a discussion on the shortage of fertilizer in eighteenth-century Chester County. Elizabeth Hitz, "A Technical and Business Revolution: American Woolens to 1832" (Ph.D. diss., New York University, 1978), 62, also suggests that in many areas of colonial America, with the possible exception of the backcountry regions, wool production was not the main reason for keeping sheep.

73. Quoted in Clark *History of Manufactures*, 202.

74. Bowden, *The Wool Trade in Tudor and Stuart England*, 8–9.

75. James T. Lemon, "Household Consumption in Eighteenth-Century America and Its Relationship to Production and Trade: The Situation Among Farmers in Southeastern Pennsylvania," *Agricultural History*, 41 (1967): 61–62, and Stevenson Whitcomb Fletcher, *Pennsylvania Agriculture and Country Life, 1640–1840* (Harrisburg, 1950), 191, both state that Pennsylvanians of this period did not eat mutton. Account Book, Jonas Ingham, 1724–1748 and Joseph Eldridge, Account Book, 1788–1795, show that both Ingham and Eldridge were paid for their services with lamb and mutton and both sold it.

76. Ledger, Jacob Bucher, Hatter, Harrisburg, Pennsylvania, 1795–1819, WRBR, manu. 75x67, shows that in the 1790s, his customers paid him with various quantities of sheep and lamb's wool for the hats he made for them; they also paid him with mutton. For sheepskin, see Bowden, *The Wool Trade in Tudor and Stuart England*, 12–13, and an entry in the Eldridge account book for May 5, 1795, shows that he sold Isaac Yarnall "a Sheep Skin apron."

77. Lemon, *The Best Poor Man's Country*, 167. Peter W. Cook, "The Craft of Demonstrations," *Museum News* (1974): 15, notes that in 1683 the town of Newbury, Massachusetts, hired a shepherd to look after the sheep. John Beale Bordley, "Purport of a Letter on Sheep," (Philadelphia, 1789), said that he

generally let his sheep run free and only fed them if there was snow. Michael L. Ryder, *Sheep & Man* (London, 1983), 685–87, describes the work involved and says that lambing was the busiest time of a shepherd's year.

78. Lemon, *The Best Poor Man's Country*, 167. See also Clark, *History of Manufactures*, 81. For a good discussion on the factors affecting the quality of sheep fleece in general, see P. J. Bowden, "Wool Supply and the Woollen Industry," *Economic History Review*, series 2, 29 (1956): 45.

79. Ryder, *Sheep & Man*, 696. Diaries, Aaron Leaming, 1750–1777, Cape May, New Jersey, vol. 2, May 27, 1761, Am. 0923, HSP, says "today drove our Sheep—we finished shearing them yesterday." Dyer's Journal, Bucks County, has entries for May 22, 1769, and May 27, 1770, noting that he washed and sheared the sheep "now abouts." Shearing was mainly done once a year, but some people, like Roger Kirk, hired a man to clip his sheep in November 1776, suggesting that a few farmers may have performed this task in both spring and fall, Roger Kirk, Mill Book. Ryder, *Sheep & Man*, 694, notes that in some places sheep were sheared twice a year. John Wiley, *A Treatise on the Propagation of Sheep* (1765), gives a good description of sheep washing and shearing in colonial America, quoted in *Homespun to Factory Made: Woolen Textiles in America, 1776–1876* (North Andover, Mass. 1977), 8.

80. Wool shears were advertised for sale in the newspapers, for example *American Weekly Mercury*, Dec. 8–15, 1737, and *Pennsylvania Gazette*, Oct. 13, 1743, 3. There is less evidence that wool shears were being imported in the later decades of the century and by then may have been available from local blacksmiths. See Ryder, *Sheep & Man*, 696–97, for an excellent description of the construction of shears and their use.

81. Percentage of households with sheep shears (rounded off): 1715–1718, 0; 1734–1737, 10; 1754–1757, 6; 1772–1776, 10; 1792–1795, 10; 1810–1813, 7; and 1828–1831, 5. Percentage of households with sheep (rounded off): 1715–1718, 43; 1734–1737, 54; 1754–1757, 51; 1772–1776, 54; 1792–1795, 52; 1810–1813, 38; and 1828–1831, 22. Inventory database.

82. Ryder, *Sheep & Man*, 694.

83. Average number of sheep owned by people who had sheep (rounded off): 1715–1718, 11; 1734–1737, 14; 1754–1757, 15; 1772–1776, 12; 1792–1795, 11; 1810–1813, 12; and 1828–1831, 12. Inventory database. Bowden, *The Wool Trade in Tudor and Stuart England*, 23. Brinton, Day Book, shows that he generally sheared between seventeen and twenty-six sheep in a day.

84. It is not clear from colonial records who sorted the wool, but it had to be someone with a sufficient understanding of fleece quality. Wiley, *A Treatise on the Propagation of Sheep*, 8–9, quoted in *Homespun to Factory Made*, 10, suggested that if each fleece had been properly rolled, "the person employed to sort the wool may with the greater ease separate the fine from the coarse, and likewise that which is suitable to be combed for worsted from that which will answer for other uses." He also recommended that the wool be washed again before further processing.

85. Aldred, Miscellany Book, 40–42, "Method of washing Merino Wool" gives a detailed description of the labor and equipment involved in this task. George Brinton, Account Book, has an entry for paying Margaret Rock to pick wool.

86. In Europe, pickers used this method, first beating the wool on a hurdle then picking it with their hands. In addition, by 1765, there were hand-operated

mills that performed this task, but it is unlikely these existed in Chester County. For a good explanation and diagrams of this process, see M. Duhamel du Monceau, *Art de la Draperie* (1765).

87. See Chapter 5 for details on cloth fulling.

88. This is especially apparent in the newspaper ads, for example, *American Weekly Mercury*, Jan. 28–Feb. 4, 1729, advertised a fulling mill for sale with "proper Utensils for Dying"; in Oct. 13–20, 1737, there was an ad looking for a person "capable of Managing the Fulling & dyeing Business." The *Pennsylvania Gazette*, Feb. 22, 1775, notes that fire destroyed "the dwelling, workshop, dye house, presses . . . of Aaron Oakford, fuller and dyer." In addition, large numbers of entries in the account books of fullers Jonas Ingham and Roger Kirk show that they were also dyers. The book of a professional dyer working early in the century had recipes for dyes with samples of the colored, unspun fleece beside them (Fig. 8). Book of Recipes for Dyeing, 1710–1714, Pim Papers, ms. #13785, CCHS.

89. Inventory database. In Chester County, of the 15 percent of the households owning wool cards, over half had more than one pair (14.4 percent of the households had cards and 8.2 percent had more than one pair). J. de L. Mann, *The Cloth Industry in the West of England from 1640 to 1880* (Oxford, 1971), 287, discusses the replacement of cards. Almost all the ship cargoes advertised for sale in the *Pennsylvania Gazette* and *American Weekly Mercury* had wool cards among the other imported goods. Daybook, Wallace and Davis, May 1, 1798, to July 14, 1798, Lancaster County, Pennsylvania, #2094 man. #69x101, WRBR, 4, 22, 55, 58, show that these merchants were selling wool cards; and CCWI #4221 shopkeeper, Francis Armstrong (d. 1792), had seventeen pairs of cards among his merchandise. See Mann, *The Cloth Industry*, 286, for a discussion of card making in England. For quantities of cards exported from England, see S. D. Smith, "The Market for Manufactures in the Thirteen Continental Colonies, 1698–1776," *Economic History Review*, 51 (1998): 692. H. Ling Roth, *Notes from the Bankfield Museum, Hand Card Making* (England, n.d., c. 1900), has a good description of the techniques of hand card making in England.

90. CCWI #6110, Calvin Cooper, fulling mill owner, had a carding machine in his inventory when he died in 1815. As soon as carding could be done by machine, this labor-intensive work was transferred from the household to the mill.

91. Henry Wansey, *The Journal of an Excursion to the United States of North America, in the Summer of 1794* (Salisbury, England, 1796), 47, quoted in *Homespun to Factory Made*, 16.

92. J. Hector St. John de Crèvecoeur, *Letters from an American Farmer and Sketches of Eighteenth-Century America*, Albert E. Stone, ed. (New York, 1981, first published 1782), 313.

93. George Brinton, Account Book, June 26, 1790.

94. E. Lipson, *The History of the Woolen and Worsted Industries* (London, 1965), 131. There is more evidence to show that wool combs were imported more in the earlier years of the eighteenth century than in the later years. See, for example, ads in the *American Weekly Mercury*, Oct. 9–16, 1729, and Oct 12–19, 1732.

95. Clark, *History of Manufactures*, 291, notes that American colonies did very little wool combing. See Bowden, "Wool Supply and the Woollen Industry," 45, for a discussion on the requirements for growing sheep that produce

long wool suitable for combing. Inventory database. Percentage of households with wool combs: 1715–1718, 1.5; 1734–1737, 1; 1754–1757, 1.3; 1772–1776, 2.5; 1792–1795, 0.4; 1810–1813, 0; 1828–1831, 0.4

96. Wool combers were among the indentured servants emigrating from Europe and could have provided some of the labor needed to work up worsted fiber. Throughout the eighteenth century there were newspaper ads selling servants who were combers of worsted wool, as well as ads for runaways of the same occupation. For combers, see *Pennsylvania Gazette*, July 23, 1741, Nov. 14, 1751, and Aug. 8, 1751. For runaways, see *American Weekly Mercury*, May 9–16, 1723, *Pennsylvania Gazette*, May 4, 1732, Oct. 29, 1741, and Feb 25, 1752. In 1774, two Irish wool combers arrived in Philadelphia hoping to set themselves up in business, *Pennsylvania Gazette*, Oct. 12, 1774.

97. All but one of the wool combers on the Chester County tax lists were inmates: In 1765, David Broonell of Nether Providence and Moses Rawson of Lower Chichester were taxed as wool combers—Broonell had no property and Rawson had only a house and lot; in 1781, the following were taxed as wool combers: Benjamin Coates and James Tompkin, Charleston; Marmaduke Wivel, East Bradford; Thomas Swainey, East Marlborough; and Abraham Sharpless, Middletown; all were inmates.

98. Arthur Harrison Cole, *The American Wool Manufacture*, Vol. 1 (Cambridge, Mass., 1926), 39.

99. Mary McKinney Schweitzer, "Contracts and Custom: Economic Policy in Colonial Pennsylvania, 1715–1755" (Ph.D. diss., Johns Hopkins University, 1983), 84–85.

100. Percentage of Chester County households with hemp: 1715–1718, 2.9; 1734–1737, 1; 1754–1757, 0.6; 1772–1776, 7.9; 1792–1795, 3.2; 1810–1813, 0.6; and 1828–1831, 0.6. Percentage of households with flax: 1715–1718, 8.8; 1734–1737, 18.6; 1754–1757, 25.6; 1772–1776, 36.4; 1792–1795, 36.8; 1810–1813, 31.3; and 1828–1831, 16.8. Percentage of households with wool: 1715–1718, 5.9; 1734–1737, 21.6; 1754–1757, 20.6; 1772–1776, 23.6; 1792–1795, 17.8; 1810–1813, 11.2; and 1828–1831, 9.3. Inventory database.

101. David J. Jeremy, *Transatlantic Industrial Revolution: The Diffusion of Textile Technologies Between Britain and America, 1790–1830s* (North Andover, Mass., 1981), 126.

102. *Homespun to Factory Made*, 56, and Clark, *History of Manufactures*, 322.

103. Inventory database. For example, by 1810 in Chester County, the average number of sheep (rounded off) per household was 4 (Essex County, 4), declining to 3 in 1830 (Essex County, 0.4). In contrast, in 1810, people who owned sheep had an average of 12 (Essex County, 16) and in 1830, 12 (Essex County, 8). The general population seemed to be relying increasingly on others for their wool.

104. Jeremy, *Transatlantic Industrial Revolution*, 41.

105. See Chapter 6 for a discussion of imported textiles.

Chapter 4. Spinning and Knitting

1. Elizabeth Sandwith Drinker, *The Diary of Elizabeth Drinker: The Life Cycle of an Eighteenth-Century Woman*, Elaine Forman Crane, ed. (Boston, 1994), 137.

2. For a good description of the spinning mule, see Anthony F. C. Wallace, *Rockdale, the Growth of an American Village in the Early Industrial Revolution*

(New York, 1972), 140–43. Spinning mules were invented in 1779 by Samuel Crompton, but they did not see widespread use until the early nineteenth century.

3. Linda Stone-Ferrier, "Spun Virtue, the Lacework of Folly, and the World Turned Upside-Down: Seventeenth-Century Dutch Depictions of Female Handiwork," in *Cloth and the Human Experience,* Annett B. Weiner and Jane Schneider, eds. (Washington, D.C., 1989), 226–27, discusses the negative connotations of men depicted as spinning in seventeenth-century Dutch painting.

4. Marilyn Palmer, *Framework Knitting* (Aylesbury, England, 1984), 9–19.

5. Dorothy K. Burnham, *Warp and Weft: A Textile Terminology* (Toronto, 1980), 129.

6. The spinning wheel has become today's icon of colonial industry; for example, Stevenson Whitcomb Fletcher, *Pennsylvania Agriculture and Country Life, 1640–1840* (Harrisburg, Pa., 1950), 423, claims that almost every household had a spinning wheel. Contemporaries made similar claims: In 1744, Alexander Hamilton observed, "They raise, [in Pennsylvania] too, a great deal of flax, and in every house here the women have two or three spinning wheels a going." Quoted in Alexander Hamilton and Carl Bridenbaugh, *Gentleman's Progress; The Itinerarium of Dr. Alexander Hamilton, 1744* (Chapel Hill, N.C., 1948), 12. See note 9 below for percentages of spinning wheels in Chester County.

7. *Pennsylvania Gazette,* March 20, 1750, advertised Irish spinning wheels for sale, and *Pennsylvania Gazette,* Oct 19, 1752, referred to a Joseph Saul, a chair and spinning-wheel maker in Philadelphia. William Smith, Petition, Orphan's Court Docket, vol. III, p. 5, Nov. 28, 1734, Chester County Archives (hereafter, CCA), and Jonathan Hays, Petition, Court of Quarter Sessions, Feb. 1755, CCA, show that both men were Chester County spinning-wheel makers who took on apprentices. Chester County Tax Lists, 1781, CCA, Samuel Pennock and Richard Painter of East Marlborough were taxed as "little wheel makers." These and less specialized artisans such as joiners probably made the wooden parts of the wheels, but they bought imported "spinning-wheel irons" for the metal elements. Throughout the 1730s, 1740s, and 1750s, spinning-wheel irons and other metal fittings used in the manufacture of spinning wheels were advertised for sale. See, for example, *Pennsylvania Gazette,* Jan. 31 through Feb. 7, 1738, and Feb. 4, 1752. Robert Todd, Spinning-Wheel Maker, Account Book, 1796–1799, Account Book, East Whiteland Township, Chester County Historical Society (hereafter, CCHS), shows that Todd made wheels for men and women, mended wheels, and made clock reels to be used with them.

8. The information about the quantities of yarn a proficient spinner can produce per hour is based on my own experience as a production spinner and information obtained from independent textile specialist, Norman Kennedy, former director of the Marshfield School of Weaving in Vermont and former master weaver at Colonial Williamsburg, Virginia.

9. Percentage of households with wool and flax wheels, rounded off: 1715–1718, 9 (6); 1734–1737, 11 (13); 1754–1757, 23 (18); 1773–1776, 36 (26); 1792–1795, 40 (22); 1810–1813, 26 (10); and 1828–1831, 16 (4). Inventory database.

10. Although Chester County spinners did not produce the extremely fine yarns found in some British textiles, they nevertheless did spin yarns of varying degrees of fineness.

11. Jack Michel, " 'In a Manner and Fashion Suitable to Their Degree': A

Preliminary Investigation of the Material Culture of Early Rural Pennsylvania," in *Working Papers from the Regional Economic History Research Center,* Glen Porter and William H. Mulligan Jr., eds. (Wilmington, Del., 1981), 35, says that upper lofts, called "chambers," "served for storage, as a secondary sleeping space, and for the domestic production of linen and yarn," and that there might also be an out shed for this work. J. Hector St. John de Crèvecoeur, *Letters from an American Farmer and Sketches of Eighteenth-Century America,* Albert E. Stone, ed. (New York, 1981, first published 1782), 313, noted that the "breadth [of the barns] afford [women] an opportunity of spinning long threads, of carding at their ease."

12. For a more detailed discussion of the technical specifications of wool and flax wheels and their operation, see Patricia Baines, *Spinning Wheels: Spinners and Spinning* (London, 1977), chapters 2 and 3.

13. Spun yarn has a twist to it and curls when tension is removed. When yarn is plied, strands spun in one direction are put together and spun in the opposite direction, thereby negating the twist. A garment knitted with a single strand of yarn would twist in the direction of the twist of the yarn.

14. Of 489 Chester County households with spinning wheels, 283 (60 percent) also had reels. Inventory database.

15. On the size and form of eighteenth-century Chester County houses, see Michel, " 'In a Manner and Fashion Suitable to Their Degree,' " 29–65.

16. The inventory of Josiah Phillips, of Uwchlan Township, who died in 1817, showed that he left his "two large spinning wool Wheels" to his wife and gave each of his "four daughters their respective little spinning wheels," suggesting that at least one reason for a household to have more than one wheel was related to the number of women who could use them, Chester County Wills and Inventories, CCA (hereafter, CCWI) #6401. See Chapter 5 for a more detailed discussion of the ratio of spinning wheels to looms.

17. Laurel Thatcher Ulrich, "Wheels, Looms, and the Gender Division of Labor in Eighteenth-Century New England," *William and Mary Quarterly,* 3rd series, 55 (1998): 17–18.

18. CCWI #1545, Hugh Boyd, West Nottingham Township, filed Sept. 19, 1754. For other examples of men leaving spinning equipment to their wives, see the following files: CCWI #562, Michael Blunston, d. 1736; CCWI #1652, John Holland, d. 1757; CCWI #2877, William Mason, d. 1774; CCWI #4251, Daniel Solberger, d. 1792.

19. CCWI #2844. Samuel Maxfield gave both his daughters, Isabel and Elizabeth, their spinning wheels. CCWI #2822., Mary Sharp left her wheels to her granddaughters.

20. CCWI #4387; Jean Simontown d. 1794.

21. Robert Todd, Account Book, 1796–1799, East Whiteland Township, CCHS.

22. See Robert Power file CCWI #1417 and James Guthery, file CCWI #2808.

23. Marylynn Salmon, *Women and the Law of Property in Early America* (Chapel Hill, N.C., 1986), 164–166.

24. Elizabeth England, Petition, Quarters Sessions, August 25, 1772, CCA.

25. For a discussion of female apprenticeship in England at the time, see K. D. M. Snell, *Annals of the Labouring Poor* (Cambridge, England, 1987), 270–319.

26. For example, CCWI #51 shows that the two spinning wheels were

located in the kitchen, which would have facilitated the incorporation of spin-ning with women's other tasks.

27. Lucy Simler, "She Came to Work/She Went to Work, The Development of a Female Rural Proletariat in Southeastern Pennsylvania, 1760–1820," (Un-published paper for meeting, "Women and the Transition to Capitalism in Rural America, 1760–1940," April 1989), 16–22, describes in detail how women spinners worked for wages.

28. George Brinton. Account Book, 1781–1800, Thornbury Township, Chester County, Pennsylvania. Box E-G, Family File, (CCHS).

29. CCWI #117, Robert Power vendue list shows that women bought fiber to spin. Elizabeth Williams bought tow and linen cloth from weaver Joseph El-dridge as well as Indian corn and buckwheat in the 1780s and 1790s, and she paid him in part in cash and in part by spinning tow and yarn for bedticks, Joseph Eldridge, Account Books, 1788–1795, man. #3786, CCHS. In 1803, "widdow grace" paid a portion of her account with fuller Calvin Cooper by spinning, Calvin Cooper Account Book, 1791–1802, W. Bradford B.H., v.1, CCHS.

30. Simler, "She Came to Work/She Went to Work," 19.

31. *American Weekly Mercury*, Apr. 9–16, 1730. For other ads selling slave women who could spin see *American Weekly Mercury*, Oct. 9–26, 1721; *Pennsyl-vania Gazette*, May 10, 1733; *American Weekly Mercury*, Jan. 11–18, 1736–1737; *Pennsylvania Gazette*, Apr. 12, 1764; *Pennsylvania Gazette*, Nov. 6, 1776.

32. *American Weekly Mercury*, Apr. 20–27, 1738; *Pennsylvania Gazette*, Feb. 2, 1744; *Pennsylvania Gazette*, July 27, 1774.

33. Sharon V. Salinger, *"To Serve Well and Faithfully": Labor and Indentured Servants in Pennsylvania, 1682–1800* (Cambridge, 1987), 137–52, and Lucy Simler, "The Landless Worker: An Index of Economic and Social Change in Chester County, Pennsylvania, 1750–1820," *Pennsylvania Magazine of History and Biography*, 114 (1990): 172–73.

34. According to Marla R. Miller, " 'My Part Alone': The World of Rebecca Dickinson, 1787–1802," *New England Quarterly*, 71, no. 3 (1998): 357, a possi-ble exception to the perception of women's work (paid or otherwise) as do-mestic, might be the craft of millinery or gown making, although even this work did not provide women with enough to make a living.

35. Merry Wiesner, *Women and Gender in Early Modern Europe* (Cambridge, 1993), 84.

36. For further comparison of textile production in Pennsylvania and New England, see Adrienne D. Hood, "The Gender Division of Labor in the Pro-duction of Textiles in Eighteenth-Century, Rural Pennsylvania (Rethinking the New England Model)," *Journal of Social History* 27, no. 3 (1994): 537–61.

37. Daniel Vickers, "Working the Fields in a Developing Economy: Essex County, Massachusetts, 1630–1675," in *Work and Labor in Early America*, Stephen Innes, ed. (Chapel Hill, N.C., 1988), 56–60, and Ulrich, "Wheels, Looms, and the Gender Division of Labor,"17–18.

38. Gloria L. Main, "Gender, Work, and Wages in Colonial New England," *William and Mary Quarterly*, 3rd ser., 51 (1994): 50.

39. Ulrich, "Wheels, Looms, and the Gender Division of Labor," 6.

40. Laurel Thatcher Ulrich, *The Age of Homespun: Objects and Stories in the Creation of an American Myth* (New York, 2001), 211.

41. For example, CCWI #2798, Robert Parke (d. 1773) had "Stocking Yarn 2/6"; CCWI #3012, William Garrett (d. 1776) had "Stocking Yarn wt 1/2

Pound—0/2/0"; and CCWI #4461, James Miller (d. 1795) had "Stocking Wool"; Mill Book, L. Brown and Kirk Family Miscellany, acc. 1429, film, reel 1, Hagley Museum and Library, (hereafter, HML), 42, shows that Roger Kirk settled an account with a customer who knit a pair of stockings. Account Books, John Graves, Stocking Weaver, West Chester, 1792–1815 and 1815–1831, ms. 7653 and 8495, CCHS, made large numbers of stockings each year; for example, in 1793, he made about 400 pairs. In the Nov. 12, 1730, issue of the *Pennsylvania Gazette*, a runaway servant was wearing knit mittens "mixt with red, blue and white," and CCWI #1637, Samuel Binning (d. 1756) had mittens listed in his inventory. CCWI #2899, Jeremiah Starr (d. 1775) had mittens as well as "a pair of knit breeches" listed in his inventory, while William Aldred's Account Book 1805–1893, ms. 76546, CCHS, had an entry for dyeing a knitted shawl. It is difficult to determine quantities of imported knit goods versus homemade ones, but import lists make it clear that knit goods were not just domestic products. See Chapter 6 for a more detailed discussion of locally made and imported textiles.

42. Unless produced by a framework knitter on a large loom-like device, most knitting was done by hand, and knitting needles could easily be too small or of too little value to be included in many inventories; hence, it is difficult to fully determine the scale of local knitting. Because of its domestic nature, knitting in early America is largely invisible and has not been well studied.

43. *American Weekly Mercury*, Oct. 19–26, 1721, advertises "A Negro Woman to be sold . . . She can Card, Spin, Knit, and Milk"; the *Pennsylvania Gazette*, July 27, 1774, and Nov. 6, 1776, had ads to sell the time of a Scottish indentured servant girl who could spin and knit and a black woman with similar skills. There are knitting needles in inventory CCWI #2800, of Jane Tennent (d. 1774) and CCWI #2932, of Sarah Jones (d. 1775).

44. Ads in the *American Weekly Mercury* throughout the 1730s and 1740s, and in the *Pennsylvania Gazette* between 1730 and 1750 and less frequently in the 1760s, show knitting needles, or "pins," for sale among cargoes of imported goods. In inventory CCWI #1643 of Thomas Morgan of Chestertown (Chester) (d. 1757), among other merchant goods he had "A Bundle of knitting needles 3/6."

45. For a detailed description of the workings of a knitting frame, see Richard M. Candee, "The Hibbert-Townsend Latch Needle Mystery Unraveled: Patent Control and Nineteenth-Century American Knitting Machines," in *Textiles in New England: Four Centuries of Material Life*, Peter Benes, ed., Dublin Seminar for New England Folklife Annual Proceedings, 1999 (Boston, 2001), 115.

46. Palmer, *Framework Knitting*, 7, 10–11. Despite the fact that the professional knitters were often called "stocking weavers" and their stocking frames called "looms," they should not be confused with weavers; the products were entirely different as was the technology. Alan Rogers, "Rural Industries and Social Structure: The Framework Knitting Industry of South Nottinghamshire 1660–1840," *Textile History* 12 (1981): 17, demonstrates that in Nottinghamshire, where framework knitting developed in the seventeenth and eighteenth centuries, there was also a well-developed weaving industry. He argues that there was a clear link between the weavers and knitters and notes that until the early nineteenth century, framework knitting was known as "weaving."

47. CCWI #20, John Hanes (d. 1715) was called a "stocking weaver" in his

inventory, CCA; ads in the *American Weekly Mercury* for July and August 1728 included servants for sale and among them were stocking weavers; CCWI #604, John Camm (d. 1737) called himself a "framework knitter" in his will, CCA; there were ads for several runaway servants who were stocking weavers in the *Pennsylvania Gazette*, for example Nov. 6, 1746, and Aug. 16, 1753; and in the 1799 tax assessment for Goshen Township, John Graves was taxed as a stocking weaver, CCA.

48. *American Weekly Mercury*, Dec. 5–10, 1723.

49. CCWI #604, John Camm (d. 1737) had a lot of farming equipment in addition to his stocking loom.

50. In the Chester County tax list for Goshen Township in 1799, Graves was listed as having a log house and a lot, indicating that he probably spent the majority of his time pursuing his trade.

51. CCWI #8907, John Graves (d. 1832) had a total personal estate valued at $970.00 and his stocking looms were worth $150.00. John Graves, Account Book, CCHS.

52. Ulrich, *The Age of Homespun*, Chapter 11, "An Unfinished Stocking," talks about hand knitting in New England, but it does not give daily, weekly, or annual production quantities.

53. Quoted in Victor S. Clark, *History of Manufactures in the United States, Volume I, 1607–1860* (New York, 1949), 206.

54. Barbara M. Tucker, *Samuel Slater and the Origins of the American Textile Industry, 1790–1860* (Ithaca, 1984), 50.

55. Quoted in Tucker, *Samuel Slater*, 59.

56. Joseph Eldridge Account Book, ms. #3788, CCHS.

57. Based on information contained in the 1810 and 1820 tax lists, CCA.

58. Percentage of Chester County households with generic spinning wheels (rounded off): 1715–1718, 18; 1734–1737, 34; 1754–1757, 36; 1773–1776, 41; 1792–1795, 35; 1810–1813, 44; and 1828–1831, 40. Inventory database.

59. Percentage of Chester County households with more than one wheel (rounded off): 1715–1718, 22; 1734–1737, 35; 1754–1757, 42; 1773–1776, 47; 1792–1795, 43; 1810–1813, 34; and 1828–1831, 30. Inventory database.

60. For women's opportunities in New England textile mills, see Tucker, *Samuel Slater*, and Thomas Dublin, *Women at Work: The Transformation of Work and Community in Lowell, Massachusetts, 1826–1860* (New York, 1979). For the shift of women's paid activities from spinning to dairying in Chester County, see Joan M. Jensen, *Loosening the Bonds: Mid-Atlantic Farm Women, 1750–1850* (New Haven, 1986), chapter 5.

61. Clark, *History of Manufactures in the United States*, 430.

Chapter 5. Weaving and Cloth Finishing

1. Chester County Wills and Inventories (hereafter, CCWI) #4344.

2. Laurel Thatcher Ulrich, "Wheels, Looms, and the Gender Division of Labor in Eighteenth-Century New England," *William and Mary Quarterly*, 3rd series, 55 (1998): 13, argues that some male artisans continued to weave throughout the eighteenth century in New England, but that their numbers declined as female household production of cloth expanded.

3. James E. McWilliams, "Work, Family, and Economic Improvement in Late-Seventeenth-Century Massachusetts Bay: The Case of Joshua Buffum,"

New England Quarterly, 74 (2001): 355–84, uses the example of one late seventeenth-century Massachusetts Bay family, the Buffums, to demonstrate the strategies that caused women to begin weaving for their own households. Early on, when the family could not afford a loom or extra help, it had to purchase imported and locally made cloth. In the middle period of the family's life cycle, assisted by live-in workers, the female members reduced the expenditure on textiles by weaving for themselves. Their resultant contribution to the Buffums' growing wealth ultimately permitted the household to stop weaving and increase its spending on luxury items and necessities, including both imported and locally made textiles.

4. Inventory database. Weavers comprised 1.5 percent of inventoried decedents' primary occupations, further confirmed by the percentage of the population taxed as weavers: 1765, 0.9; 1881, 2.2; and 1799, 3.4. Chester County tax lists for the years 1765, 1781, and 1799 (hereafter, Tax-list database), CCA.

5. E. Lipson, *The History of the Woolen and Worsted Industries* (London, 1965), 135, estimates that in Britain "one loom gave work to half a dozen spinners or more." Gay L. Gullickson, *Spinners and Weavers of Auffay: Rural Industry and the Sexual Division of Labor in a French Village, 1750–1850* (Cambridge, 1986), 69, says that although estimates on the spinner/weaver ratio vary, she feels that eight to ten spinners to one weaver would be a fair estimate. The discrepancy can be accounted for because Lipson is describing wool spinning and Gullickson is speaking about cotton. Generally, wool was thicker, requiring less labor. The ratios between linen and wool spinning and weaving would also reflect these differences. In Chester County, both linen and wool were spun and woven.

6. Ratio of spinning wheels to looms: 1715–1718, 9:1; 1734–1737, 9:1; 1754–1757, 10:1; 1773–1776, 14:1; and 1792–1795, 12:1. Inventory database.

7. Gullickson, *Spinners and Weavers of Auffay,* 69, calls spinning a "soft occupation" because it was regarded as women's work in Europe.

8. See Rita J. Adrosko, "Anatomy of a Quilted Counterpane," *Weaver's Journal,* 32 (1984): 113–14, for a discussion on the size of eighteenth-century looms. I also worked on many different early North American looms and spinning wheels over the course of my weaving career that provided insight into the skills needed for cloth production.

9. Many of the equipment terms in the following discussion are defined in more detail in Rita J. Adrosko, "Eighteenth-Century American Weavers, Their Looms and Their Products," in *Imported and Domestic Textiles in Eighteenth-Century America,* Patricia L. Fiske, ed. (Washington, D.C., 1976), 105–25; see also Marcus Wilson Jernegan, *Laboring and Dependent Classes in Colonial America, 1607–1783: Studies of the Economic, Educational, and Social Significance of Slaves, Servants, Apprentices, and Poor Folk* (Chicago, 1931), and Marion L. Channing, *The Textile Tools of Colonial Homes* (Marion, Mass., 1969). Many of the terms are also defined in Dorothy K. Burnham, *Warp and Weft: A Textile Terminology* (Toronto, 1980).

10. Channing, *The Textile Tools of Colonial Homes,* 113.

11. It was possible to identify 115 Chester County decedents with looms in their inventories. Of these, approximately forty-eight had some or all of the tools described, which could have been used for loom making, ranging from "carpenter's tools," to saws, chisels, augers, gimlets (for boring holes), hammers, lathes, small stores of iron, leather, and boards.

12. CCWI #3630, 583, 6764.

13. *Pennsylvania Gazette*, May 3, 1750, Philip Goodman was making and selling weavers' looms with everything belonging to them. Throughout the century, looms were advertised for sale in the newspapers either privately or at auction. See, for example, *American Weekly Mercury*, May 4–11, 1721, and *Pennsylvania Gazette*, Aug. 9, 1733, Jan. 28, 1735, Aug. 13, 1741, Apr. 18, 1745, Oct. 2, 1746, May 3, 1750. Isaac Ashton, Account Book, Philadelphia, 1777–1791, #1424, man. #62x60.1, Winterthur Museum and Library, Rare Book Room (hereafter, WRBR), shows that cabinet maker Isaac Ashton made treadles for a loom, swifts, and a spooling wheel for one of his customers in 1788.

14. For example, the following wills clearly specify that the looms and/or weaving equipment be left to an individual: CCWI #401 (1731); #727 (1741); #990 (1746); #1274 (1749); #2064 (1763); #3533 (1780); #4424 (1792); #4298 (1793); #4344 (1794); #6365 (1816); and #6401 (1817).

15. CCWI #5546.

16. Joseph Hobson of New Garden (d. 1797) CCWI #4615, had looms and "Cane for Reeds" in his inventory, and Thomas Bell left his entire estate to his "friend John Craig weaver" who would then have been able to make his own reeds. In the March 15, 1764, edition of the *Pennsylvania Gazette*, George Lechler, a reed maker in Philadelphia, advertised reeds for sale, the mending of old reeds, and that "His reeds are likewise sold in the country at the following places" followed by a list of those selling reeds for him.

17. See *Pennsylvania Gazette*, June 7, 1733, for a brush maker's ad. Brushes were also imported.

18. Based on data contained in 115 Chester County inventories from 1717 to 1820 where weaving equipment existed and the values were given. For this discussion and any following in which the life stages of the artisans are of importance, I have based my analysis on the stages through which households evolve on those delineated by Mary M. Schweitzer, *Custom and Contract: Household, Government, and the Economy in Colonial Pennsylvania* (New York, 1987), 25–34. According to Schweitzer, households moved through five stages: (1) a single youth who was beginning to acquire capital with which to set up his own farm; (2) a married youth with no offspring; (3) a young family with only minor children (young household); (4) people of mixed ages, including minors, adolescents, and young adults (mature household); and (5) grown children who were dispersing to set up their own households (dispersal).

19. Based on data contained in forty-six Essex County inventories (hereafter, ECWI) of loom owners over the eighteenth century, the average value of looms compared to the entire estate was 1.2 percent, which was much lower than in Chester County.

20. ECWI #4895.

21. Among other things, one needed to (1) have a feel for the appropriate tensions to be applied to the threads and the rhythms required to weave efficiently and evenly; (2) be able to thread the warp ends through the right sequence of heddles to obtain the desired patterns; (3) know how to make and repair the equipment involved; (4) understand the different ways of handling the various fibers being woven; (5) be able to coordinate one's hands to throw the shuttle while simultaneously depressing the appropriate foot treadle to lift the warp threads in sequence to create a flawless pattern; (6) wind the warp spools and bobbins for the weft thread so that they unwound smoothly; and (7) be able to make the necessary repairs on the threads when they broke because of bad spinning or inattention on the part of the weaver.

22. The following, representing only the single craft of weaving, suggest the presence of a system of apprenticeship both understood by the general population and supported by the local government: James Wiley, Petition, Quarter Sessions, Aug. 31, 1731, Bound Volume of Servants and Apprentices, CCA, James Wiley petitioned the court to be allowed to view the indenture of his son who had been bound to Robert Beard to learn to weave, but Beard had sold him for plantation work; Petition of Divers Inhabitants of Newtown to Court of General Quarter Sessions, Chester County, Pennsylvania, May 1741, CCA, from a group worried that "a man weak in his understanding" had been taken as an apprentice to learn to weave and was being treated as a laborer instead; CCWI #727, Thomas Garret[t?] of Darby (d. 1748) left money and much of his estate to his former apprentice; CCWI #1669, William Lewis of Newtown (d. 1757) had listed among his property "The Remain of A Ladds Apprent and Weaving Implements"; Deposition of Samuel Oakes, Court of Quarter Sessions, May 1774, CCA, is from a father who charged that his son, apprenticed to "learn the weaving trade," had been sold to a farmer; Indenture of Apprenticeship Between Abishai Ottey and James Baker, May 7, 1788, ms. 28062, CCHS, shows Ottey was to learn the "Art trade and mistery" of weaving and coopering.

23. For more detailed analyses of the system of apprenticeship in North America, see Jean-Pierre Hardy and David-Thiery Ruddel, *Les Apprentis Artisans à Québec, 1660–1815* (Montreal, 1977); Jernegan, *Laboring and Dependent Classes in Colonial America;* Richard B. Morris, *The American Revolution, a Short History* (Princeton, N.J., 1955); Ian M. G. Quimby, *Apprenticeship in Colonial Philadelphia* (New York, 1985); W. J. Rorabaugh, *The Craft Apprentice: From Franklin to the Machine Age in America* (New York, 1986); Sharon V. Salinger, *"To Serve Well and Faithfully": Labor and Indentured Servants in Pennsylvania, 1682–1800* (Cambridge, 1987), 6–8; Schweitzer, *Custom and Contract,* 34–41.

24. Although a few loom owners had slaves (3 out of 115), they were rare. A survey of the 115 Chester County loom owners shows that 13 owned indentured servants, the peak periods being the middle decades of the eighteenth century, declining sharply after the 1760s. Percentage of loom owners with indentured servants: 1710–1729, 7.8; 1730–1749, 15.4; 1750–1769, 46.1; 1770–1789, 30.7; and 1790–1800, 0. According to Salinger, *"To Serve Well and Faithfully,"* 137–52, this follows the pattern within the artisan population in Philadelphia. John J. McCusker and Russell R. Menard, *The Economy of British America, 1607–1789* (Chapel Hill, N.C., 1985), 202–03, give a good synthesis of the periods of immigration to Pennsylvania.

25. Salinger, *"To Serve Well and Faithfully,"* 10.

26. The *American Weekly Mercury* and *Pennsylvania Gazette* are full of ads throughout the eighteenth century for boatloads of servants for sale who were weavers and for runaway servants who were weavers. There are too many to enumerate fully, but for examples of the former, see *American Weekly Mercury,* Oct. 31 throught Nov. 7, 1728; *Pennsylvania Gazette,* July 9, 1741; *Pennsylvania Gazette,* Aug. 14, 1755. For examples of the latter, see *American Weekly Mercury,* Apr. 4–11, 1728; *Pennsylvania Gazette,* July 8, 1742; *Pennsylvania Gazette,* Sept. 20, 1764; *Pennsylvania Gazette,* Apr. 19, 1775.

27. It is extremely difficult to determine the ethnicity of bound labor. Two things give some indication of this: ads for runaway servants usually mention their country of birth, and arriving ships advertised servants for sale and designated the port from which they embarked. Ads for runaways must be used

with caution, as it is possible that one group had a greater propensity for running away than others. However, many shiploads of servants during the 1720s to 1750s originate from England and Ireland, which seems to correlate with the ethnicity of runaway servants (although Germans could have gone through these ports as well). Given that there was a large influx of Germans to Pennsylvania at this time, it is surprising not to see more indication of weavers from this group. Either there were no German weaver servants or they were less likely to run away. Otherwise, there seem to be few discernible ethnic differences in cloth production, a similar conclusion reached by others who have studied this region. See Lucy Simler, "The Landless Worker: An Index of Economic and Social Change in Chester County, Pennsylvania, 1750–1820," *Pennsylvania Magazine of History and Biography*, 114 (1990): 186.

28. Simler, "The Landless Worker," discusses the transition to wage labor.

29. Rorabaugh, *The Craft Apprentice*, 83.

30. CCWI #401, William Lewis of Newtown had two sons who were not minors (and several who were) but left to his eldest son, William, his "Two Looms with their Utensils & Appurtenances with what Money he has earned by weaving"; and #2064, Thomas Fryer, weaver, of Thornbury had two sons but left his eldest son Thomas his "Loom & geers with all the tackling thereunto belonging." CCWI #727, George Garrett (d. 1741), CCWI #990, John Davis (d. 1749), and CCWI #1274, Charles Linn (d. 1746) divided their weaving implements between the two eldest sons.

31. CCWI #4324; see also CCWI #4298, the will of Roger Davlen who made similar stipulations.

32. ECWI #7560.

33. Robert W. Malcolmson, *Life and Labour in England, 1700–1780* (London, 1981), 64, says that in eighteenth-century England, only a small percentage of children were apprenticed to masters outside their own families and that it was common for sons of craft workers to be taught a trade by their fathers, older brothers, or another relative. Using the craft of weaving as an example, Malcolmson says that after the male children were trained they "continued to work in the family shop until, on the death of the father or at the time of their marriage, they set up their own households in which, as a rule, weaving was their principal means of support. Some parents may have helped their children purchase a loom."

34. From a sampling of 825 probate files, only 111 (13.5 percent) belonged to women. This is similar to the findings in British probate material where about 15 percent of the decedents are women, according to Lorna Weatherill, "A Possession of One's Own: Women and Consumer Behavior in England, 1660–1740," *Journal of British Studies*, 25 (1986): 133.

35. Samuel Garrett was elderly when he died, so has no weaving equipment listed in his inventory. However, it is likely that he gave it to one or more of his sons while he was still living (see family tree, page 86). Hannah Garrett married William Lewis, whose father and son were weavers. Other wool comber-weavers were working at this time; see, for example, *Pennsylvania Gazette*, Sept. 30 through Oct. 7, 1736, where a John Robins advertised that he would do weaving and "Worsted-Combing."

36. Samuel Garrett's will and inventory, CCWI #879.

37. Of 115 people identified as loom owners 35 (30.4 percent) had more than one loom.

38. CCWI #1031 (Samuel Garrett) and #1097 (Thomas Garrett). Thomas left his entire personal estate to his brother Nathan, and, although there is not sufficient evidence to say with certainty that Nathan wove, in 1782, his son was taxed as a weaver, Chester County Tax Assessments, 1782 for Darby Township.

39. CCWI #2579, Joseph Garrett.

40. According to data from Chester County tax lists, Samuel had 145 acres and buildings in addition to 32 acres of woodland (1765); in 1765, Joseph paid tax on 220 acres and buildings, 280 acres of woodland, and was a "weaver to trade."

41. James probably lived and worked with his father for wages until his father died and left him property. In the 1765 tax list for Goshen, he has no property, but, in 1782, he was taxed on 150 acres and also taxed on his occupation of weaving.

42. J. Smith Futhey and Gilbert Cope, *History of Chester County Pennsylvania* (Evansville, Ind., 1986), 530. Simler, "The Landless Worker," 176, says that artisans who lived as cottagers or inmates of a landholder paid rent by working at their trade. If they did field work, it was for wages.

43. Joseph Eldridge, Account Books, 1788–1795, man. #3786, CCHS. Entries in this book actually begin in 1786.

44. Eldridge Account Book. The fact that his customers were neighbors and relatives is clear from an analysis of the names on the Garrett/Eldridge family tree and tax assessments for the townships around Goshen where Eldridge lived, in particular Willistown, East and West Whiteland, and Westtown.

45. Eldridge Account Book, 77. Jesse Oakes settled his account with Eldridge "By weaving 31 yd of Tow Linen."

46. This is what had happened with Yarnall's predecessor, James Alcorn, who worked for Eldridge in 1794. After Eldridge settled accounts with Alcorn for his year's work, he hired Yarnall with a similar agreement. Both Alcorn and Yarnall were single and trained as weavers. It appears that Yarnall worked for Eldridge for several years because in the tax assessment of 1798 for Goshen, Yarnall was taxed as a weaver and freeman living with Eldridge.

47. A survey of the Chester County loom owners with either servants or apprentices shows that the peak periods for servant owners was in the middle decades of the eighteenth century, declining sharply after the 1760s (Table 1). According to Salinger, *"To Serve Well and Faithfully,"* 137–52, this follows the pattern within the artisan population in Philadelphia.

48. The data were taken from the wills and inventories of 115 loom owners who died in eighteenth-century Chester County, and an analysis of all the taxable population in the townships of Darby, East Fallowfield, Goshen, East Nottingham, Pikeland, Thornbury, and Tredyffrin contained in the Chester County tax lists for the years 1765, 1781, and 1799. Tax-list database.

49. For those taxed as weavers in the tax-list database, 26.2 percent had property, while 30.8 percent were identified as inmates, 16.3 percent as freemen, and 19.1 percent as renters. It is difficult to know whether the nonlandholders worked full time at weaving, but the designation and taxing of an occupation suggests that it occupied the majority of a person's time.

50. See Joan M. Jensen, *Loosening the Bonds: Mid-Atlantic Farm Women, 1750–1850* (New Haven, 1986), 43–45, for a discussion of the work of female inmates.

51. The information on Benjamin Simcock is from a Deposition from Simcock, May 29, 1788, and an Order of Removal, April 16, 1788, Court of Quarter Sessions, CCA; I would like to thank Lucy Simler for bringing this case to my attention. John Lea's inventory (CCWI #241), shows that he died in January 1727, leaving three looms, one of them a broad loom, and a great deal of miscellaneous weaving equipment.

52. See, for example, CCWI #1958, William Downard (d. 1761 at about age seventy) who was called a "yeoman" in his bond of administration, but in 1736 when he was about forty-five years old he was called "weaver," *Pennsylvania Archives,* ser. 1, vol. 1, 512; CCWI #2834, John Taggart (d. 1774 in Vincent township) was called "yeoman" on his inventory, but in 1765 he was taxed as a weaver living in Uwchlan Township; CCWI #5283 William Mann (d. 1806 in Sadsbury) called himself a farmer in his will, but in 1799, he was taxed as a weaver in the adjacent township of East Fallowfield.

53. Out of fifty-six people taxed as weavers in the tax-list database, only fourteen (25 percent) were taxed on property holdings while forty-two (75 percent) were inmates, freemen, and nonlandholders. Clearly, those property holders identified as weavers were still carrying on their trade full-time. Moreover, weavers owned an average of 80.5 acres of land, but if the two men who had very large holdings (500 and 315 acres) are eliminated, the others owned an average of 26 acres, well under the average eighteenth-century Chester County holding of 125 acres (see Chapter 2).

54. CCWI #697.

55. The estate papers of Robert Chalfont has a plan of his plantation that shows a weaver's shop, 1792, Orphan's Court, CCA (Fig. 19). Dimensions for other weavers' shops were specified in the West Caln tax assessment for 1799 as 16 x 20, 18 x 18, 10 x 15, and 14 x 12 feet.

56. CCWI #5448.

57. Based on information contained in the inventories of loom owners and people whose shops appeared on tax lists, the average size of land holding for twelve people identified with weaving shops was 287 acres, compared with the 125-acre average for the population as a whole.

58. For example, weaving shops turn up in 1717, CCWI #65; 1756, CCWI #2362; 1770, CCWI #2564; 1772, CCWI #2720; 1773, CCWI #2771; 1774, CCWI #2819; and 1792, CCWI #6401.

59. The women with weaving equipment were identified through bequests made in their husband's wills: Mary Hutton (d. 1736), CCWI #553; Martha Hobson (d. 1776), CCWI #2975; Mary Smith (d. 1743), CCWI #442; Hanna Shortledge (no probate); and Rebecca Davis (d. 1772), CCWI #2720.

60. Martha Hobson was the only one who specifically mentioned her loom, willing it to her grandson, Francis Hobson.

61. Gullickson, *Spinners and Weavers of Auffay,* 104–5, finds that in the region of France she examined, women were not recorded formally as weavers until 1808. Although she has little proof, she feels that women probably wove on the equipment of a male relative on an informal basis before that time. John Smail, "Manufacturer or Artisan? The Relationship Between Economic and Cultural Change in the Early Stages of the Eighteenth-Century Industrialization," *Journal of Social History,* 25 (1992): 802, thinks this was also the case in early eighteenth-century West Riding woolen cloth production.

62. Several ads in the *Pennsylvania Gazette* suggest that when a weaver died his widow hired someone to continue the business. See, for example, *Pennsyl-*

vania Gazette, Sept. 16–23, 1736, where a widow placed the following ad: "a Hand is wanting in the business of Weaving Hair-Cloth [a durable fabric made with hairs from a horse's tail, suitable for sieves or upholstery]. The proper Loom and all other Utensils belonging to that Business are ready, and a Piece in the Loom half done, by which one not before used to that Sort of weaving may have an Insight of the Method of Working." In this case, it is clear that the widow did not know how to do the weaving.

63. When John Pennick, weaver, of Concord Township, died in 1717, his widow sold the loom to Joseph Townsin, CCWI #47. In an ad in the August 13, 1741, issue of the *Pennsylvania Gazette,* a widow was selling six looms and everything that went with them, including several servant weavers.

64. Gervase Markham, *The English Housewife* (Kingston, Ont., 1986), 152.

65. For a description of the economic and demographic transformation in New England, see Gloria L. Main, "Gender, Work, and Wages in Colonial New England," *William and Mary Quarterly,* 3rd ser., 51 (1994): 39–66.

66. For a description of increasing numbers of women into textile production in New England and how they worked, see Ulrich, "Wheels, Looms, and the Gender Division of Labor," and Laurel Thatcher Ulrich, *The Age of Homespun: Objects and Stories in the Creation of an American Myth* (New York, 2001).

67. Cloth finishing could be done using hand or foot power, but the extent to which this occurred in Chester County is difficult to evaluate because of the informal nature of the work. See Beverly Gordon, *The Final Steps: Traditional Methods and Contemporary Applications for Finishing Cloth by Hand* (Loveland, Colo., 1982), for a description of the techniques of hand and foot fulling, which might have been used in eighteenth-century Chester County. The fact that throughout the period there were fullers who operated mills scattered throughout the county and that people of English descent were used to taking their fabric to public mills, suggests that unless one was very poor, it would have been unnecessary to finish cloth oneself. M. J. Dickenson, "Fulling in the West Riding Woolen Cloth Industry, 1689–1770," *Textile History,* 10 (1979): 127–31, describes the kinds of public mills in existence in parts of Britain and argues that they probably took the place of home fulling.

68. In Britain at the time, the term *clothier* had a variety of meanings. According to Herbert Heaton, *The Yorkshire Woollen and Worsted Industries from the Earliest Times to the Industrial Revolution* (Oxford, 1965), 299–301, in Yorkshire most clothiers were involved in making (as weavers and employers of weavers) and selling the woolen cloth. Because they did not have the equipment with which to finish it, however, they took their fabric to a fulling mill and paid someone to do the work. In another region, the West Riding of Yorkshire, Lipson, *The History of the Woolen and Worsted Industries,* 41, says that clothiers "assumed the function of the *entrepreneur*—that is, they directed the industry and left to others the execution of its details. . . . The West Country Clothier was in short an employer, not a manual worker." In eighteenth-century Pennsylvania, the term meant neither of these; rather, it was synonymous with the term *fuller.* For example, Phillip Tanner (d. 1795, CCWI #4441), was called a "clothier" in his will but had a fulling business complete with tools and associated materials that he bequeathed to his son. In the *Pennsylvania Gazette,* Feb. 16, 1764, there was an ad for a clothier who understood all aspects of the fulling business, but shearing in particular.

69. Dickenson, "Fulling in the West Riding Woolen Cloth Industry, 1689–1770," 127.

70. It is possible that some mills, especially the earlier ones, were made of wood, but it seems that most were stone. Information about the size and structure of fulling mills can be found in *Pennsylvania Gazette*, Oct. 31, 1751, ad to sell a fulling mill in New Jersey with a gristmill under the same roof, the dimensions of which were fifty by thirty-three feet; the 1799 tax assessment for East Caln, where the mill was twenty feet square; *Pennsylvania Gazette*, March 23, 1774, ad to sell a Chester County fulling mill that was three stories high and made of stone; the 1799 county tax assessment occasionally specified the materials of which fulling mills were built and they were always stone. The larger mills probably accommodated both grist and fulling operations.

71. Jennifer Tann, "The Textile Millwright in the Early Industrial Revolution," *Textile History*, 5 (1974): 80. Many of the townships in the Chester County tax lists in which there was a fulling mill also had at least one person who was a millwright. In the *Pennsylvania Gazette*, Sept. 20, 1780, Isaac Perkins offered a reward to capture whoever burned down his mills, one of which was a fulling mill, as indicated in *Pennsylvania Gazette*, May 17, 1780, 4, adding that he needed a millwright to rebuild the mills.

72. Definitions of these terms are from Isabel B. Wingate, ed., *Fairchild's Dictionary of Textiles* (New York, 1970). For a good description of the process of cloth finishing and its application in eighteenth- and nineteenth-century New Jersey, see Harry B. Weiss and Grace M. Ziegler, *The Early Woolen Industry of New Jersey* (Trenton, N.J., 1958).

73. Examples of mills with the facilities to do the jobs represented by all this equipment can be found in an ad in the *Pennsylvania Gazette*, Sept. 4, 1746, selling a fulling mill in Philadelphia County and asserting that the mill was in good repair and had all the utensils needed for fulling, dyeing, tentering, shearing, pressing, and so on; and Mar. 21, 1765, a fulling mill for sale in Gloucester Co., with a press shop, dyehouse, tenter bars, and all other tools needed to carry on the fulling business.

74. These represent the ideal and not all fullers would have had all these structures, equipment, or materials. This composite picture was created from information found in newspaper ads, wills, and inventories relating only to eighteenth-century Chester County.

75. For example, Reese Peters of Aston Township had 402 acres valued at £1,608 and a fulling mill at £600 or 37.3 percent of his property. Of the three years examined in the tax lists, 1765, 1782, and 1799, the 1782, tax assessments were the most specific and consistent in stating separate valuations for mills and property, so they are the only ones used for this calculation.

76. In 1765, there were nineteen mills; in 1782, nineteen; and in 1799, sixteen. These figures represent fulling mills that were in townships that existed in all three years. Because many townships were no longer part of Chester County after 1789, there were in fact more mills than these numbers represent: in 1765, there were twenty-four; in 1782, twenty-four; and in 1799, twenty-five. Between 1765 and 1782, three mills disappeared and one new mill appeared; between 1782 and 1799 five mills disappeared and four new mills appeared. The fact that more mills seem to have disappeared further suggests the costly investment of these operations.

77. CCWI #4897.

78. Richard Downing, in the 1788 tax assessment for East Caln, had interests in merchant, saw, hemp, and fulling mills. The first three were housed in a single structure, but the fulling mill was a separate building. Dickenson,

"Fulling in the West Riding Woollen Cloth Industry," 131, notes that because the basic gears and shafts of all water mills were fairly similar it was easy to convert a fulling mill to a gristmill, for example. K. H. Rogers, *Wiltshire and Somerset Woollen Mills* (Edington, Wiltshire, 1976), 10, says that in eighteenth-century Wiltshire, England, the dual function of fulling and gristmilling was accommodated in many individual mills "sometimes separately occupied, and sometimes worked by the same man."

79. Fifty-five people owned fulling mills, and fifteen (27.3 percent) of those with mills were also identified as fullers. The numbers should be adjusted slightly upward to accommodate the fact that trades were not consistently taxed, but it is clear that many people owned cloth-finishing mills but did not participate fully in their operation.

80. See Victor S. Clark, *History of Manufactures in the United States, Volume I, 1607–1860* (New York, 1949), 176–79 for a description of saw and flour milling during the colonial era.

81. Most of the specialized dyers working in eighteenth-century Pennsylvania lived and worked in Philadelphia. See, for example, ads by Michael Brown, *American Weekly Mercury*, July 11, 1734; Anthony Duche, *Pennsylvania Gazette*, Feb. 4, 1752; and James Clark, *Pennsylvania Gazette*, June 21, 1775. There were servants who were dyers coming from Britain (see *Pennsylvania Gazette*, June 21, 1750, and June 26, 1766) who might be purchased by a fuller in Chester County, but there was probably less specialization by the fullers in this rural area than by the dyers in the city. For very specialized work, people could take their material to Philadelphia.

82. The account book of Calvin Cooper, fuller, of West Bradford, 1791–1800, CCHS, shows that he did most of these things: milling (fulling), dyeing, dressing, and pressing. It would seem that he did not nap or shear the cloth, but most of the fabric he processed would not have required these steps. Fuller Roger Kirk of West Nottingham did everything: dyed, scoured, fulled, dressed, napped, sheared, and pressed the various pieces of cloth that were brought to him to finish, Mill Book, L. Brown and Kirk Family Miscellany, Acc. 1429, film, HML. There is some indication, however, that there were specialized workers because in the *Pennsylvania Gazette*, Nov. 6, 1746, Jonathan Ingham, a fuller, says that some cloth had been stolen from him, probably by a journeyman fuller or shearman. An ad to sell Irish and English servants in the *Pennsylvania Gazette*, June 26, 1766, had dyers and shearers among them.

83. Tax-list database. There were eight weavers to every fuller. See also an indenture between Andrew Gibson, fuller, and Simon Hutton, March 8, 1785, ms. 13596, CCHS.

84. See CCWI #6911 Calvin Cooper (d. 1815), West Bradford. Cooper's account book indicates that he and his father were working together, Calvin Cooper, Account Book, Chester County, 1791–1802, W. Bradford B.H., CCHS.

85. For example, the following left their fulling operations to their sons: CCWI #1281, John Marshall (d. 1749); CCWI #1412, Job Harvey (d. 1751); CCWI #4509, John Fulton (d. 1796); CCWI #4897, Samuel Painter (d. 1802). CCWI #3543, Reese Peters (d. 1784) left his fulling mill to his grandson. No one left their businesses to their daughters.

86. Martha Harvey, Petition, Orphan's Court, Samuel Harvey Estate Papers, 1784. Lisa Wilson Waciega, "A 'Man of Business':The Widow of Means in Southeastern Pennsylvania, 1750–1850," *William and Mary Quarterly*, 3rd series,

40 (1987): 40–64, argues that widows often took over and ran their late husbands' businesses and it appears that Martha Harvey attempted this with her husband's fulling operation. Running the business, however, is very different from doing the actual work involved.

87. Eighteen people were identified as having more than one milling operation, eight (44.4 percent) were also fullers and ten (55.5 percent) had no assigned occupation.

88. Among all of the fulling-mill owners there were fifteen saw mills (60 percent), seven gristmills (28 percent), one hemp mill (4 percent), one papermill (4 percent), and one boulting mill (4 percent). Among just the fulling-mill owners who were identified as fullers, there were seven sawmills (63.6 percent), two gristmills (18.2 percent), one papermill (9.1 percent), and one boulting mill (9.1 percent).

89. In the tax assessments of 1765, 1782, and 1799, the acreage was always specified. In addition, out of twelve inventories identified as belonging to fulling-mill owners, eleven (91.7 percent) had livestock and/or agricultural products and implements, indicating that farming was an integral part of their livelihood.

90. In the winter, ice interfered with the mill operation; in the summer, the rivers might dry up.

91. There are three account books of fullers from which the details of the following discussion have been taken: Jonas Ingham, Hunterdon Co., New Jersey, 1724–1748, acc. 890 III, HML; Mill Book, L. Brown and Kirk Family Miscellany, Chester Co., acc. 1429, film reel 1, HML; and Calvin Cooper, Chester County, 1791–1802, W. Bradford B.H., CCHS. Although Ingham was from New Jersey, his account book has been used in this analysis because it is unusual to find one of this early date, and it is unlikely that the operations would have differed greatly from those in Chester County.

92. For example, according to the 1765 tax assessment for Goshen Township, Ellis Davis was a fuller with a mill. On July 23, 1741, he advertised in the *Pennsylvania Gazette* to recover his runaway servant who was a fuller by trade and who also understood plantation work. Other ads for runaway servants who were fullers can be found in the *Pennsylvania Gazette*, Sept. 15, 1743, and Jan. 15, 1751. In addition, there were servants for sale who were trained cloth workers; see, for example, *Pennsylvania Gazette*, July 9, 1741, June 21, 1750, and June 26, 1766.

93. *American Weekly Mercury*, Apr. 5, 1744. There were numerous similar ads trying to rent fulling businesses in other counties; see, for example, *Pennsylvania Gazette*, Apr. 30, 1731, July 11, 1734, April 18, 1754, Feb. 28, 1765, Aug. 31, 1774, May 17, 1780, Oct. 20, 1784. One ad in the *American Weekly Mercury*, Aug. 5–12, 1736, tried to find a person to rent a fulling business in New Castle County, but in the event that failed the advertiser was interested in hearing from "any good careful Workman of the Business [who] is inclined to go out on hire."

94. *Pennsylvania Gazette*, Feb. 28, 1765.

95. This is based on an analysis of the 1765 and 1799 Chester County tax assessments. In 1765, there were five fullers without mills living in the townships of East Caln, London Britain, Tredyffrin, and Vincent, and in each of these townships there were fulling-mill owners, three of whom were not fullers, who would have employed these men. In 1799, there were eight fullers without mills, working in townships where there were mills; four of the

owners were not fullers. Of the thirteen men who were fullers without mills, five were single and five were inmates, indicating that they were working for, and probably living with, the mill owners in the township. In the case of John Culbertson, a storekeeper and fulling-mill owner in 1765, his son, John Jr. was a fuller who ran the business, Chester County tax assessments, 1765, for East Caln Township.

96. Percentage (rounded off) of weavers in relation to the overall population: 1765, 1; 1781, 2; and 179, 3. Percentage (rounded off) of weavers who did not own property: 1765, 49; 1781, 74; and 1799, 71. Tax-list database.

Chapter 6. From Loom to Market

1. *American Weekly Mercury,* August 8–15, 1728. *Oznabrigs* were coarse, unbleached linen cloths suitable for work clothes, sacks, or bags; *garlicks* were partially or fully bleached linen cloths that were used for household textiles and aprons; *duroys* were worsted wool suiting fabrics that were plain or patterned, depending on where they were woven, and were glazed (pressed and with a sizing applied to make them shiny); *shalloons* were a cheap worsted wool cloth with a twill weave that were used for lining clothes; *strouds* were woolen cloths, usually red, often used as Indian trade goods; *duffels* were heavy woolen cloths with a long nap, used as trading goods or for warm outerwear (see Glossary).

2. William Smedley, Account Book, 1751–1800, ms. #77049, Chester County Historical Society, West Chester, Pennsylvania (hereafter, CCHS). Chester County Wills and Inventories, Chester County Archives, West Chester, Pennsylvania, (hereafter, CCWI), #2255, and CCWI #2335.

3. Paul G. E. Clemens and Lucy Simler, "Rural Labor and the Farm Household in Chester County, Pennsylvania, 1750–1820," in *Work and Labor in Early America* Stephen Innes, ed. (Chapel Hill, N.C., 1988), 124.

4. For inventories designating yarn for specific projects, see CCWI #1544, William Huey (d. 1754); CCWI #1627, George Pierce (d. 1756); CCWI #4286, Patrick Anderson (d. 1793); CCWI #4364, Isaac Pimm (d. 1794); and CCWI #4476, James Carter (d. 1795).

5. Some of the fullers/dyers sold modest amounts of dyestuffs to their customers that would have been suitable for home dyeing small quantities of yarn. For example, Jonas Ingham, Account Book, 1724–1805, acc. 890 #3, Hagley Museum and Library (hereafter, HML), sold one ounce of indigo to a customer in 1720 and two ounces to someone else in 1726; he also sold four ounces of madder (a red dye). According to Mill Book, L. Brown and Kirk Family Miscellany, acc. 1429, film reel 1, HML, and Calvin Cooper, Account Book, 1791–1802, W. Bradford B.H., CCHS, Roger Kirk sold an ounce of indigo and Calvin Cooper sold twelve ounces of madder in the late eighteenth century.

6. According to Mill Book, L. Brown and Kirk Family Miscellany, Roger Kirk dyed cotton yarn for a customer in 1774 and one and a half pounds of yarn red for someone else in 1776. Calvin Cooper, Account Book, 1791–1802, 29, 41, shows that Cooper also dyed small quantities of yarn.

7. Mill Book, L. Brown and Kirk Family Miscellany, shows that, in addition to the small quantities of yarn (two and three pounds) that Kirk dyed for most of his customers, he dyed much larger amounts for weaver Michael Randle in

the 1770s: 10 pounds of yarn red; 20 pounds yellow in 1774; 32 pounds yellow and 32 pounds red in 1775. Red cost twice as much as yellow. Joseph Eldridge, Account Book, 1788–1795, ms. #3786, CCHS, 33, has an entry indicating that weaver Eldridge charged his client Lewis Williams for the cost of "Blue Dying at Fitzpatricks" for which Eldridge had paid.

8. Joseph Eldridge, Account Book, 1788–1795, 47, charged George Brown nine shillings for weaving 17.5 yards of tow linen and 1s 5d for spooling it.

9. CCWI #4467; in her will in 1795, Abigail Davis bequeathed her "web [warp] of Linsey ready for the weaver" to a friend. Mary M. Schweitzer, *Custom and Contract: Household, Government, and the Economy in Colonial Pennsylvania* (New York, 1987), 49–56, argues that from as early as the 1720s wage labor in a variety of forms existed and was compatible with the local economy, and that wages were high by British standards. Thus, people who chose to produce fiber and yarn or do some dyeing and other work would have known what that work would have cost to pay someone else to do it.

10. Advertising in the *Pennsylvania Gazette* provides evidence of specialty weavers in Philadelphia: May 10, 1739, a sieve weaver; Oct. 4, 1739, a tape weaver; Apr. 21, 1743, a plush weaver; and May 5, 1743, a lace weaver. Many immigrant servant weavers had specialized in a single branch of the business: *Pennsylvania Gazette*, May 28, 1741, had linen weavers for sale (as servants); the July 8, 1742, issue advertised for a runaway servant who was a weaver specializing in fine work; Feb. 19, 1751, had a woolen weaver for sale; and on June 26, 1766, among a group of servants were linen, worsted, yarn, broadcloth, stocking, tape, and girth-web weavers.

11. Joseph Eldridge, Account Book. It is impossible to state the exact yardage of cloth made from the various fibers because some entries just denote the pattern of cloth and not its fiber content.

12. Caleb Wickersham, Newlin Township, B.H. (CCHS).

13. For the quantities of woolen cloth imported to the thirteen colonies, see S. D. Smith, "The Market for Manufactures in the Thirteen Continental Colonies, 1698–1776," *Economic History Review*, 51 (1998): 689.

14. CCWI #241; Lea had both "single and double gears" on which he could weave cloth of the most simple weave structure with two shafts and more elaborate cloth with four. He also had "3 pair of broad Double gears."

15. CCWI #727. Most looms had two or four shafts; it took special training to weave on a loom with more than four shafts (see Chapter 5). The presence of the two other looms indicates that Garrett was also weaving plainer cloth.

16. CCWI #3510, Andrew Snider (d. 1783). CCWI #5247. *Huckaback* was a type of weave structure usually found in linens that produced a small overall pattern suitable for table linens and, because of its absorbency, towels.

17. See Arthur Harrison Cole, *The American Wool Manufacture*, Vols. 1 & 2 (Cambridge, 1926), 28–29; Rolla Milton Tryon, *Household Manufactures in the United States, 1640–1860* (Chicago, 1917), 202–06; and Elizabeth Hitz, "A Technical and Business Revolution: American Woolens to 1832" (Ph.D. diss., New York University, 1978), 72–73. Hitz, 73, says "So far, no records of American master weavers of superfine broadcloth have come to light. . . . [W]hatever fine cloth there was would have had to have been narrow cloth as there is no evidence of any kind of the existence of broadlooms."

18. Joseph Eldridge, Account Book. Entries for the years 1786 through 1789 that were specified as "linen" totaled 866 yards, while the yardage for "tow" was only 367 yards. The degree of fineness of a fabric was determined

by the size of the reed used to maintain the appropriate spacing of the warp threads across a forty-five inch width. According to Ellen J. Gehret, *Rural Pennsylvania Clothing* (York, Penn., 1976), 6, "tow was woven through the reeds with from 350 to 800 dents [openings] and would have had from fifteen to thirty-five threads per inch in the warp direction. . . . All flaxen cloth woven through a 900 reed or finer was called linen."

19. 1799 Tax Assessment, CCA. There were two coverlet weavers in London Britain (one was an inmate who probably worked for the other) and one in West Nottingham. The hairsieve weaver lived in New Garden. Until 1799, cloth makers were always taxed just as "weavers" and, with the exception of stocking weavers, there was no indication of product specialization.

20. J. R. Commons, "American Shoemakers, 1647–1895," *Quarterly Journal of Economics,* 24 (1909): 49. Commons argues that there are four stages of craft production and that this bespoke production represents the first stage.

21. Joseph Eldridge, Account Book, 1788–1795, has several payments in wool and flax fiber, although the quantities were not large (one to two pounds of wool). The following people paid for cloth made by Eldridge with spinning: Elizabeth Williams, Rachel Abbot, Dinah Willett, Gershen Bates.

22. Eldridge Account Book. Eldridge sold small quantities of both wool and flax fiber, often to women who were spinning for him. He also sold yarn. Mill Book, L. Brown and Kirk Family Miscellany, shows that several weavers wove for Roger Kirk to pay him for cloth-finishing services.

23. For late seventeenth- and early eighteenth-century households, Lorna Weatherill, "Consumer Behaviour, Textiles and Dress in the Late Seventeenth and Early Eighteenth Centuries," *Textile History,* 22 (1991): 298, contends that it was the second-largest expenditure after food. Using Gregory King's contemporary figures for clothing expenditures, N. B. Harte, "The Economics of Clothing in the Late Seventeenth Century," *Textile History,* 22 (1991): 290, estimates that about 25 percent of personal income was for clothing.

24. Tryon, *Household Manufactures in the United States,* 91–93; Jonathan Prude, "To Look on the 'Lower Sort': Runaway Ads and the Appearance of Unfree Laborers in America, 1750–1800," *Journal of American History,* 78 (1991): 124–59; and Rita Susswein Gottesman, compiler, *The Arts and Crafts in New York 1726–1776: Advertisements and New Items From New York City Newspapers* (New York, 1938).

25. Inventories are limited as a source for clothing estimates because they do not usually list individual items; instead, entire wardrobes usually appear simply as "wearing apparel." In a sampling of 120 inventories from 1715 to 1795, only 12 (10 percent) specify any detail about clothing, but this often represents important pieces rather than comprehensive lists; 50 (41.7 percent) specify wearing apparel or clothing with no further information; and 58 (48.3 percent) give no mention of clothing. The following estimates, therefore, are based on the few listings of clothing found. For a further discussion, especially relevant for seventeenth-century Massachusetts, see Pat Trautman and Donna Bartsch, "Probate Documents: American Costume History Research," *Clothing and Textiles Research Journal,* 6 (1988): 26–36.

26. For a discussion of the issues of the psychological, social, and economic impact of textile goods on eighteenth-century Philadelphia County residents, see Susan Prendergast Schoelwer, "Form, Function, and Meaning in the Use of Fabric Furnishings: A Philadelphia Case Study, 1700–1775," *Winterthur Portfolio,* 14 (1979): 25–40.

27. Gehret, *Rural Pennsylvania Clothing*, 101, 126, 158, 169.

28. Billy G. Smith, *The 'Lower Sort': Philadelphia's Laboring People, 1750–1800* (Ithaca and London, 1990), 106. How people in early America, particularly those on the margins, thought about clothing, and how they acquired it are topics that need more study. These subjects have been better studied for Britain; see, for example, Beverly Lemire, "Consumerism in Preindustrial and Early Industrial England: The Trade in Secondhand Clothes," *Journal of British Studies*, 27 (1988): 1–24; Beverly Lemire, "The Theft of Clothes and Popular Consumerism in Early Modern England," *Journal of Social History*, 24 (1989): 255–76; and John Styles, "Clothing the North: The Supply of Non-Elite Clothing in the Eighteenth-Century North of England," *Textile History*, 25 (1994): 139–66.

29. CCWI #3976.

30. Based on an analysis of the clothing listed in seven inventories from 1726 to 1803. I have chosen only the items that the majority of the decedents all had listed in common. Other things that were mentioned less often included undershirts, cloaks, stocks, drawers, suits, and vests. See CCWI #241, John Lea (d. 1726/7); CCWI #609, Joseph Hibberd (d. 1737); CCWI #3381, Captain Henry Barker (d. 1782); CCWI #3510, Andrew Snider (d. 1783); CCWI #3976, David Henry (d. 1788); CCWI #4145, William Smith (d. 1791); and CCWI #5247, Samuel Sellors (d. 1803).

31. Prude, "To Look on the 'Lower Sort,' "144.

32. Women's inventories are more likely to itemize clothing than are men's, as it often constituted a major part of their property. Even so, out of a sampling of 572 Chester County inventories between 1715 and 1776, 70 belonged to women and of these, only 8 (11.4 percent) even mention specific items of clothing and only 4 (5.7 percent) give detailed lists.

33. CCWI #1315, based on the list of items Jacob Hibberd (d. 1750) bequeathed to his daughter; CCWI #2019, Margaret Smith (d. 1762); CCWI #2751, Elizabeth Taylor (d. 1773); CCWI #2880, Sebbellah Parker (d. 1774); CCWI #2891, Jane Hanna (d. 1775); CCWI #3785, Hannah Calvert (d. 1786); and #4294, Hannah Davis (d. 1793). These consist of the four inventories found in the sampling of seventy women's inventories that listed clothing, supplemented by three others that I found randomly. Too few inventories are available to be able to trace changes over time or because of wealth differential.

34. The clothing items were determined from information contained in Chester County Wills and Inventories, from the description of the clothes worn in eighteenth-century Pennsylvania in Gehret, *Rural Pennsylvania Clothing*, and clothing worn by English country people in the eighteenth century as described in Anne Buck and Phillis Emily Cunnington, *Clothes and the Child: A Handbook of Children's Dress in England, 1500–1900* (Carlton, Bedfordshire, 1996),120–46. Although the numbers of sheep and/or flax acreage were often specified in wills to provide for some of a widow's cloth needs, as were some items of clothing, lengths of cloth did not appear in the wills analyzed for this study.

35. Family size was determined from an analysis of the 1783 tax list (CCA) for five townships: East Bradford (households, 89; population, 568); Goshen (households, 123; population, 757); Westtown (households, 42; population, 222); East Whiteland (households, 59; population, 352); and Willistown (households, 107; population, 662). In total, there were 420 households with a population of 2,561, averaging 6.1 people per family.

36. The list of textiles is based on items found in eighteenth-century Chester County inventories.

37. Grace Rogers Cooper, *The Copp Family Textiles* (Washington, D.C., 1971), 23, describes a complete set of late eighteenth-century, checked, linen bed furniture from the Copp family in Connecticut. These would have been similar to such a set in Chester County at the time, although not everyone would have had them.

38. Schoelwer, "Form, Function, and Meaning in the Use of Fabric Furnishings," 26–27.

39. Neil McKendrick, John Brewer, and J. H. Plumb, *The Birth of a Consumer Society: The Commercialization of Eighteenth-Century England* (Bloomington, Ind., 1982), 1.

40. The percentages of fabric occurring in twenty Chester County inventories for each sampled year are as follows. Sheets: 35 percent (1717–1718), 40 percent (1737), 55 percent (1757), 60 percent (1776), and 65 percent (1795). Blankets: 40 percent (1717–1718), 25 percent (1737), 55 percent (1757), 30 percent (1776), and 15 percent (1795). Tablecloths: 15 percent (1717–1718), 35 percent (1737), 30 percent (1757), 50 percent (1776), and 55 percent (1795). Pillowcases: 5 percent (1717–1718), 20 percent (1737), 15 percent (1757), 35 percent (1776), and 40 percent (1795). Napkins: 10 percent (1717–1718), 15 percent (1737), 5 percent (1757), 5 percent (1776), and 25 percent (1795). Towels: 5 percent (1717–1718), 5 percent (1737), 5 percent (1757), 10 percent (1776), and 10 percent (1795).

41. It is also possible that the absence or presence of a textile item in a particular year is just a reflection of the limited sampling.

42. Lois Green Carr and Lorena S. Walsh, "Changing Lifestyles and Consumer Behavior in the Colonial Chesapeake," in *Of Consuming Interests: The Style of Life in the Eighteenth Century*, Cary Carson, Ronald Hoffman, and Peter J. Albert, eds. (Charlottesville, Va., 1994), 59–166, argue that the desire to be fashionable at all levels of society encouraged the acquisition of consumer goods in the Chesapeake during the eighteenth century. Undoubtedly, this was also true of Pennsylvania residents.

43. For some itemized listings of clothing in inventories, see CCWI #509, #2019, #2800, #2418, and #4294. For more details on eighteenth-century men's and women's dress, see Linda Baumgarten, *Eighteenth-Century Clothing at Williamsburg* (Williamsburg, Va., 1986), and Anne Buck, *Dress in Eighteenth-Century England* (New York, 1979).

44. There is very little work on early American clothing and attitudes to fashion, especially in the rural areas. For Quaker dress, see Adrienne D. Hood, "Quakers as Consumers: Museum Collections, Material Culture, and Early American History" (unpublished paper, 2002); Leanna Lee-Whitman, "Silks and Simplicity: A Study of Quaker Dress as Depicted in Portraits, 1718–1855" (Ph.D. diss., University of Pennsylvania, 1987); and Deborah E. Kraak, "Variations on 'Plainness': Quaker Dress in Eighteenth-Century Philadelphia," *Costume*, 34 (2000): 51–63. For more general works on eighteenth-century clothing, see Baumgarten, *Eighteenth-Century Clothing at Williamsburg*; Linda Baumgarten, " 'Clothes for the People': Slave Clothing in Early Virginia," *Journal of Early Southern Decorative Arts*, 14 (1988): 27–70; Linda Baumgarten, "Plains, Plaid and Cotton: Woolens for Slave Clothing," *Ars Textrina*, 15 (1991): 203–22; Karin Calvert, "The Function of Fashion in Eighteenth-Century America," in *Of Consuming Interests: The Style of Life in the Eighteenth Century*,

Cary Carson, Ronald Hoffman, and Peter J. Albert, eds. (Charlottesville, Va., 1994), 252–83; Gehret, *Rural Pennsylvania Clothing;* Tandy Hersh and Charles Hersh, *Cloth and Costume 1750–1800: Cumberland County, Pennsylvania* (Carlisle, Penn., 1995); Prude, "To Look on the 'Lower Sort' "; Timothy J. Shannon, "Dressing for Success on the Mohawk Frontier: Hendrick, William Johnson and the Indian Fashion," *William and Mary Quarterly*, 3rd series, 53 (1996): 13–42; Laurel Thatcher Ulrich, "Cloth, Clothing, and Early American Social History," *Dress*, 18 (1991): 39–48; and Shane White and Graham White, "Slave Clothing and African-American Culture in the Eighteenth and Nineteenth Centuries," *Past and Present*, 148 (1995): 149–86.

45. For New England, see Gloria L. Main, "The Distribution of Consumer Goods in Colonial New England: A Subregional Approach," in *Early American Probate Inventories*, Peter Benes, ed. (Boston, 1989), 153–68, and Gloria L. Main, "The Standard of Living in Colonial Massachusetts," *Journal of Economic History*, 43 (1983): 101–08.

46. For a good discussion of the concept of comfort as a justification for consumption in the early republic, see John E. Crowley, "The Sensibility of Comfort," *American Historical Review*, 104 (1999): 725–82, and John E. Crowley, *The Invention of Comfort: Sensibilities and Design in Early Modern Britain and Early America* (Baltimore, 2001).

47. Smith, "The Market for Manufactures in the Thirteen Continental Colonies, 1698–1776," 702.

48. Inventory database.

49. This statement is made with the understanding that the absence of sheep in an after-death inventory may not have meant there were no sheep during the owner's lifetime.

50. In addition to the discussion of women's work in Chapter 4, much evidence shows that people sold some or all of the fiber and yarn they produced. For example, Calvin Cooper, fuller, of West Bradford, Account Book, 1791–1800, CCHS, shows that Cooper was paid for his services as a fuller by Mordecai Hayse between June 1791 and June 1794 by 30.5 pounds of wool, 4 pounds of black wool, and 5.25 pounds of coarse wool, and in 1793 Cooper credits John Ford for spinning done by Ford's wife. Jonas Ingham, Account Book, Hunterdon Co., New Jersey, 1724–1748, acc. 890 III, HML, indicates that Ingham was also paid by several clients in wool and flax fiber and spinning. Aaron Leaming, Account Book, 1764–1784, man. #69x74, Winterthur Museum and Library, Rare Book Room (hereafter, WRBR), shows that Leaming, who was running a sawmill in Cape May, New Jersey, was paid in quantities of fiber such as 32 pounds of flax in February 1772.

51. Smedley's household contained at least four members of his immediate family and several dependent outsiders. Because it is difficult to know how many people he actually provided for, I will continue to base my estimations on the average family size of six. Smedley, in fact, may have furnished clothing and basic textile goods for a larger number of people. For a more detailed discussion of the Smedley household, see Clemens and Simler, eds.,"Rural Labor and the Farm Household in Chester County, Pennsylvania, 1750–1820," 121–27.

52. Joseph Eldridge, Account Books. These figures are rounded off for the sake of clarity. His yearly production in yards was: 1786, 613.3; 1787, 661.5; 1788, 949.4; and 1789, 274.5. I have based his annual output on the fact that he would have worked six-day weeks. Robert Blair St. George, "The Decentralization of Skill in New England Society, 1620–1820," paper presented at

"The Social World of Britain and America, 1600–1820: A Comparison from the Perspective of Social History" (Williamsburg, Va., September 5–9, 1985), suggests that most people at this time worked (or were expected to work) a six-day week.

53. Eldridge, Account Book, v. 1, p. 2, notes that James Garrett owed him £1s15 for "Work Done in harvest and at other times." CCWI #4344; James Garrett's will refers to his infirmity.

54. Barbara M. Tucker, *Samuel Slater and the Origins of the American Textile Industry, 1790–1860* (Ithaca, 1984), describes the setting up of the first American spinning mill in Pawtucket, Rhode Island, in 1790, and shows (pp. 57–64) that by the late 1790s, as a result of aggressive marketing techniques, professional weavers in New England and the Mid-Atlantic were ordering quantities of cotton yarn from Rhode Island. By the early years of the nineteenth century, therefore, weavers like Eldridge would no longer need to rely solely on locally produced raw materials.

55. Commons, "American Shoemakers, 1647–1895," 49.

56. J. Smith Futhey and Gilbert Cope, *History of Chester County Pennsylvania* (Evansville, Ind., 1986), 530.

57. Based on an average family size of 6.1. see n. 35.

58. In 1787, when Eldridge was weaving full-time, he had twenty-three customers. In 1809, with a journeyman and his two sons working for him, his clients totaled twenty-four.

59. Tench Coxe, *A View of the United States of America, in a Series of Papers Written at Various Times, in the Years Between 1787 and 1794* (New York, 1965): 63–64.

60. Between 1786 and 1789, Eldridge had forty-nine customers, of whom it was possible to identify thirty-three (67.3 percent) on the 1783 tax lists either directly or by the presence of a family name. The majority (twenty-four, or 72.7 percent) of these lived in Goshen Township where Eldridge lived and worked, while the others came from the contiguous townships of East Bradford (three, or 9.1 percent) and Willistown (six, or 18.2 percent). He was related to many of his customers who were either cousins, related by marriage or through his stepmother, and included names such as Garrett, Griffiths, Hoopes, White, and Davis. The three townships from which Eldridge's customers could be identified had 319 households, according to the 1783 tax list, indicating that he clearly was not weaving for everyone.

61. Schweitzer, *Custom and Contract*, 123, argues that when farmers bought goods on credit, they were in effect taking out a loan, the cost of which was included in the price of the goods rather than as a separate interest payment.

62. Between 1786 and 1789, Eldridge received forty-nine payments totaling £29s3d9. Of these, almost twice as many (thirty-two) were in cash with a value five times greater (£24s2d5) than the payments made in goods and services (£5s1d4).

63. Jonas Ingham, Account Book, 1724–1739. For the year 1728, payments received by Ingham for a variety of goods totaled £84s18d9 in cash and £77s9d10 in goods and services. This is in accord with the findings of Schweitzer, *Custom and Contract,*, 131, who demonstrates that in account-book entries between 1727 and 1731 the majority of transactions were paid in Pennsylvania currency.

64. This concept is well typified in Carl Bridenbaugh, *The Colonial Craftsman* (Chicago, 1950), 34–35.

65. *American Weekly Mercury,* Aug. 8–15, 1728, advertised imported cloth for sale that could be "paid for next Spring in Country Produce."

66. Laurel Thatcher Ulrich, "Wheels, Looms, and the Gender Division of Labor in Eighteenth-Century New England," *William and Mary Quarterly,* 3rd series, 55 (1998): 15.

67. Robert Parke, Chester, to Mary Valentine, Ireland, December 1725, folder 87, Chester County Papers, 1684–1897, HSP.

68. Most of the fabric goods people brought with them that were specifically mentioned in correspondence and newspapers were clothing. This may be due partly to the fact that fabric furnishings were subsumed under broad categories such as "household goods." For example, the term "bed furniture" included textile hangings, in addition to the bed.

69. See ads by Michael Brown in the *Pennsylvania Gazette,* May 10, 1739, and *American Weekly Mercury,* July 28 through Aug 4, 1743.

70. Schoelwer, "Form, Function, and Meaning in the Use of Fabric Furnishings," 36 and 37 (tables 7 and 8), notes that traditionally scholars have thought that wrought silver represented the most important component of eighteenth-century household investment among wealthy Philadelphians, but her conclusions suggest that textiles outranked silver. Even for householders in the lower levels of society the fabric furnishings they owned "constituted a significant economic investment."

71. For example, Aaron Leaming, Account Book, 1764–1784, has numerous entries showing that sawmill owner Aaron Leaming took cloth in payment for his services and in turn resold it. *American Weekly Mercury,* Mar. 1–10, 1742–1743, had the following advertisement: "A Promisary Note for 55 Yards of Ten-Hundred Linen, or the Value thereof, at 2s per Yard, in Cash, was lately found."

72. Beverly Lemire, *Dress, Culture, and Commerce: The English Clothing Trade Before the Factory, 1660–1800* (New York, 1997), 145.

73. CCWI #352, Nathaniel Newlin (d. 1729) of Concord Township was a storekeeper who had a fulling mill in the adjacent township of Birmingham. On the tax lists for 1765, John Culbertson of East Caln had a fulling mill but was "a Store Keeper by Profession." Jonas Ingham, Account Book, 1724–1748; in the 1720s, fuller Jonas Ingham also sold meat, writing paper, wool, dyestuffs, soap, and woolen and linen cloth. Mill Book, L. Brown and Kirk Family Miscellany; Roger Kirk, working in the 1770s and 1780s, sold agricultural products, flour, dyestuffs, and a variety of fabrics. Calvin Cooper, Account Book, 1791–1802, sold meat, vegetables, dyestuffs, leather, thread, and hats.

74.Richard Hayes, Ledger, 1708–1740, Am. 073, HSP.

75. Mill book, L. Brown and Kirk Family Miscellany. At least thirteen people paid Kirk by weaving during the decade 1775–1785.

76. Mill Book, L. Brown and Kirk Family Miscellany, 97, 104, 132.

77. CCWI #4013, Thomas Marshall (d. 1789) was a fuller with a mill who also had a loom in his inventory. CCWI #2376, William Kirk (d. 1767) had a fulling mill and two looms.

78. See also advertisement in *Pennsylvania Gazette,* Jan. 11, 1732, by Solomon Fussul, who "designs to work any woollen Cloth or Clothes that want turning, to raise a Frise or Nap . . ."

79. Mill Book, L. Brown and Kirk Family Miscellany.

80. James Benezet to T. Matlack, New Town, Bucks County, July 31, 1777,

in *Pennsylvania Archives*, vol. 5 Samuel Hazard, ed. (Philadelphia, 1853), 469. Benezet says, "According to my directions from Colonel Kirkbride I have sent by Samuel Rees, Waggoner, One hundred of the Best & cleanest Blankets of those Collected in our County, the remainder, about 200, shall send (this morning) to Thomas Jenks's Fulling, who says if the Weather continues Dry he will compleat them in a Week."

81. For the secondhand clothing trade in England, see Lemire, "Consumerism in Preindustrial and Early Industrial England," 1–24.

82. This might seem surprising given the existence of the many documents detailing the origin and types of products imported to eighteenth-century Philadelphia, and several compilations of trade statistics about goods from abroad, in particular textiles, destined for America. Such data can be found in contemporary newspaper advertisements to sell ship cargoes lately arrived from abroad, merchants' correspondence, port records, both in North America and England, and household inventories of residents and storekeepers in Pennsylvania. For published trade statistics, see Raymond Leonard Sickinger, "The British Textile Trade and Britain's Trading Partners, 1772–1792: A Quantitative Study" (Ph.D. diss., University of Notre Dame, 1978); Elizabeth Boody Schumpeter, *English Overseas Trade Statistics, 1697–1808* (Oxford, 1960); Helen Louise Klopfer, "Statistics of Foreign Trade of Philadelphia 1700–1860" (Ph.D. diss., University of Pennsylvania, 1936); and Marc Egnal, "The Pennsylvania Economy, 1748–1762: An Analysis of Short-Run Fluctuations in the Context of Long-Run Changes in the Atlantic Trading Community," (Ph.D. diss., University of Wisconsin, 1974).

83. Florence M. Montgomery, *Textiles in America, 1650–1870* (New York, 1984), takes a large step in overcoming this problem, but helpful as it is it has not eliminated all the difficulties with terminology.

84. The use of fabrics designated as "homespun" is most apparent in newspaper advertisements for runaway servants and slaves throughout the eighteenth century. See Tryon, *Household Manufactures in the United States* 91 and 203, for a breakdown of the homespun cloth worn by runaways during the period. Bridenbaugh, *The Colonial Craftsman*, 35, states, "By 1750 nine tenths of Pennsylvania's farmers fabricated their own wearing apparel." He backed his contention with Tryon's data on runaways and also used excerpts from several government reports, concluding that "[p]rior to 1765 the average family was forced into making fabrics for its own use simply because it did not have the money to buy them."

85. Out of 825 Chester County wills and inventories sampled for the eighteenth century, only six, or 0.7 percent, had textile entries specifically designated "homespun" or "homemade"; these were scattered throughout the century.

86. During the last years of the eighteenth century, the Chester County authorities attempted to set up a farm for the poor, many of them women. One of the objects of this endeavor was to create a situation in which poor women could help maintain themselves by spinning yarn for sale. This did not represent an attempt to set up a manufactory, however; rather, it was viewed as an extension of the household environment with the residents replicating as closely as possible the lives of local farm families, Joan M. Jensen, *Loosening the Bonds: Mid-Atlantic Farm Women, 1750–1850* (New Haven, 1986), 62–66.

87. Ideally, cloth from the period should help clarify what contemporaries understood by the term "homespun," but a survey of several collections at

both the national and local level failed to provide enough clearly attributed eighteenth-century artifacts to make this possible. The Department of Textiles at the American Museum of History and Life in Washington has several scraps of what are felt to be mid-eighteenth-century, American handwoven textiles, which were found inside a quilt, described by Rita J. Adrosko, "Anatomy of a Quilted Counterpane," *Weaver's Journal*, 32 (1984): 42–46. Winterthur Museum has some coverlets dated from the late eighteenth century, as does Chester County Historical Society and Germantown Historical Society, but these examples are too few and too late to provide any concrete sense of what weavers produced throughout the century in Pennsylvania.

88. Cole, *The American Wool Manufacture*, 27.

89. The homespun fabrics worn by runaways, as indicated in newspaper ads include a wide variety of wools, linens, and mixed cloths of many colors, sometimes patterned with stripes or checks.

90. Ann Smart Martin, "Shopkeepers' Accounts in the Chesapeake: Textiles and Clothing at Eighteenth-Century Virginia Stores," paper presented at the Third Textile History Conference (1990):10, also finds imported homemade checks in the inventories of rural Virginia storekeepers in the mid-1770s.

91. Gervase Markham, *The English Housewife* (Kingston, Ont., 1986), 150, writes that most seventeenth-century English housewives spun all their yarn alike while the more experienced could spin several types of yarn. Clearly, the skill of the spinner had a great deal to do with whether a textile was called "homespun."

92. From a sampling of 250 eighteenth-century Essex County inventories, ten (4 percent) listed homespun items among the other property spread out fairly evenly over the period. Among the items were "blue homespun Curtains Couverlid & blankets" (1715); homespun shirts, blankets, napkins, tablecloths, ticking, and blankets (1735); homespun camlet and aprons (1754); homespun thread and coat, "blue homespun Wast Coat" (1773); brown homespun gown, homemade woolen blankets (1792).

93. The *Pennsylvania Gazette* had constant advertisements to sell shiploads of textiles from numerous countries; for example, Oct. 2, 1729; Dec. 1–8, 1737; June 21, 1750; and Feb. 21, 1781. In addition, information contained in some merchants' records provides further details about the variety of fabrics being shipped from abroad for sale in the American colonies. For example, Philadelphia Merchant (probably John Yeates), Account Book, Invoice, London, July 3, 1750, HML, acc. 823, v.2; Andrew Clow and Co., Account, Philadelphia, 1790–1791, acc. 1097, folder 2, HML; Greenberry Dorsey, Invoice, Philadelphia, October 16, 1790, man. #55x761.1, WRBR.

94. Montgomery, *Textiles in America, 1650–1870,*, 258 and 312, defines "holland" as "once specifying the country of manufacture for a wide variety of linen goods. 'Holland' later became the generic name for linen cloth, often of fine quality"; and "osnaburg" as "coarse, unbleached linen or hempen cloth first made in Osnabruck, Germany."

95. Aaron Leaming, Account Book, 1764–1784, has several entries to show that "Dutch Linsey" was being woven for him by a neighboring New Jersey artisan.

96. Quoted in Montgomery, *Textiles in America, 1650–1870,* 345.

97. Montgomery, *Textiles in America,* 218–20.

98. Jonathan Nesbitt to John Brown, l'Orient, March 24, 1781, John Brown Papers, Philadelphia, 1781–1784, acc. 348, HML. Writing from "the Orient,"

Nesbitt detailed the textiles he bought for John Brown. See John Irwin and Katharine B. Brett, *Origins of Chintz, With a Catalogue of Indo-European Cotton-Paintings in the Victoria and Albert Museum, London, and the Royal Ontario Museum, Toronto* (London, 1970), 3–6, for a description of the variety of fabrics purchased in India by the East India Company agents for sale in Europe in the seventeenth and eighteenth centuries.

99. That storekeepers stocked and sold a wide variety of imported textiles is apparent in the inventories of several Chester County store keepers, CCWI #352, Nathaniel Newlin, Concord (d. 1729); CCWI #1643, Thomas Morgan, Chester (d. 1757); CCWI #2711, John Trimble, Concord (d. 1772); CCWI #2758, George Ashbridge, Goshen (d. 1773).

100. Numerous ads detailed imported textiles for sale throughout much of the eighteenth century, listed in the *Pennsylvania Gazette*. Virginia retailers also sold a similar array of cloth; see Martin, "Shopkeepers' Accounts in the Chesapeake," 15.

101. Thomas M. Doerflinger, *A Vigorous Spirit of Enterprise: Merchants and Economic Development in Revolutionary Philadelphia* (Chapel Hill, N.C., 1986), 87.

102. Based on inventories of Chester County shop keepers. CCWI #352, #1350, #1643, #2711, and #2758. The cloth was divided into three categories: that which was clearly imported and never listed in account books or probate records as products of local weavers; that listed as both being made by local weavers and found on import lists; and that specifically called "homespun."

103. This is not to say that all of the inhabitants were wealthy, just that in terms of textile manufacture, there was not a widespread home production.

Chapter 7. Weaving Moves into the Mills

1. Victor S. Clark, *History of Manufactures in the United States, Volume I, 1607–1860* (New York, 1949), 529. See also Kenneth L. Sokoloff and David Dollar, "Agricultural Seasonality and the Organization of Manufacturing in Early Industrial Economies: The Contrast Between England and the United States," *Journal of Economic History*, 57 (1997): 288–321, for a comparison of the British and American shift from domestic to factory production with its intermediate stage of putting out.

2. Daniel Vickers, *Farmers and Fishermen: Two Centuries of Work in Essex County Massachusetts, 1630–1785* (Chapel Hill, N.C., 1994), 209–11.

3. Vickers, *Farmers and Fishermen*, 254.

4. Benno M. Forman, "The Account Book of John Gould, Weaver, of Topsfield, Massachusetts, 1697–1724," *Essex Institute Historical Collections*, 105 (1969): 37.

5. Based on a sampling of 117 Essex County household inventories from 1650 to 1699. Probate wills and inventories, Essex County Court House (hereafter, ECCH), Salem, Massachusetts.

6. Forman, "The Account Book of John Gould," 41.

7. James E. McWilliams, "Work, Family, and Economic Improvement in Late-Seventeenth-Century Massachusetts Bay: The Case of Joshua Buffum," *New England Quarterly*, 74 (2001): 373.

8. Laurel Thatcher Ulrich, "Wheels, Looms, and the Gender Division of

Labor in Eighteenth-Century New England," *William and Mary Quarterly,* 3rd series, 55 (1998): 15; Vickers, *Farmers and Fishermen,* 254; and Philip J. Greven, *Four Generations: Population, Land, and Family in Colonial Andover, Massachusetts* (Ithaca, N.Y., 1970), 224.

9. Inventories and wills survive for a group of weavers from Ipswich throughout the eighteenth century, beginning with John Dennison (d. 1683) who identified himself as a weaver and had a shop with three looms and equipment. (ECCH #7558). He was from a long line of weavers who passed their equipment on to their sons until we lose track of them in 1761, when the last Dennison died without children and left his looms to his wife. See ECCH #7560, John Dennison (d. 1720); ECCH #7562, John Dennison (d. 1761). Numerous other weavers are identified as such and with specialized equipment in Ipswich as well. See ECCH #13971, John Hovey (d.1720); ECCH #6647, Stephen Cross (d. 1735); ECCH #5512, Samuel Clark (d. 1757); ECCH #4464, Daniel Caldwell (d.1759); ECCH #13503 John Hodgkins, Jr. (d. 1792).

10. Essex County database. Based on a sampling of 408 Essex County wills and inventories (hereafter, ECWI).

11. In Chester County, of the ninety-seven households owning looms between 1715 and 1830, twenty-five (26 percent) owned two or more, Chester County Wills and Inventories (hereafter, CCWI). In Essex County for the same dates, of the sixty loom owners only five (8 percent) had more than two, ECWI.

12. Ulrich, "Wheels, Looms," 27.

13. For a full discussion of this system, see Tucker, *Samuel Slater,* 55–74.

14. Gail Fowler Mohanty, "Experimentation in Textile Technology, 1788–1790, and Its Impact on Handloom Weaving and Weavers in Rhode Island," *Technology and Culture,* 29 (1988): 1–31, has a good description of the Providence hand-loom weavers.

15. Thomas Dublin, "Rural Putting-Out Work in Early New England: Women and the Transition to Capitalism in the Countryside," *New England Quarterly,* 65 (1991): 531–73.

16. Barbara M. Tucker, *Samuel Slater and the Origins of the American Textile Industry, 1790–1860* (Ithaca, N.Y., 1984): 57.

17. Dublin, "Rural Putting-Out Work in Early New England," 538.

18. Thomas Dublin, *Women at Work: The Transformation of Work and Community in Lowell, Massachusetts, 1826–1860* (New York, 1979), 17–21.

19. Dublin, "Rural Putting-Out Work in Early New England," 534–35.

20. See Dublin, *Women at Work,* 26.

21. Essex County database. In 1811, 20 percent of households had looms; in 1830, only 10 percent.

22. *Pennsylvania Gazette,* Feb. 22, 1775, Supp. p.1.

23. Chris Aspin, *The Cotton Industry* (Aylesbury, Bucks., UK, 1981), 9–11.

24. *Pennsylvania Gazette,* May 29, 1776, 1; and Clark, *History of Manufactures in the United States,* 190.

25. David J. Jeremy, *Transatlantic Industrial Revolution: The Diffusion of Textile Technologies Between Britain and America, 1790–1830s* (North Andover, Mass., 1981), 159, notes that between 1824 and 1831 more than twice as many textile immigrants landed in Philadelphia than in Boston.

26. Shelton, *The Mills of Manayunk,* 33. By the 1850s, the immigrant population was about 30 percent of Philadelphia's population, according to Philip

Scranton, *Proprietary Capitalism: The Textile Manufacture at Philadelphia, 1800–1885* (Cambridge, 1983), 44.

27. Scranton, *Proprietary Capitalism*, 76.

28. Scranton, *Proprietary Capitalism*, 84, 86, 100.

29. Shelton, *The Mills of Manayunk*, 51–53.

30. Between 1799 and 1810, the population increased by 48 percent, the average size of landholding declined from 107 acres to 85, while at the same time 30 percent more people owned land, suggesting that larger parcels were being divided among a greater number of people. In addition, there was a 5 percent growth in the landless population and a 14 percent increase in the number of smallholders with fewer than twenty acres. Based on an analysis of all taxables on Chester County tax lists for 1799 and 1810 in East Fallowfield, Goshen, East Nottingham, Pikeland, Thornbury, and Tredyffrin townships. Total taxables: 1799, 917; 1810, 1,357. Taxables with land: 1799, 562; 1810, 730. Taxables with twenty acres or fewer: 1799, 504; 1810, 577. CCA.

31. Loom ownership declined from 10 percent in 1795 to 6 percent in 1810. Inventory database.

32. Between 1795 and 1830, fifty-two households had looms and ten of these (19.2 percent) had two or more. Inventory database.

33. Based on an analysis of the 1820 Manufacturing Census (manuscript) for Philadelphia and Chester Counties (hereafter, 1820 MC).

34. Tucker, *Samuel Slater*, 57–58.

35. Based on information contained on the 1785, 1810, and 1820 tax lists, CCA.

36. Anthony F. C. Wallace, *Rockdale: The Growth of an American Village in the Early Industrial Revolution* (New York, 1972), 161.

37. John Bradley, *The Dickey Family and the Growth of Oxford and Hopewell* (Elkton, Md., 1990), 8, provides the information about the Hopewell mill.

38. 1820 MC.

39. Clipping file, Lower Oxford Industries, CCHS.

40. Joan M. Jensen, *Loosening the Bonds: Mid-Atlantic Farm Women, 1750–1850* (New Haven, 1986), part II.

41. The information on the Charlestown factory comes from a series of newspaper clippings collected in the Clipping File, Industries, CCHS.

42. Inventory database. Households owning flax declined from 37 percent in 1795, to 31 percent in 1813, to 17 percent in 1830; households with wool declined from 18 percent in 1795, to 11 percent in 1813, to 9 percent in 1830. More work needs to be done to determine how extensively weavers may have been producing cloth to stock and sell; however, with more yarn available, it was a possibility in a way it had not been in the past.

43. Clipping File, Industries, CCHS.

44. Pat Hudson, *The Industrial Revolution* (London, 1992), 111–12.

Index

Acknowledgments

Any project that takes as long to come to fruition as this one generates many debts of gratitude. Spanning several life stages and careers, it began during the years in which I worked as a weaver. At that time, two wonderful people imparted their extensive knowledge of textiles to me. Dorothy Burnham, as curator of textiles at the Royal Ontario Museum (ROM), opened her library and generously shared her expertise of cloth production. She was always an unfailing supporter of my quest to learn more about the production and use of fabric in past cultures. At the same time, I had the wonderful experience of working with Norman Kennedy, master weaver, singer, and storyteller. Over the years that we wove, traveled, and taught together, I learned more about the tools and techniques of hand weaving than I had thought possible. Without my experiences with Dorothy and Norman, I would never have chosen to extend my interest beyond practice to study history.

My formal research into the world of early American textiles began at the University of California, San Diego (UCSD). I must thank my adviser, Roy Ritchie, for supporting what seemed like a somewhat unconventional project and to go on to provide support and advice at all the appropriate moments. In addition, from my UCSD days, I thank Victoria Brown, Vikki Bynum, Thomas Dublin, and Mary Lou Locke.

Part of the delay in completing this book stemmed from my ten-year job as a curator in the textile department at the ROM in Toronto. It did, however, allow me to explore in depth the world of cloth. Moreover, as administrator of the Veronika Gervers Memorial Fellowship, I was able to encourage other historians to use the textile collection in their own work. In addition to the many art historians, ethnographers, and curators who received the fellowship over the years, several intrepid social historians took up the challenge. As I worked closely with many of the fellows, showing them how to examine and "read" the textile artifacts, I could see that the exercise changed (often profoundly) their approach to history; my knowledge, too, broadened and deepened. Three people stand out in this process. Beverly Lemire's analysis of eighteenth-century quilted petticoats helped her to understand women's role in England's ready-made clothing industry, described in her book *Dress, Culture, and Commerce: The English Clothing Trade Before the Factory, 1660–1800;* material culture continues to play a major role in her scholarship. The early North American textiles in the collection provided Laurel Thatcher Ulrich with yet another tool with which to explore early American history through the lives of New England women; indeed, material culture fully informs her most recent book, *The Age of Homespun: Objects and Stories in the Creation of an American Myth.* Moving into a later period, corsets and underwear formed the "foundation" of Jill Field's dissertation, "The Production of Glamour: A Social History of Intimate Apparel, 1909–1952" and subsequent articles. I think all of us would agree that working closely with the textiles and each other had a lasting impact on our approach to history. I thank Beverly, Laurel, and Jill for the opportunity to exchange ideas. Many of the scholars with whom I worked at the ROM have gone on to publish their books; I have taken longer to complete mine. Museums are wonderful repositories of material culture, but in these days of funding and staff cuts it is difficult to find the time for one's own research and publishing. Nevertheless, my colleagues at the ROM deserve a great deal of thanks for their support, especially David Barr, Shannon Elliott, Greta Ferguson, Anu Liivandi, Angela Sheng, Gene Wilburn, and the library staff.

Not until I made my most recent career change—to teach history at the University of Toronto—was I finally able to turn this manuscript into a publishable form. Thanks to my many colleagues and students in the Department of History and Victoria College for support over the last few years. With the opportunity to combine my research interests with teaching I have finally been able to finish this project.

I am indebted to the many people who read all or parts of the manuscript at one time or another, in particular Jim Lemon, Laurel Ulrich, Marc Egnal, Stevie Wolf, Joe Ernst, Nancy Grey Osterud, Jay Fliegelman, and Ned Cooke. I am especially grateful for the close readings at the earliest stages by Thiery Ruddel and, later, by Beverly Lemire. Everyone made important and helpful suggestions for improvements, and any failure to incorporate their advice is mine.

Many libraries and their staff assisted in the completion of this project, beginning with the UCSD library, as well as the libraries at the ROM and the University of Toronto. In addition, I thank the Historical Society of Pennsylvania, Essex Institute, Hagley Museum and Library, and Winterthur Museum and Library. At the American Textile History Museum thanks go to Clare Sheridan, Anne Cadrette, and Diane Fagan Affleck for help with images. Special thanks go to Archivist Laurie Rofini at the Chester County Archives for generous advice, assistance, and support over the many years I worked there; Assistant Archivist Barbara Weir was always helpful, especially when it came to genealogical issues. I thank Ellen Endslow and Rob Leukens at the Chester County Historical Society and Library for access to the collections and assistance with images, and Rosemary Phillips, Diane Rofini, and Pamela Powel for help in using the library collections. Above all, I thank Lucy Simler for sharing her extensive knowledge of the history of Chester County with me over many years, and providing access to, and information about numerous things I could never have discovered on my own. Without her, I would not have realized the richness of the historical evidence available on textile production in the area.

Funding over the years came from the Social Sciences and Research Council of Canada, the Royal Ontario Museum, the Arthur H. Cole Grant-in-Aid for Research in Economic History, the Sullivan Fellowship from the Museum of American Textile History (now the American Textile History Museum), the Philadelphia Center for Early American Studies (now the McNeil Center for Early American Studies), and Victoria College at the University of Toronto. I thank them all for their financial support.

I have been very fortunate in being able to work with the team at the University of Pennsylvania Press. I would like to thank both series editors, Richard Dunn for his initial support and Daniel Richter for working so closely with a manuscript he did not initiate; I realize how difficult it is for one editor to inherit the project of another. Bob Lockhart provided unfailing encouragement and enthusiasm at all stages of a long process—a very welcome asset in an editor. Particular thanks go to Noreen O'Connor for her excellent editing job at several stages of the manuscript preparation. It has been a pleasure to work with a team that strives so hard for excellence.

As with any project like this, friends and family make important contributions that simply cannot be enumerated: Lynn Appleby, Beverly Lemire, Grant McCracken, Trudy Nicks, Cheryl Robertson, Thiery Ruddel, Stevie Wolf, and many others were there when I needed them. For providing distraction and perspective, thanks go to Joanne White,

Paddy, Reuben, and Bristol. My family—Wharton Hood, Mary Emmett Hood, Ginny Hood, and Lou and Shoshana Cole—was always understanding; my grandmother, Dora Ridout Hood, instilled in me her love of books and her appreciation of history. No one, however, deserves more thanks for patience, advice, and encouragement than my husband, Edward Cole.

www.ingramcontent.com/pod-product-compliance
Ingram Content Group UK Ltd.
Pitfield, Milton Keynes, MK11 3LW, UK
UKHW030034120225
454972UK00002B/102/J